*f*P

*Un*Godly

THE PASSIONS, TORMENTS, AND MURDER OF ATHEIST MADALYN MURRAY O'HAIR

Ted Dracos

Free Press

New York   London   Toronto   Sydney   Singapore

*f*P
FREE PRESS
A Division of Simon & Schuster, Inc.
1230 Avenue of the Americas
New York, NY 10020

Copyright © by Theodore Michael Dracos
FREE PRESS and colophon are trademarks of Simon & Schuster, Inc.

For information regarding special discounts for bulk purchases, please contact Simon & Schuster Special Sales
at 1-800-456-6798 or business@simonandschuster.com

Designed by Karolina Harris

Manufactured in the United States of America

10   9   8   7   6   5   4   3   2   1

Library of Congress Cataloging-in-Publication Data
  Dracos, Ted.
  Ungodly : the passions, torments, and murder of atheist Madalyn Murray O'Hair / Ted Dracos.
    p.   cm.
  Includes index.
  1. O'Hair, Madalyn Murray. 2. Atheists—United States—Biography. I. Title.
  BL2790.038 D72 2003
  211'.8'092—dc22
  {B}   2003049303

ISBN 0-7432-2833-2

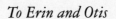

To Erin and Otis

Contents

UnGodly

ONE

The Secret Place

---

*I*f you think in terms of a side of beef, then the Hill Country is prime filet of Texas. It is God's country. There are places left where pure spring waters merge in the hills, becoming delicate valley creeks that flow over ancient limestone beds with real dinosaur tracks—if you know where to look. There are many wild things: turtles, turkey, fox, javelina, bobcats, armadillos, cougar, tusked boar, herds of white-tailed deer and enough bird life to attract fanatic watchers all the way from Europe. Towns are named Utopia and ranches High Heaven. If there is a location in America that could still be comfortably called *graced*, it is the Texas Hill Country.

The peak of the hill closest to the secret burial site of the world's most famous atheist is adorned with a white cross. The sign that Madalyn Murray O'Hair feared and hated above all others was the only symbol of humanity that could be seen from the wildness of her grave. And it was here that a twenty- by twenty-foot excavation of this God-smitten landscape would disclose a fresh revelation of the extent of human cruelty and of hell on earth.

• • •

A year after the turn of the millennium, a classic Hill Country gentleman-rancher's vehicle would be a four-wheel-drive white

Chevy Suburban with metal brush guards in front, a custom dia-mond-plate rear bumper, and oversized black fiberglass wheel-well moldings to keep the mud down. You'd also need dark-tint windows, and a corkscrew cell phone antenna dead center on the roof. When a passenger emerged from just such a vehicle late on a Saturday morning at the five-thousand-acre ranch, he easily could have been a rich Houston executive looking for a place to spot a deer feeder on his hunting retreat.

The man's sharp, handsome features were heartland Amer-ica. Brushed back boldly, the salt-and-pepper hair was thick and well groomed—the kind of mane you might see in an ad for men's shampoo. The large aviator-style glasses he had on gave him a look of coolness and intelligence. He wore his casual cloth-ing well too, as might be expected from a broad-shouldered and trim man. His shirt was a muted brown madras plaid, covered by a dark, indigo-colored windbreaker. The jeans he wore were stonewashed blue—maybe a little young looking for a fifty-three-year old man. Then again, he looked at least a decade younger than his age.

But the executive image was ruined by the clinking steel on his ankles and wrists. His manacled hands were locked to a metal waist-belt that prevented him from lifting them higher than chest level. His ankles were shackled too—joined by a two-foot length of chain. And, in a final insult to his sartorial style, the prisoner was wearing cheap black sneakers—the kind a poor Chi-nese peasant might have, or maybe a street clown. They were laceless and their tongues lolled drolly upward and outward.

There couldn't have been any worse footwear for hiking around a rugged Hill Country ranch, and that was exactly how the government agents wanted it. They intended for their pris-oner to concentrate on the task at hand and put all fantasies of escape out of mind. The two-foot chain between his ankles was also a continual reminder—a painful reminder—of exactly what the situation was. Every time the prisoner forgot and took a normal step, the chain would go taut and the steel cuffs would dig into his ankle bones. He had to constantly catch himself and take abnormally small, mincing, shuffling steps as he walked from the Suburban that was the lead vehicle in a convoy of government cars.

Toward the dry creek bed the prisoner clanked. No, this wasn't it, he nodded negatively. He returned to the SUV, with the agents ducking his head, and the caravan started to roll once again. If he felt panic rising inside him, he didn't let it show. He conversed sotto voce with the tall, burly, Texas-sized attorney who sat next to him in full camouflage gear.

The procession went through a gate and the prisoner asked the agents to stop. Again he walked the ground—and there it all was. There was the caliche gravel mound. There was the dried-up creek bed. There was the Y in the ranch road with the gate behind to the south. There was the flat, terraced area. This was it. But it had been more than five years since he'd buried them, riding on a mind-twisting methamphetamine high, and he wasn't sure of the exact spot.

There was another quiet conference with the big lawyer who had stayed by his side. Finally, not being able to gesture with his hands, which were shackled to his waist, the prisoner looked at the dry-wash terrace and, pointing with his head, said in a soft voice, "If I were you, that's where I'd start digging." An agent took a thin rod with a yellow plastic flag attached to it—the kind used to mark body parts at an airline disaster—and sunk it into the ground in the approximate center of the terraced area toward which the prisoner had motioned.

Two cadaver dogs were released by their handlers. Both showed interest in a tuft of cheat grass near the center of the dry-wash terrace toward which the prisoner had nodded. With rotors whup-whupping noisily overhead, news choppers got aerials of the grave site from the cold overcast January sky, as the professor of forensic anthropology hired by the FBI, assisted by his students, made a grid of the terrace using plastic tape and thin poles much as you might see in a National Geographic documentary. After two hours of delicate digging—at about noon on Saturday, January 27, 2001—one of the excavators found something.

The professor got down on his side and started removing the soil around the object with the tools of his trade—first a mini-trowel, then a dental pick, and finally a soft-bristled three-inch paintbrush. The article of interest was mocha-colored and oblong—too smooth to be a root but lying horizontally much like one. As the professor patiently continued his work, a hush fell over the site.

Everyone watched as he pecked and tapped and brushed. It soon became clear that a bone had been found. But it was gigantic and more likely a part of the skeletal remains of some long-dead cow, the professor reflected to himself, hiding his initial disappointment from his rapt audience. Finally he was able to gingerly extract the bone from the ground.

As the onlookers silently gaped, the professor turned it over in his hand and stared at it. At last, one of the cadaver dog handlers blurted out: "Is it human?" The professor nodded a somber affirmation. It was human, a femur from a very large person, probably a male—and it had been cleanly sawed in half.

The professor set up an assembly line for careful soil removal from the dig site. Soon a ghostly image began to evolve in the pit—that of two human female skeletons. The bodies had obviously been dumped there haphazardly, but somehow the bones had become intertwined in a kind of ghastly lovers' embrace. There were fragments of blue cotton flower-print material scattered amongst the remains, and one of the females had the rubber remnants of her panty waistband still around her pelvic area. Both had their femurs—thigh bones—sawed off just below the hips.

As the professor continued to cautiously excavate, he found that beneath the females, as though cradling them protectively with his massive bones, were the skeletal remains of a male human. The first bone found had been his. The stubs of the man's huge, sawed-off leg bones stood straight up from his hips, giving his skeleton somewhat the look of a picked-over Thanksgiving turkey carcass.

At the front gate of the ranch at 4 P.M., the regional FBI agent-in-charge faced the massed representatives of the media with a phalanx of law enforcement operatives involved in the investigation behind him. He was the ranking officer and, as such, he would conduct the news conference that would get global coverage. A few hours earlier, a stainless steel apparatus found in the excavation had been identified. It was a hip replacement joint.

The primary investigator in the case, an IRS agent, had been prescient enough to have the medical records of one of the victims subpoenaed and he had obtained a model number for a prosthetic hip joint that she'd had implanted. The device recovered from the grave had matched the model number of the victim's. This allowed the FBI chief to announce that the remains of Madalyn Murray O'Hair, her son Jon Garth Murray, and her granddaughter, Robin Murray O'Hair, had been positively identified—and the international mystery finally solved.

• • •

David Glassman was a man blessed. He loved his work. Sure, some might think that forensic anthropology was more than a bit ghoulish, but that was their problem. Besides, it really couldn't be that bad if he averaged at least a call a day from somewhere in the United States from a student wanting to get into his program at Southwest Texas State University in San Marcos.

It was fun. Working with smart and eager young men and women hungry for knowledge was a continual satisfaction. The direct intellectual rewards were even greater. You never do the same dig twice. Every excavation, every set of bones, was really a huge database, a complete history of the rise and fall of a human being, if you knew how to decode the bits and pieces. After almost three decades of work, including studying with the world-renowned William Bass at the "Body Farm" in Knoxville, Tennessee, Dr. Glassman could tease the most tenuous information out of a pile of old bones.

Per usual, there were interesting findings from the excavation. As he had suspected they would be, the remains were all skeletal, the complete bone sets of three adults: two Caucasian women and an extremely large-boned Caucasian male. As well, there was an additional finding—an extra adult male Caucasoid skull with a bullet hole, and a set of hands.

Glassman arranged all three complete skeletons on his large laboratory tables like some giant, devilish jigsaw puzzle. By far the most eye-catching aspect of the six hundred plus bones that Glassman lined up for the skeletons was that each femur had been sawed into two pieces.

The victims had been literally butchered, perhaps to make their corpses fit into containers such as a fifty-gallon drum, he speculated. All the remains showed signs of "light charring" too, indicating that each body had been partially subjected to a short and hot fire, possibly gasoline, or lighter fluid.

The eeriest part of the entire analysis for Dr. Glassman surrounded the remains of the younger Caucasian female: Robin O'Hair, the granddaughter of Madalyn. Her skull still had the hair attached. It was a beautiful blond-reddish color—perfectly brushed and braided and carefully tied with white bows, as though she'd been about to go to a party.

Madalyn Murray O'Hair's remains, like her granddaughter's, showed no signs of trauma intentionally inflicted while she was alive. Glassman couldn't determine a cause of death for either of the women. It was nothing more than a guess, but Glassman believed they had been manually strangled. If garrotes had been used to kill them, a telltale small bone in their necks would have been broken, but there were no fractures of this type that the professor could find.

The skeleton of Madalyn's son, Jon Garth Murray, held the most ominous information for the forensic anthropologist. The details told of what probably had been a frightful ending for the president of the American Atheists. His skull had been recovered from the grave wrapped in a plastic garbage bag. It was hard to see at first, but almost the entire circumference of his cranium had small hairline fractures. With a surprisingly unprofessorial concision, Dr. Glassman summed up his observations on Jon Garth by simply saying, "They beat the shit out of him before he died."

There could only be speculation on how Madalyn Murray O'Hair died—but not about how she had lived. For decades her life must have been a marathon of pain endurance. Four of her neck vertebrae were fused or partially fused. Her backbones were fusing and were festooned with bone spurs that could have produced excruciating pain. Her joints were disintegrating—being consumed by her immune system attacking its own connective tissue in a massive, arthritic self-assault.

Even breathing must have been torture at times for the elderly woman. Glassman observed that the cartilage in her rib cage had become calcified—it was turning to bone—and thus there may have been times when every breath that she drew, except perhaps for the most shallow, would produce a sharp stabbing pain.

As living life must have been physical hell for Madalyn, her death and the deaths of her children—they were held captive for a month while their bank accounts were systematically looted, they were restrained for long intervals with handcuffs and duct tape, multiple sexual predations were inflicted on Robin O'Hair, and the final murders were conducted so that some family members were alive and conscious when their loved ones were being killed—were perhaps the ultimate in human horrors. Yet the evil revelations held by her grave were not without a dreadful, divine irony, for Madalyn had spent her entire adult life trying to convince the world that only fools believed that there was a Hell.

TWO

The Making of an Atheist Amazon

---

*T*he *Phil Donahue Show* was to begin on November 6, 1967, and the lineup for the first week was crucial. The competition—Bob "Come on Down" Barker and Monty Hall with *Let's Make a Deal*—could be killers. Content was going to make or break Donahue, since the show was going to be pretty much a visual disaster. The TV station was a converted ice-skating rink and the studio, not so long ago, had been the rink itself. While the station owner—Powel Crosley, the manufacturer of the first compact car in the United States—might have been a business visionary, he wasn't exactly like a sailor on a drunk with his capital-expenditure money.

Not to worry. Donahue, even though a broadcasting youngster comparatively, was already a shrewd and skilled media tactician with a genius eye for what would hold people's attention. He wasn't going to let the set concern him. His shtick was, and always would be, *controversy*—high-energy, no-lube controversy, sprinkled with enough old-fashioned prurience to make a double-whammy draw for high ratings.

The Phil Donahue Show lineup for each day of the first week would be: a man discussing the uses of anatomically accurate dolls, an undertaker who would have Donahue recline in a casket brought to the set, a couple of handsome Midwestern studs discussing what they looked for in a woman, and an actual childbirth showing a human female's private parts in live action as never seen before on commercial TV anywhere in the world. ("You could see the baby's crown in the birth canal!" Donahue would cackle happily afterward.)

And the *very* first Donahue show—a show that would inaugurate a new type of television programming, which would eventually penetrate and then dominate every market in the United States—would star a venomous, anti-Catholic, and incredibly eloquent atheist named Madalyn Murray. For her debut appearance, Madalyn was primly dressed, wearing a black-and-white two-piece suit with a somewhat weird black blouse with white lightning streaks. By forty-eight years of age, she had already become "stout and stocky," by her own admission, but her physical aura was kind, jovial, and grandmotherly.

In fact, her appearance was deceptive and cagily cultivated to magnify the shock value of her views. It certainly would be hard to believe from looking at her that this pleasant-looking middle-American grandma had recently been featured only two years earlier in a major interview in *Playboy* magazine, speculating that nuns had fantasies in their rooms at night of "Christ taking their maidenheads" using his staff as a wooden dildo.

Few, if any, women in the audience had ever heard of Madalyn Murray, and Donahue himself, despite his good Irish background, had a reputation in Dayton, Ohio—a predominantly Roman Catholic, blue-collar town with a distinctly conservative bent—for being a bit "strange." Donahue was the replacement for a popular local musical variety show, whose host had just left for a try at the big time in Hollywood. Unfortunately for Donahue, the ladies in his audience hadn't been informed of the change and they were all primed to sing songs and then wave into the studio cameras at their kids bouncing excitedly on the living room sofa watching their very own mommy on the big Sylvania.

When Donahue introduced his guest and related that she

was responsible for prayers being banned from public schools, there were rumblings from the audience—undisguised sighs and muffled mutterings. But the comfortable herd of middle-class *Hausfrauen* listened alertly as Madalyn began her ungodly rap— that is, until Madalyn whipped out the old Bible she had brought on set with her—and ripped out a page!

Nobody even heard what she was saying while she tore the Bible. Everybody—floor crew, staff, the audience—went into mass fibrillation, struck dumb and still by the horror of this live-and-in-color desecration. However, when the commercial break came, the women had recovered their wits and then some. Donahue stepped down amongst the palpitating females all perched on the edges of their folding chairs. They plastered him with questions to throw at his guest. Good questions. Tough questions. Better questions than his. Madalyn started answering them with the cameras still off, sprinkling her glib, erudite responses with profanities including even the unbelievable—the F-word.

It was wild. It was heaven. Donahue was in semicontrolled ecstasy. He told his director-producer to have the floor crew get him a hand microphone. He wanted to wade into the mass of agitated women when they came out of the commercial break and went back live. From that moment on, for decades hence, Donahue would be out of the host chair and into the aisles, waving his mic like a large black phallus through rows of countless females. A new type of TV programming had been brought forth with Madalyn as the midwife.

On Palm Sunday, April 13, 1919, Madalyn Elizabeth Mays was born to John and Lena Mays. Those with sensitivities toward such things might say that aspects of Madalyn's birth—besides its being on the thirteenth—foreshadowed all the events that were to follow. According to her mother, Lena, who claimed to have psychic powers, the entire body of the newborn Madalyn was covered with a "dark membrane" like a "black shroud" of mourning. Nobody could explain the phenomenon, but the attending physician gave part of the membrane wrapping to Lena—a freakish memento that she kept for many years.

The birth of their first child could not have been considered a blessed event by either father or mother. Lena and John Mays had married young to escape from families cinched in Appalachian poverty with a dozen siblings each. According to Madalyn's eldest son, Bill Murray, who chronicled part of Madalyn's early life in his own autobiography, *My Life Without God,* "Their lack of enthusiasm for children is shown by an incident that occurred in 1918 when Grandmother was several months pregnant with Madalyn. Hoping to abort the fetus, Grandmother jumped from a second-floor window of the family home in Pittsburgh. The hard landing must have not damaged either the baby or the mother, because Grandmother carried Madalyn full term."

In the newly forming suburbs of Pittsburgh in the 1920s, John Mays, an uneducated but intelligent handyman, opened a "construction firm" and prospered to the point of being able to build a nice two-story brick house for his young family. The interior was handsomely finished with hardwood floors and moldings, and cabinets from Germany. The yard was landscaped, and two pear trees were soon bearing fruit. As if to reinforce the image of the plenteous times for the Mays family, Lena bore a son, Irving Mays.

The Pittsburgh period was to be the family's social and economic high-water mark. John Mays's construction firm tanked soon after the stock market did. The Depression years would mean a steep slide into working as a bootlegger and perhaps even a part-time pimp for Madalyn's father. Details are sketchy, but Madalyn recalled sitting on top of a hidden moonshine tank when her father went on his bootlegging runs.

Finally John Mays settled his family in Akron, Ohio, the

location where Madalyn claimed to have had her first atheist epiphany at twelve or thirteen years old. She told *Playboy* some thirty years later that, for some reason, when they moved to their new home she didn't have access to the public library, and all she had to read were a dictionary and a Bible. She said she "picked up the Bible and read it from cover to cover one weekend—just as if it were a novel—very rapidly." She claimed she was intellectually traumatized: "The miracles, the inconsistencies, the improbabilities, the impossibilities, the wretched history, the sordid sex, the sadism in it—the whole thing shocked me profoundly. I remember I looked in the kitchen at my mother and father and I thought: Can they really *believe* in all that?"

After graduating from high school in Rossford, Ohio, Madalyn attended the University of Toledo. Then when the family moved briefly back to Pittsburgh, while juggling a full-time credit load at the University of Pittsburgh and a part-time secretarial job, Madalyn met and fell in love with a young steel worker named John Henry Roths. They eloped on Thursday, October 9, 1941, by running off to a hamlet in the Maryland Appalachians that may well have been a stop on the bootlegging runs of Madalyn's father during Prohibition.

Their togetherness was to be short-lived. The Japanese attacked Pearl Harbor less than two months later. Roths immediately joined the Marines, went through boot camp, and was shipped out to the South Pacific. Madalyn, equally patriotic, enlisted in the Women's Army Corps. She went to officers candidate school and was cleared for top-secret cryptographic duties in North Africa and Europe.

Her actual military service as a Wac is somewhat disputed, but whatever Madalyn's duties and accomplishments were, there is no doubt that she liked military life and was influenced by her tour of duty. But even though Madalyn was already a confirmed workaholic, her World War II military service wasn't all labor and striving. Madalyn fell in love with a young, connected and brave Eighth Army Air Corps B-24 pilot—William J. Murray Jr. For Madalyn Mays, wrong-side-of-the-tracks, factory row-housing girl, the dashing, courageous bomber pilot from a politically well-placed Long Island family was the catch of a lifetime.

In what may have been an act of unguarded celebration on the part of Captain Murray and perhaps a more calculated activity by Lieutenant Mays, in September 1945—the month of the official Japanese surrender—Madalyn became pregnant by him. Unfortunately Murray was already married and a devout Catholic to boot. The young officer was at least a semigentleman. He told Madalyn he wanted to marry her, but that his Catholicism prevented him from divorcing his wife. Whether this was a blow-softening device or an expression of true religious conviction for Murray can't be judged. In any case, Madalyn mustered out of military service, pregnant with another man's child and with her Marine husband about to come home to her.

Back in Ohio, Madalyn found her parents living in a "dirt-floor" shack—her father having squandered on alcohol the paychecks that she'd sent back to put into savings. Madalyn was devastated. To go from a storybook romance, a dream love affair in war-torn Europe from the pages of a Hemingway novel, to a disgusting hovel—and to be pregnant under the most difficult circumstances imaginable—might have shattered the toughest woman.

Not Madalyn. As she paced inside the dirt-floored shack heavy with child, surveying the shambles of her young adulthood, Madalyn was to have her second and grandest antiepiphany. As Bill Murray related in his poignant and fiery autobiography, one evening in the early spring of 1946 an intense Midwestern electrical storm with Old Testament fury exploded outside the flimsy walls of the house. As a bolt of lightning hit nearby, followed by a huge crash of thunder, the pregnant Madalyn announced she was going to go out into the maelstrom and "challenge God to strike me and this child dead with one of those lightning bolts."

With family members gathered, she went into the stormy night, looked up—her face illuminated by pulses of lightning, perhaps wet with rain as well—and she shook her fist at the sky, cursing God. She cursed Him violently and extravagantly so that He would have no choice but to strike her down for her blasphemies. But, for whatever reason, God was reluctant to take His cue from Madalyn, and she swaggered back into the house, elated, proclaiming her survival as incontrovertible proof that God did not exist.

If Madalyn could face down God, she certainly could handle her ex-Marine husband. She waited calmly for him to find her. When Roths finally hunted down his errant wife and discovered that she was about to deliver another man's child, the cuckolded Marine reacted with what can only be described as gallantry above and beyond the call of duty. Roths not only offered to stay with Madalyn, but he wanted to adopt the pilot's child. She refused. Instead she initiated and pursued divorce proceedings against him.

Not long afterward, Madalyn delivered a son, William Joseph Murray III, on May 26, 1946. It was a thirty-five-mile drive to the hospital, and when the doctor delivered the newborn into his mother's arms she said that she was shocked at how battered and blue he was. Nonetheless, she was overwhelmed with maternal joy. In her diary she wrote, "He almost did not make it. I was so proud and happy."

The willful new mother named her bastard son after the father, who denied his paternity. As if to reinforce her never-to-be-consummated wish of marriage to her wartime lover and, as well, to point an accusatory finger of guilt at him, Madalyn changed her own name to Murray. She then filed what would be the first lawsuit of a lifetime of filings across the United States—a paternity action against the absent father, William J. Murray Jr. With what would become legendary litigious audacity, Madalyn entered into evidence a pair of the war hero's pants to substantiate her claim. The jury found for her and the judge ordered Murray to pay child support of fifteen dollars a month until their son was eighteen.

Madalyn's comeback continued. With a Veterans Administration loan, she bought a house for the whole family—mother, father, brother Irv—in a tiny Ohio town named Hayesville in the north-central part of the state. Madalyn would ever after mythologize their residence into a bucolic "farm." But according to residents, it was just a simple two-story home on Main Street with a modest yard. The only relation the home would have to a farm was the cow that Madalyn bought and put in the front yard—much to the consternation of the neighbors.

With GI Bill education funds available, Madalyn reenrolled in college. Her choice was determined by geography. The only college within daily commuting distance of Hayesville and the "farm" was Ashland College, a pleasant thirty-minute drive to the north. But geographical considerations or not, it was a mind-boggling choice considering Madalyn's triumph over God the night of the maelstrom.

Ashland College was a religious school. Not just religious—*evangelical*. Founded and administered by the Brethren Church, the college welcomed nonbelievers to the student body with the hope of possible conversion. Although the faculty was laid-back and mellow in their approach to religion, students were required to attend chapel. It was mandatory—so mandatory that when Madalyn enrolled at the college, there was a factory time clock at the chapel entrance, and the students would punch in and out to mark their daily attendance.

By the time that she received her B.A. in history from Ashland College in May 1948, Madalyn was ranked second in her class of forty-three. Her yearbook picture shows a confident and quite attractive woman. Even though she never would particularly care about her appearance, Madalyn at twenty-nine years old was perhaps at her zenith of natural charms. The overeager and horsy teenage look she once had had been supplanted by the sexy wholesomeness of the postwar 1940s. Her hair was thick and well coiffed. Her high cheekbones were accented by the ever-so-slightly Asian cant to her eyes. The smile, with seemingly perfect teeth, was a bit sardonic but pleasantly mature compared to the self-conscious grins of her younger college classmates.

But bills were piling up at home, and the "farm" idyll was rapidly coming to an unhappy conclusion. Brother Irv and "Pup" (Madalyn's lifelong nickname for her father) couldn't find work to make ends meet. Even with Madalyn working full-time as a secretary at the Akron Rubber Company, the family couldn't make the low mortgage payments that the VA allowed.

Pup decided to head for the rumored fount of big blue-collar paychecks—the greener pastures provided by the Texas oil fields—believing that, as an unlicensed electrician and jack-of-all-trades, he would find somebody to put him to work. The rest of the Murray-Mays clan joined up with Pup in Texas within the year. Abandoning most of their furniture, they loaded as many of their belongings as possible on top of two automobiles and headed down to Houston in a kind of Okie-from-Ohio caravan.

There, with her capacities for hard work running at full open, Madalyn got a job as a probation officer and enrolled in night school at South Texas College of Law. As with Ashland College, her choice of a school again demonstrated that pragmatism dominated principle, for the South Texas College of Law was owned and operated by none other than the Young Men's Christian Association. It must have been crunch time for Madalyn, juggling the responsibilities of motherhood, riding herd on a case-load of hard cons, and learning the law—all at the same time. Perhaps it was too much to ask. She graduated from law school in 1952, but evidently took and failed the Texas bar exam.

Passing or failing the exam didn't make much difference for Madalyn because the family was on the move again. Pup had been talked into going to Baltimore by a sister-in-law, with the lure of starting an intrafamily business of some sort. By November 1952, the Mays-Murray clan had moved once again, this time to a brick row house in north-central Baltimore. It must have seemed like depressing déjà vu, since the Baltimore row house was close to a clone of the family's factory row house in Ohio: brick, shared common walls, two-story, and cookie-cutter same as the neighboring structures.

To deepen the family demoralization, the Mays-Murrays had abandoned almost all their furniture in the moves from Ohio and Texas. They hardly had anything with which to furnish the dark and dispiriting interior of their new home. Lena Mays pawned her diamond ring so that basics, such as chairs and tables, could be purchased. Worse, at least for young Bill Murray, was that there weren't enough rooms to go around, so he had to sleep next to his grandparents' double bed.

Irv Mays, Madalyn's brother, was unable to find regular employment in Baltimore, and in fact he was never to hold down a full-time job again. John Mays never would either. Pup bought a big TV set in 1953, turned up the volume, and sat in front of it. He would keep the sound up so high that normal conversation in the home was an impossibility until he died ten years later.

• • •

Madalyn became pregnant soon again, this time by a "local Italian man," as Bill Murray would put it, who happened to be a talented aeronautical engineer. Madalyn's thoughts about her

neighborhood lover would later provide possibly the most touch-
ing expression of personal emotions that she would ever make
publicly. She told *Playboy* interviewer Richard Tregaskis: "I loved
him madly for some time. I don't think anybody in the world
thought he was gentle, but he was gentle with me. And he
treated me like a woman, which is all I really ask or want. I felt
handled by him, and this is a good feeling. . . . I loved him very
much."

Later in her life, the unfeminine sloppiness of dress, the lack
of makeup, the lumpy figure, the aggressive voice spewing out
profanities would point for some toward Madalyn being lesbian.
But they were wrong. Her expressions were those of a committed
heterosexual. In the *Playboy* interview, she went on to say: "I just
want a man—a real, two-balled masculine guy—and there aren't
many of them around, believe me. But I do want somebody my
own age, and somebody who has brains enough to keep me interested and to earn enough money to support me in the style to
which I've become accustomed. And I want a big man physically
as well as intellectually. I want a man with the thigh muscles to
give me a good frolic in the sack, the kind who'll tear hell out of
a thick steak. . . ."

Certainly the physical attraction that Madalyn felt for her
"tall, dark, and handsome" neighbor was evidenced by the birth
of her second bastard son, Jon Garth, to whom she also gave the
Murray name, out of ease and perhaps to spare her local lover
embarrassment. Whatever the case, Madalyn evidently did not
take to motherhood with Jon Garth any more than she did with
her elder son, Bill, who would write perhaps the most chilling
passage in his book when describing his brother's early childhood
in the Baltimore row house:

He was held and touched only when he was fed or changed.
He was rarely removed from his crib in the dining room,

except when relatives came to visit. Suffering from this cruel isolation, as he grew older Jon Garth sought attention by banging his head against the headboard of his crib. Some days he would keep this up for what seemed to be hours. I heard the thudding of his head, even above the television set. . . .

THREE

Jihad!

How come it's so quiet in here?" Madalyn asked Bill as they walked down the corridor of his junior high school. Madalyn, registering Bill in person a few days late, glanced into an open classroom. The students were standing quietly with their heads bowed, reciting the Lord's Prayer. "Do they do this every day or is this something special?" she demanded. "Every day," her son replied. Madalyn Murray's eyes turned to hazel slits.

She threw off a wake of negative high-energy particles as she stalked rapidly down the silent hallways of Baltimore's Woodbourne Junior High School to the administrative offices in September 1960. There was no way these sons-of-bitches were going to get away with forcing her son to say that groveling, wormlike, gawd damn Lord's Prayer. No sir.

With Bill in tow, she barreled into the admission counselor's office in full battle mode. There, a pleasant young man's smile quickly turned into an appalled stare as Madalyn semicoherently snarled something about prayers. "Is your son a student here?" the man stuttered, vamping for time to gather himself before the onslaught of this pear-shaped banshee. Madalyn got right up in his face. "He will be starting today. I'm an atheist and I don't want him taught any gawd damned prayers."

The counselor started filling out forms for Bill as Madalyn seethed. As he worked, he commented that Baltimore public schools had had students saying daily prayers since before the American Revolution, and he doubted that would change because of a confrontation with her. Purpling with rage, Madalyn signed the late-enrollment forms and leveled a final broadside: "This won't be the last time you hear from me about your gawd damn prayers in this school!" The counselor, with hackles now raised, told her that if she didn't like prayer in the public schools she ought to enroll her son in a private one.

"It doesn't matter where I put him. You people have to be stopped," she rejoined.

"Then why don't you sue us?" he said.

Madalyn bored into him through her eye-slits in silence as her brain quickly absorbed the concept. Given her superior intelligence, her legal background, and her extraordinary—but so far untapped—political intuition, it is likely that during that momentary silence she saw a vista of her life before her.

It was an illumination. Yes. Of course! She would sue—and it wouldn't make a damn bit of difference if she won or lost. It would be a great suit—a challenge to the system that would force a legal soul-searching right down to the very foundations of the nation's principles. It was about freedom and the rights of individuals in a democracy. Madalyn saw herself mounting a sacred war to secure and uphold these ideals. She was going to be a female freedom fighter the likes of which had never been seen before in American history—a godless Joan of Arc.

But first, the initial campaign had to be launched. This meant the enlistment of her son. Madalyn ordered Bill to log everything that he observed his classmates doing that had any religious overtones, starting with his second day back in school. Unfortunately for the campaign, Bill's spiritual spy log was slim. After weeks of observation, the only religious event that Bill would be able to record was the morning prayers.

No matter. On the Sunday preceding his third week of

school, Madalyn sat her son down to discuss her war plan for changing public religious practices in the United States. Pounding the table, she told Bill that she planned to pull him out of school unless he was allowed to leave his homeroom when the prayers were being said. The plan sounded great to Bill—as it would to any fourteen-year-old facing a pile of homework. The next day, Madalyn informed the school that her son, being an atheist, must be excused from the morning prayer ritual.

You could almost hear Madalyn's peremptory demand crashing through the tiers of Baltimore's horrified educational bureaucracy. Good gracious. This was ridiculous. Incredible. Pupils had been reciting the Lord's Prayer for centuries. It wasn't discretionary by school or classroom—it was rule of law with clear specifications: Recitations were to come only from the King James Version of the Holy Bible. Its exclusive use had been specifically approved for schools in Maryland in 1839, at the very birth of the state public school system, and adopted by the Baltimore Board of Commissioners, which officially codified the regulation in 1905.

On October 12, 1960, Madalyn's godless jihad was opposed by Baltimore school officials, in what was to be one of a series of foolish, bollixed decisions that played right into the hands of the cagey heretic. The superintendent of secondary schools told Madalyn on the phone that her son would definitely not be excused from the morning prayers. "Bill will, Bill shall, attend these services," Madalyn was told. Not only would he not be excused, he would have to stand, to bow his head in an attitude of "respect and reverence." As a special dispensation, he could "refuse to say the prayer," Madalyn was informed, but he will be required to "move his lips as if he were saying it."

The grand, stupid arrogance of the superintendent's position filled Madalyn with glee. The fool thought he was a medieval cardinal issuing a bull to an unwashed, ignorant peasant. Immediately Madalyn hunched over her typewriter. Speed-slamming the keys, she created the message that would begin her public journey to the mountaintop. She wrote to the Baltimore *Sun*.

Dear Sir:

I have had enough. When the last infamous epithet is cast and when the speaker or writer gropes for an even more vile indictment of a person or a system, invariably the word then hurled is "Atheist."

I have had enough, for I am an Atheist, and I will no longer be maligned and abused by identification with all that is evil, corrupt and noxious. . . . What of us who are Atheists, agnostics, humanists, non-believers, and those who are unchurched? There are 68,000,000 (sixty-eight million) Americans who do not belong to a church. We have no spokesman in Congress, no liaison representative at the White House, no organized lobby or pressure group in Washington, D.C. Who speaks for us? Who defends us?

. . . When we go to a public meeting why are we subjected to prayer, in the efficacy of which we do not believe? When we handle money, why, since 1955, are we confronted with money minted with In God We Trust on it? Why should our mail be stamped "Pray for Peace"? As we pledged allegiance, why should this pledge be extorted from us to a nation "under God"? Is your belief so thin that you must force it upon others?

. . . I have had enough. Therefore, I have withdrawn my fourteen-year-old son from Woodbourne Junior High School, in an act of civil disobedience, in defiance of Maryland Code, Article 77, Section 231, because the State of Maryland, in the persons of the Board of Education of Baltimore City, has violated both the First and the Fourteenth Amendments of the Constitution of the United States by requiring daily Bible reading and recitation of the Lord's Prayer in their public classrooms.

And may my conscience now Rest In Peace.

Madalyn went over the letter/manifesto with Bill. He approved. They drove together to the main post office where, with a dramatic pause, Madalyn flicked it through the mail slot and Bill—by now a full collaborator as well as an inveterate wiseacre—made the sign of the cross.

The next morning Madalyn rushed out to get the *Sun,* but there was nothing. There was nothing the day after, nor the day after that. Finally, six days later, a reporter for the newspaper knocked on the door of the Mays-Murrays' row house. Stephen Nordlinger introduced himself with a soft voice and a limp handshake. He was almost half a foot shorter than Bill, who was already well over six feet tall at fourteen. Nordlinger had a diffident, quiet air common to intellectually oriented reporters. Over cups of steaming tea and with Pup's TV set blaring, he took copious notes as Madalyn traced her surprisingly cogent arguments for herself, her son, and atheism. Nordlinger was impressed. Halfway through Madalyn's monologue he called the newspaper and requested a photographer.

Two days later, Nordlinger's story broke, with the headline writer indulging in an mini-orgy of alliteration—"Boy, 14, Balks at Bible Reading"—over the lengthy three-column piece. The low-keyed Nordlinger had drawn the battle lines skillfully with multiple levels of conflict: Young versus Old, David (Bill) versus Goliath (the superintendent), Freedom versus Conformity, even Communism versus Capitalism (an essay Bill had submitted in praise of the Soviet system had evoked serious anger from one of his teachers).

Nordlinger's story was a watershed. Not only would it launch Madalyn on the path to world fame, it marked a sea change in her view of the rules of the game. Madalyn had never been in contact with top-notch, big-city daily journalism. She clearly held Nordlinger in high esteem—in some degree of awe. Like the rest of the public, she had no idea how articles were written, even though she read the newspaper every day. The piece gave her an inside look for the first time, and she was shocked by what she saw.

Casual conversation that she assumed was off-the-record was used in-depth. According to Madalyn's accounts, statements made by school officials were altered and made less inflammatory. The article had Bill making statements that he never made. She was aghast—and she was profoundly impressed.

Before she had finished reading Nordlinger's story, the phone started ringing. First were local radio and TV news reporters looking for sound bites for morning newscasts and cut-ins. Then came the light heavyweights—the regional TV news affiliate stations calling for interviews. And finally, the full monty—network news producers from Manhattan, ringing to set up coverage arrangements with her. They wanted her on the national nightly news! By Madalyn's count, within three weeks more than one hundred individual articles about her and Bill appeared in the three Baltimore dailies alone. She and Bill were on the local news every night for more than a week straight. Madalyn said she soon lost track of the number of radio interviews she did—but there were many dozens.

She loved it. Madalyn would accommodate any and all. Endless pots of coffee and tea were brewed for the newsmen. Beer by the case was available for the often thirsty scribes. Madalyn was a savant at rapidly summing up and providing for their professional needs along with the personal ones. She became not only the subject of the news but an active and ready partner in creating it: She produced and edited herself on herself.

Madalyn decided that Bill, after missing eleven days of school, would go back the next day and gainsay the religious ceremonies in direct fashion—by refusing to participate in the homeroom prayer services. He would walk to Woodbourne Junior High by himself. It would make *wonderful* visuals: the young, strong, tall boy, challenging the powers that be, in a lone walk to his school—a pubescent version of *High Noon,* the famous film starring Gary Cooper. Besides, she had received enough serious threats from anonymous callers that she felt that Bill's return to school not only would provide the requisite drama for the media vultures, but might afford Bill some protection against possible violence.

Oh, yes! The news guys LOVED Madalyn's script for them. Madalyn was to arrange the media circus with the deftness of a budding impresario: ENG (electronic news gathering) vehicles with photographers, field producers, and reporters would keep pace behind Bill moving at three to four miles per hour, and two print journalists would follow on foot a few dozen yards behind him on the sidewalk.

A little before seven-thirty in the morning on a fine fall day, Bill, feeling like "shark bait," walked through a crowd of hostile, milling neighbors toward school two miles away. Behind Bill and the news media, Madalyn, like a battalion commander monitoring the deployment of troops according to the drawn order of battle, trailed at a distance in her car.

Even though she was now a celebrity, Madalyn archly refused to dress up for the occasion. She wore a wraparound housedress and a big corduroy car coat that belonged to brother Irv. Of her attire for the event, Madalyn was to earnestly write that she would not, could not—in good conscience—don "the accouterments of the female in polite society: an unendurable girdle, high-heeled shoes to totter in, a mask of makeup and sprayed-up beehive hair with no brains underneath."

Unfortunately for the gathered news media, Bill was not brained by a rock during his dramatic walk to Woodbourne

Junior High. There were a few catcalls as he approached the
school, but nothing more. And school officials—in perhaps the
only intelligent move they made during the entire four-year
affair—trumped Madalyn. They doused the anticipated show-
down by having Bill report to the office rather than homeroom.
It was an effective strategy that was to frustrate Madalyn—but
only momentarily.

This was Holy War. It would be like all Madalyn's wars:
nasty, personal, psychological *mano a mano*. The enemy would be
vilified in order to inspire her legions. The Baltimore Establishment would be a fascistic monolith dominated by religious
zealots right out of the Inquisition. The school administrators—
who really *were* clueless and arrogant—would become imbeciles
not worthy of regard—subhuman reflexive idiots. Bill's principal
at Woodbourne would be described by Madalyn as a wanton,
painted lady of the night who desired to physically seduce her
young male students.

It was wild stuff. The media loved it. Madalyn could sell
newspapers. Even the most grizzled daily reporters hadn't seen
anything like her in all their years of beating shoe leather. You
could love her or hate her, but either way you *had* to read about
her. She was terrific—the beers, the scripted sequences, the
housecoats and bawdy talk. Oh, that Madalyn, she could provide
a mother lode of hot copy—on demand.

On November 2, 1960, Bill on his own initiative defeated the
school district's plan. Instead of reporting to the office first thing
in the morning as usual, Bill slipped into his homeroom just
prior to the prayer's being said. With his "heart pounding," he
stood when the teacher asked all the pupils to rise for the morning prayer. She immediately noticed Bill—as he was quite tall—
but said nothing, evidently thinking that the office had approved
of his return. The other students stared at their classmate in the
hushed room, as the teacher paged through the Bible. Before a

passage could be read, Bill, his face flushed, uttered, "This is ridiculous," grabbed his books and coat, and left for the office.

Madalyn was already giddy when she heard the news from Bill. Coincidental to Bill's actions, the Maryland attorney general, C. Ferdinand Sybert, had issued a ruling backing up the school board and its prayer policy as well as threatening Madalyn with criminal prosecution for contributing to truancy. Sybert had also recommended that the school board excuse any child who objected to the opening exercises from attendance in homeroom. This last point was a nod toward Madalyn—an attempt at injecting some fairness and balance into his opinion. But it was always unwise to give Madalyn-the-Mujahiddin any daylight. As things would turn out, the attempt to appease her would be a momentous legal mistake—and she knew it.

But to exploit any gaffes by the enemy would require that Madalyn retain good—preferably great—legal counsel. This wasn't easy. She was nearly destitute. She had repelled her only legal ally—the American Civil Liberties Union—by divulging to them that she had financial backers who were rabidly anti-Semitic. Madalyn could not argue in court as an attorney for her son because she either flunked or refused to take the Maryland bar examination. Nor did she want to humble herself to the legal community by shopping her case.

Necessity would lead Madalyn to one of the stranger bedfellows in her life of strange bedfellows—Leonard J. Kerpelman. Kerpelman was a thirty-something Orthodox Jewish attorney, born and raised in the Baltimore area. He apparently was a believer in the school of self-advertisement via taking on wacky, high-profile cases—one of which involved securing the right of a South American entrepreneur to hold a bullfight in the Baltimore Memorial Stadium.

Kerpelman showed up at one of Madalyn's well-publicized confrontations with officials at Bill's junior high school. She claimed that, during a lull in the skirmish, Kerpelman sidled up to her and whispered that he would take her case for free, if she'd hire him. After that, Madalyn said that Kerpelman called her continually at home, pestering her to allow him to represent Bill.

When she vetted his status with other attorneys in Baltimore, Madalyn reported that they literally laughed in her face at the mention of Kerpelman's name. But regardless of Kerpelman's standing, Madalyn had no other choice but to hire him. It was a decision driven by circumstance. Kerpelman was a freebie and even though the case looked like it had Supreme Court potential, no other lawyer in Baltimore would touch it. There was another reason to hire Kerpelman. Although she would kvetch unceasingly about Kerpelman—"his cheap clothing, his dandruff, his dirty collars"—Madalyn was actually secretly delighted with the arrangement, since Kerpelman would allow her to participate in the legal drafting and strategy, accommodating the needs of her ravenous ego.

As attorney Kerpelman came on board, the Mays-Murray household was functioning in a state of siege. Their cars were egged, their flower beds trampled, their windows broken by rocks. But if anything should have been worrisome, it was the mail Madalyn was receiving. The very first letter she opened after the Baltimore Sun's initial story read: "Dear Commie, I think you are a Slut. Why don't you go back to Russia where you belong." It would turn out to be one of the more benign missives she received. Others read:

> . . . You must be an insidious creature, without even a brain. No wonder you're crazy. You probably have no children either, let alone a man. Your hooked, ugly nose, triple chin and fat body are enough to make you godless.

> You will repent, and damn soon a .3030 [rifle bullet] will fix you nuts. You will have bad luck forever. You atheist,

you mongrel, you rat, you good for nothing shit, you damn
gutter rat. Jesus will fix you, you filthy scum.

Madalyn's personal favorite was a letter that had the printed
message "This is my toast for you—here's crud in your eyes—and
I hope somebody drops poison in your beer." Pasted on the page
was a picture of Madalyn from one of the newspapers—smeared
with feces. Madalyn would keep this horrid keepsake for years,
producing it, still reeking, for select journalists.

Nevertheless, by Christmas 1960 all things were rosy for
Madalyn. Her jihad was rolling along with the court filings. She
was becoming an international figure and couldn't have cared less
what her neighbors thought. As far as the poison-pen letters were
concerned—fact be known—she loved them deeply and patho-
logically. At this point, the post office was delivering Madalyn's
mail in canvas bags, given the great quantity, and now coming
alongside the thousands of letters of hate mail was *fan* mail. Fan
mail with cash and checks. Praise gawd!

This life was good—even if it had its moments of utter
incongruity, as when a crowd appeared before the Mays-Murray
home in the evening a few days before Christmas. It was a choir,
in all likelihood from a local congregation, that had come to carol
the newly media-anointed atheist high priestess.

Paradoxically, Madalyn loved Christmas carols and would
always have them playing during the holidays in the privacy of
her home. In any case, the choir sang carol after carol in front of
the row house. Finally they began the universally moving "Silent
Night," and Madalyn was enraptured. Bill broke the spell by asking permission to go out and thank the carolers. "No," Madalyn
told her son. "They came out of hatred to taunt us with it. They
would be appalled to learn that we love music too. Let them go.
They have filled their mission of hating—and we had a pleasant
hour here. Let's all have some hot spiced brandy. It was so lovely!"

O fficers Larry Wight and Bob Lee couldn't have been too happy when they heard the dispatcher tell them to respond to a late-night domestic disturbance. Any patrol cop will tell you the same thing: the worst calls to make are for family disputes. You just never know what you're getting into. It might be anything from a minor family spat with raised voices to a homicide in progress. You could get offered a cup of coffee, or get blown away at the doorstep. But there was one good thing about the call for the two young patrolmen: It broke the cold monotony of dogwatch in the "Adam" patrol sector, a tattered blue-collar district of Peoria, Illinois.

As Wight and Lee approached the decrepit two-story residence, they knew the call wasn't going to be for a coffee klatch. Sitting on the porch was a young man—late teens to early twenties—cradling his head and moaning over and over, "He hit me." He was bleeding badly from a wound on his forehead. It looked like his skull might have an indentation fracture. The window on the front door of the duplex was smashed. There was blood all over the entryway, and the officers could hear shouting coming from the kitchen of the ground floor apartment.

They cautiously entered. There a middle-aged woman was holding a large knife, with a small boy huddling next to her. When she saw the officers she screamed, "He's trying to kill me," pointing to a well-built, hippie-type male—early twenties—holding a claw hammer. The man had shoulder-length, greasy black hair and a pearl stud earring. Neither was a common style for Peoria in the mid-1970s. The man's facial features were an eerie multiple overlay of Asiatic, Negroid, and Caucasian. His eyes were wild, with wired pinhole pupils.

Officer Wight ordered them both to put down their weapons. The woman quickly complied, laying the large knife on the kitchen counter. But the man held on to the hammer and turned toward the officers. Raising it he said, "I'm gonna kill you."

The patrolmen started backing up. As they did, they drew their revolvers and leveled them at the man. Wight shouted at him to "Drop it!"—but he kept coming. The officers retreated into the entrance hallway. There Wight stopped, took aim, and fired into the man's chest. A barrage of shots by both officers followed. The hammer wielder fell to the floor dying. Behind him in the kitchen, the young boy was gushing blood from his thigh—shot by one of the rounds that missed their target.

The woman with the knife turned out to be the dead man's mother. Betty Waters told the police that he was trying to hit her and a younger brother with the hammer, and she had drawn a kitchen knife to defend them. She told police that her son was high on drugs and that he had just burglarized a drugstore. She added she also thought he was a degenerate who was living with "queers" and "shooting downers." She didn't blame the officers at all for shooting him. She said, "If I had a gun I would have shot him and he's my son."

At the funeral home where the body was taken, police investigators found track marks on both of Steven Plumley's arms, and noted that he was wearing a roach clip necklace. They took a blood sample from the corpse. The pathology report indicated that Plumley was legally drunk and stoned on barbiturates when he was shot by police. The investigation into his background determined that the young man had a long history of problems, mostly psychiatric in nature. He'd been convicted of armed robbery—stealing three dollars and some cigarettes from a cabbie—and had served time for resisting arrest. His late teen years were spent in the Peoria state mental hospital.

On the eve of his shooting death by police, Steven Plumley was homeless. Evidently, on a freezing-cold winter night he had come to his mother's house to sleep where it was warm. When she refused him, he became enraged, and when a neighbor came to check on the disturbance, he hammered the neighbor in the head. But he couldn't bring himself to strike his mother. Instead, it appears that Steven Plumley committed what is known as suicide-by-police in front of her—a relatively well known phenomenon in law enforcement.

His mother, Betty Waters, had a long arrest record herself for a variety of crimes—theft, battery, solicitation for prostitution. In her first arrest as a young adult, police had broken up a wild late-night party at Betty's apartment by hauling everybody down to the station. In their report, besides leads on stolen property, the police noted that some of the celebrants were only partially clothed. They also found two toddlers who had slept through the party cuddled together on a bed. Police left the little boys in the care of neighbors and charged Betty Waters with criminal endangerment of her sons, two-year-old Steven Plumley and a five-year-old, named David Waters, who would morph from a sweet, quiet child into a frozen-hearted murderer capable of snuffing out the lives of the world's only atheist royalty without an iota of remorse.

FOUR

Celebrity, Money,
and Cultural Combat

*T*he *Realist,* the most infamous counterculture magazine the United States had ever seen, was usually written, edited, pasted up, and published single-handedly by Paul Krassner. The shaggy-haired radical would work from funky New York office space with minimal trappings, since he needed to be able to shut things down instantly and move, if a serious libel judgment threatened or arrest was imminent for other illegal activities.

Like the redoubtable Dr. Hunter S. Thompson, he was alleged to have been a voracious user of hallucinogenic drugs. And like Thompson, Krassner was a man who could write and edit—despite his drug usage—with powerful rationality against the mainstream of his own culture. It was an unlikely melding of abilities—but then genius, regardless of variety, often flourishes amidst the exotic fauna of the chosen.

Naturally Krassner prattled with the other Olympian radicals, revolutionaries, and visionaries of that wildly fecund era. Ram Dass, Timothy Leary, Abbie Hoffman, Allen Ginsberg, Mort Sahl, Ken Kesey, and Lenny Bruce (whose autobiography Krassner edited) were some of the illuminati of Krassner's milieu. Along with his ability to thrill his fellow counterculturalists with spine-tingling journalistic nose-thumbs at the Establishment, Krassner had a sharp instinct for spotting and cultivating new radical talent.

So it wasn't surprising when Krassner, in 1961, sent a letter of inquiry to a Baltimore housewife who was heavy-duty hassling the local government with a lawsuit demanding an end to prayers in school. Krassner, a professed atheist along with being a professed anti-everything-except-anarchy, asked Madalyn Murray if she'd like to write about her experiences.

Madalyn declined, saying she wasn't a writer. But Krassner was an aggressive editor-publisher, unmellowed even by massive doses of THC. He prevailed by asking her to "just send me letters" and he would edit them into articles. This was done. Krassner began publishing his "Malice in Maryland" series—taking Madalyn to the very tip of the counterculture spearhead in one swift leap.

She was ready for the call when it came—although she didn't fit the mold that well. She was stout, bordering on obese, and the counterculturist female icons of the era were skinny, with the exception of big Mama Cass. Nor did Madalyn like illicit drugs. Her thing was booze. (Bill, her son, would recount how, at ten years old, he would join his mother and grandmother drinking warm tea and wine after dinner to the point of inebriation.) The Fugs? The Beatles? Bob Dylan? Jazz? Gawd, no. Madalyn's tastes in music were cloyingly bourgeois. A good aural high for Madalyn might be Mantovani with strings doing "The Blue Danube."

But all that was tangential. Madalyn had a type of personal power that can't be precisely defined except to say it is present in every star human. In her case, her persona was augmented by creative biles and loquacious toxins that gave her instant, undisputed entree and automatic good standing with the elite of the American counterculture. Of course, it helped to have the imprimatur of being published in Krassner's *The Realist*.

It was a given that Madalyn would come out swinging for the fences in her first professional journalistic foray. The opening paragraph was classic Madalyn. "Some people have interpreted my position to mean that I am against religious ceremonies in schools," she wrote.

> This is not true. I am against religion. I am against schools. I am against apple pies. I am against "Americanism." I am against mothers. I am against adulterated foods. I am against nuclear fission testing. I am against commercial television. I am against all newspapers. I am against 99-and-44/100% of the magazines. I am against Eisenhower, Nixon, Kennedy, Lodge. I'm even against giving the country back to the Indians. Why should the poor fools be stuck with this mess?

The rest of the five-thousand-word article touched on Madalyn's mythic themes of personal heroic self-sacrifice—professions of inordinate maternal love (mixed with peculiar codes of discipline for her *exceptional* children) and of course descriptions of her ongoing martyrdom at the hands of Christian zealots. It was a self-portrait for public consumption that Madalyn would only touch up cosmetically until her death nearly forty years later.

Krassner was gassed with his discovery. She was a perfect contributor to *The Realist:* a housecoat-wearing, atheist-feminist martyr who used the right recipe of hip intellectual socialist patois mixed with incendiary issues—God, kids, and religious freedom. Yeah, she was a mind-blower.

It was with pleasure that Krassner launched Madalyn on her career as firebrand atheist. He was also the first to establish that she had surpassing abilities at raising money. In a special dispensation for a contributing writer, Krassner allowed Madalyn to publish her Baltimore address, along with pitiable pleas for financial support from readers to cover the costs of her school prayer lawsuit. "This is sheer insanity," she wrote about her suit. "I don't have $15,000." She then cheekily claimed that she really needed only $14,985—because she was contributing the $15 fee she received from Krassner for the article toward the fund.

The fact was, she didn't need the money for the lawsuit at all. Two other atheist organizations had already covered the filing costs and other incidentals, and her attorney, Leonard Kerpelman, was working pro bono. But Madalyn did need money. She'd been fired from what was to be her last salaried job—as a welfare casework supervisor—and she had to support two young sons, her now deadbeat father and brother, and her mother as well.

Madalyn not only prevailed on Krassner, her discoverer-editor-publisher, to allow her to use his magazine to solicit funds, but she hit him up personally for financial support. Even more amazing is that Krassner, a man who always lived with the specter of utter financial ruin sweeping him away at any moment, acquiesced to underwriting the mortgage on Madalyn's Baltimore row house for an unlimited period of time.

What Krassner didn't know, and what Madalyn neglected to tell him, was that she was receiving thousands of dollars a month in donations—cash and checks with no strings attached.

Or *almost* no strings attached. Madalyn's biggest and earliest sugar daddy was an atheist-nudist wheat farmer from Kansas named Carl Brown. The first letter he wrote Madalyn contained a check for five thousand dollars. He also told her that if she won her lawsuit he'd send substantial stock certificates to her sons for their birthdays. (He was later to keep his word.)

Brown was a believer that man was "simply an animal and should live accordingly." He lived the lone life of a frugal bachelor on his Kansas wheat farm, but was also a sort of civic benefactor for his small town. He single-handedly paid for a municipal swimming pool—perchance to gaze more easily on his neighbors closer to their natural state.

When Brown told Madalyn that he might like to donate his

land for an atheist university, and asked if she'd like to discuss the possibility by flying out with her two boys to Kansas on his nickel, she responded enthusiastically. Madalyn met with Brown at his farm. There he told her that he meant "no harm"—but would she allow him to show her some of his pictures?

A rock-ribbed Republican, Brown had traveled extensively after each farming season was over—regularly attending nudist international conferences in England, Denmark, Japan, Italy, and France—and he wanted to put on a slide show for Madalyn. Madalyn couldn't *really* decline, and she was treated to hours of color slides of "Carl completely nude except for his shoes" in cottages in the English countryside, the woods of France, the hills of Italy, and assorted locations all over the Far East.

Madalyn paid the randy side of farmer Brown no heed, and he was to be one of her staunchest financial supporters during her ascent. According to Madalyn, there were many other contributors. Even if they weren't of the caliber of Carl Brown, Madalyn welcomed all comers who bore money or gifts of value: communists, humanists, Orthodox Jews, antigovernment right-wingers. (Interestingly, Madalyn gloated to *Time* magazine that her biggest financial supporters by occupation were physicians.)

But it wasn't just money that came to the new atheist diva; fruit baskets, flowers, boxes of chocolates, and well-wisher cards poured in from every compass point. Of course, getting all the goodies was balanced by the chance of receiving hate mail smeared with shit, but that was the acceptable price of public love/hate for Madalyn.

• • •

Judge J. Gilbert Prendergast knew it was going to be unpleasant. First, there was all this publicity. Second, there wasn't any precedent in the State of Maryland for the case. School prayer had never been challenged since it was established a century and a half ago. Making things worse was that he had to deal with a weirdo plaintiff and counsel—some communist-sympathizing, atheist militant and a publicity-hound lawyer.

However, on Thursday, March 2, 1961, the judge patiently listened to a weak argument by the attorney for the school board and a disturbingly tight line of reasoning from Leonard Kerpelman, plaintiff Murray's counsel. Prendergast could see that he wasn't going to get much help from the defendant's table, so he grilled Kerpelman himself, leveling question after question at him: How were the King James and the Douay Versions of the Bible sectarian? What was it specifically about prayer that made it religious? How could there be an objection under the First Amendment, as it applied to religion, if the plaintiff was obviously without religion? Kerpelman responded as though he'd been pondering each question for months. Prendergast took the case under advisement.

Kerpelman's startlingly adept presentation notwithstanding, on April 29 Judge Prendergast dismissed Madalyn's suit. He opined that granting her claims and banning prayer from Baltimore's schools would be to "subordinate all pupils to atheist belief." He went on to state, "If God were removed from the classroom, there would remain only atheism." Further warming to the task and warping legal realities with abandon, Prendergast boomed, "Any reference to the Declaration of Independence would be prohibited because it concludes with the historic words of the signers, '. . . with a firm reliance on the protection of Divine Providence, we mutually pledge to each other our Lives, our Fortunes, and our sacred Honor.'" The judge went on to finally fret that it was "even possible that United States currency would not be accepted in school cafeterias because every bill and coin contains the familiar inscription IN GOD WE TRUST."

The Baltimore Board of Education had won the battle—and was to lose the war. What appeared as a great victory for the board enclosed the kernel of its defeat. In fact, the lawyers for the City of Baltimore had made a serious strategic error—as bad as that contained in the opinion of the state attorney general. They had filed what is called a demurrer as a response to Madalyn's claims in Prendergast's court, and when Madalyn saw what they had done in prehearing, she danced a jig.

A demurrer is a haughty legal maneuver that effectively says that you believe your opponent's case is so weak that you don't even deign to answer it. Technically, it is an objection to the presentation of an argument by the complaining party, stating that their case is so insufficient that it can't sustain a favorable action in a court of law. In layman's terms, it puts much of the case in the lap of the judge—but gives the judge no helpful legal ammunition to rule for the demurrer.

In Maryland at the time, filing of a demurrer had a special and relevant effect. It could be viewed as an admission by the respondent that all the allegations of the complaining party were *true*—essentially saying to the court, "Even if everything the complainant says is true—so what?"

Not only was the foolish and arrogant demurrer going to contribute heavily to the eventual defeat of the school board, it also allowed Madalyn to continue her legal guerrilla warfare with minimum resources. Before the demurrer, Madalyn had worried that the cost of transcriptions alone might overwhelm her limited financial resources, and now her enemy had delivered her from the brink. If Madalyn had been forced to prove all her allegations in open court, it would have meant days of testimony, endless summonsing, and hours of expert double-talk. It also might have further demonstrated the weakness of her counsel—who Madalyn feared might fatally screw up at any moment.

It was, as Madalyn put it, "all too good to be true." Now all she and her attorney would have to do was organize and present oral arguments and minimal briefs. She directed Kerpelman to immediately file with the Maryland Court of Appeals—the state's highest court.

FIVE

Pup's Death

On January 9, 1962, Madalyn took Jon Garth and Bill out of school to observe oral arguments on her prayer suit before the Maryland Court of Appeals. The court, located in the historic town of Annapolis, was set in a perfectly maintained circle of Colonial-style brick government buildings on a rolling green. The interior chamber with its arching vaults contained a giant hall of cool marble accented with ornate hardwoods. The panorama was unified by a graceful grand stairway that Y'ed to the second floor where visitors could ogle the scene of judicial splendor from above.

The chambers, where the legal affairs of the State of Maryland were performed, were also elegant—bordering on opulent. The waiting rooms had commodious leather armchairs and enormous mahogany tables surrounded by walnut paneling. The hearing room of the Court of Appeals itself was no less dazzling. There was gunstock-quality wood everywhere, and thick crimson carpeting covered the floors beneath a stained-glass dome.

According to Madalyn's recollections, the setting not only awed Leonard Kerpelman, it addled him with terror as he stood before the appellate bar. Her lawyer "was frightened out of what little wits he had," Madalyn was to write. They had worked for months on the appeal. "I sat there in the court, waiting for the ground to open up and swallow me in order to preclude anyone from seeing my embarrassment for him," Madalyn continued. "One reporter whispered to me, 'You have a little gem in that one.' Another one grinned and said, 'Rots of ruck with your counsel.' Even my mother, a dumb broad—if I must categorize her at all—said, 'My, he isn't doing too good is he?'"

In fact, the performance by Kerpelman couldn't have been *that* bad. The court asked for a second round of arguments so that the full panel of justices could hear the constitutional issues involved before considering the case. Nevertheless, when the Maryland Court of Appeals issued its ruling a few months later, it found for the Board of Education against Madalyn. The majority opinion blandly held that the First and Fourteenth Amendments weren't intended "to stifle all rapport between government and religion."

However, the vote was a close four-to-three decision. Not only was the court seriously divided, Chief Judge Frederick Brune was dissenting with what seemed to be a knowing eye toward the United States Supreme Court. Brune noted the religious content of the opening prayer and wrote that it "seems to plainly favor one religion and in doing so against other religions and against non-believers in any religion." The dissenting justices weren't swallowing the school board's seemingly contorted contention that the prayers weren't religious in nature.

True to her word, on May 15, 1962, Madalyn had Kerpelman file an appeal with the United States Supreme Court, to the surprise of her opponents who thought she would quit. It was foolish thinking, since every step of the way there was "a new blast of publicity," as Madalyn would put it. And of course all the media attention converted handsomely into more cash and check donations.

There was also another lucky financial convergence that the lawsuit's publicity brought for Madalyn. The publisher of a small atheist magazine offered to let her take over his business gratis. It wasn't much: basically a masthead, seventy-five dollars in the bank, and a mailing list of some six hundred subscribers. But with her money-sniffing nose keen as a cadaver dog's for decomposing flesh, Madalyn jumped at the chance to obtain a mailing list of hard-core and radicalized atheists.

She sent Bill out to purchase a small A. B. Dick printing press—which he installed in the basement of the row house—and they were in business. Madalyn titled her new magazine *The American Atheist.* The first issue came out on July 1, 1962. The three-page magazine/newsletter contained an outline of her suit filed with the Supreme Court, along with verbiage on the harassment that she and Bill had experienced in Baltimore. But the main theme, as Madalyn readily admitted, was "We're broke!" On the last page she left readers with instructions for seven different methods of contribution and support—checks preferred.

The newsletter was a smashing success. For twelve days the responses poured in—some 225 letters. A fund-raising star was born. The bonanza was on for Bill as well. He may have spent his nights printing flyers and newsletters for his mother in the dank basement of the row house, but he was getting paid royally. Madalyn boosted his allowance from seven dollars to fifty dollars a week, which was definitely serious money for a teenager at the time. Within a year of becoming Madalyn's printer's devil, Bill would be tooling around Baltimore with his own wheels—a fine late-model Oldsmobile Cutlass.

Less than two weeks into 1963, Madalyn had a knock-down drag-out with her father, John Mays, or Pup. Nobody could remember the cause, but the fight started with harsh words over the breakfast table. As she left the house she screamed: "You old bastard. I hope you drop dead." Bill noticed his grandfather's hand shake when the old man put his coffee cup to his lips, as Madalyn slammed the door behind her. That afternoon, John and

Lena Mays went to the A & P to return some pop bottles for a refund. Pup went over to say hello to a favorite checkout cashier, and as he reached out to touch her arm with his hand, he grabbed at his chest instead, and fell to the floor—stone dead.

When Madalyn returned to the house later, not seeing Pup in his favorite armchair in front of the blaring TV, she called out to her mother, "Where's the old man?" Lena walked into the living room, looked directly at her daughter, and said evenly, "You got your wish." She then tersely explained what had happened an hour earlier. According to Bill's account, Madalyn matched her mother's aplomb with her own. She responded, "Well, I'll be. Where's the stiff?"

Since funeral arrangements hadn't been made, Madalyn brusquely ordered her sixteen-year-old son to "call up some undertakers and find the cheapest one. Then have them pick up the stiff from Memorial Hospital." Bill got on the phone and called funeral homes to retrieve his beloved grandfather's corpse, as Madalyn prompted in the background, "Tell 'em we want a cheap wood box." When Bill reported that state law required that Pup's body had to be embalmed within twenty-four hours, Madalyn groused darkly, "Just a bunch of shit to make money for the undertakers."

However, by the time that she and the rest of the family reached the mortuary, Madalyn had been overwhelmed by a tidal wave of remorse. She told the undertaker there had been a mistake. She wanted the most expensive casket that the funeral home could provide for her father. She then kept "a solitary vigil" next to the coffin for two full days. After she paid the mortician for all the funeral expenses, she took the receipt, wrote "PAID IN FULL" on it, and placed it next to Pup's body.

Eighteen months later she'd tell *Playboy* the heartrending story of her father's death: "The neighborhood children, of course, were forbidden by their parents to play with my little boy, Garth, so I finally got him a little kitten to play with. A couple of weeks later we found it on the porch with its neck wrung. And then late one night our house was attacked with stones and bricks by five or six young Christians, and my father got very upset and frightened. Well, the next day he dropped dead of a heart attack."

But it was neither the "young Christians" nor Madalyn's parting words that killed John Mays. At sixty-nine, he was a man worn out from hard drinking, smoking, and too many rashers of bacon with his eggs. Nonetheless, the beatification of Pup would become a propaganda fixture for Madalyn. As a superlative political operative, she would use Pup's death for her own cause, even though she knew full well that he would have hated being her conscript-in-death. Madalyn's autobiographical book on the Baltimore school prayer battle, *An Atheist Epic,* is dedicated to her father with these words:

This book is for
Pup
who died in Baltimore, Md.,
. . . and for
those glorious Christians,
known to us by name,
who killed him.

SIX

Victory on High:
Madalyn at the Supreme Court

Oral arguments before the Supreme Court were delivered on a brisk and clear late February day a month after Pup's death in 1963. It was the era, and the kind of Washington weather, that might bring to mind an image of Camelot and Jackie Kennedy clad in a neo-czarist Oleg Cassini outfit: high-hemline wool suit with modest heels, dark hose, a chicly sculpted A-line coat, and an adorable sable hat perched ravishingly on her very own Jackie-do.

God knows where Madalyn came up with her outfit for the Supreme Court, but it appeared to be a Cassini knockoff—a hideous one that could only catalyze suicidal ideation in the original designer. Her hat and coat were made of a cream-colored synthetic fur. The hat was as formless as one that a duffer might throw in his golf bag in case of a sudden downpour. The bulky coat, accentuating the mass of Madalyn's figure, was a buttonless and beltless faux sable—an even sadder replica of what a rich, middle-aged Palm Beach matron might throw over her shoulders for an air-conditioned cocktail party. The appearance of Madalyn's thick hair—one of her finest natural attributes, along with her surprisingly shapely and long legs—was sacrificed to the horrid hat plopped askew on her head like some drunken afterthought.

Madalyn, her son Jon Garth, and her son Bill—the actual focal point of the day's activities—had all piled into the deceased Pup's gargantuan Olds 88 for the drive to D.C. Along the way, they picked up Leonard Kerpelman. Madalyn claimed that he needed a ride because the "beat up, hundred dollar" Cadillac he owned never would make the short trip from Baltimore to the Supreme Court in Washington. As Bill sat in the back seat, fantasizing about chicks and hoping for an end to the nightmare of conflict and publicity his adolescence had degenerated into, Madalyn drove the Olds and manically babbled her usual narcissistic political drivel in between cross-examining Kerpelman to see if he had his arguments lined up.

Madalyn's suit against prayer in the Baltimore public schools had been joined by the clerks at the Supreme Court with another similar action. For expediency, if two cases before the Court have congruent legal issues, oral arguments for each are given to the justices on consecutive days. The other suit that the high court was considering was brought by a suburban Philadelphia man, Ed Schempp, against his son's high school for forcing students to read Bible verses as well as recite the Lord's Prayer.

Schempp never claimed to be an atheist. To the contrary, he played up his family's attending a local Unitarian church. But according to Madalyn, after visiting Schempp she believed that he was a crypto-atheist—but just too scared to show his true colors because doing so might hurt his small electronics business. Madalyn further held that the Unitarian church was an infidel nest of Milquetoast freethinkers, agnostics, and scared-rabbit atheists looking for comfort from the "cover of a church outline." (However, Madalyn was not to be critical of Unitarians a few months later, when a church minister in Hawaii would give her refuge as a fugitive facing more than a hundred years in prison.)

No, Madalyn wasn't impressed with the Schempps. She observed that they had hidden their anti-nuclear-war signs "behind bushes at their side door." Even worse, she alleged with disgust, was that Ed Schempp had posed his family for the media in their living room—all sitting quietly reading the Bible. When she saw the senior Schempp at the Supreme Court on the first day of oral arguments, according to her accounts, she kept repeating to herself over and over again, "Ed Schempp, how could you!! How could you? Is economic life so dear, or peace so sweet?"

Regardless of Madalyn's views on Schempp's character, his suit was in better shape and was in well-regarded legal hands. While her petition was an appeal against the unfavorable ruling of Maryland's highest court, Schempp's attorney, Henry W. Sawyer III, had won his case. A three-judge Federal District Court panel in Pennsylvania had ruled for Schempp and against the Abington Township School District, forcing them to appeal to the Supreme Court.

One of the main reasons Madalyn allowed Kerpelman to represent her was that he had no problem letting her participate in crafting the brief. It may have been good gratification for her ego, but Madalyn—while extremely bright—was hardly a legal scholar. Thus their Supreme Court brief was to be a loose amalgam of Madalyn's superficial legal research and some obvious and unsophisticated arguments by Kerpelman.

Yet their major points had solid legal precedents regardless of the ineptitude of the presenters. The two central questions that Madalyn laid before the Supreme Court were simple and primary: Can the State force religion on any of its citizens? Can individuals in the United States worship or not worship as they wish? In fact, Madalyn—via her son Bill—had inserted herself into perhaps the most controversial area of human law and governance. The issues of "separation of church and state" and "freedom of religion" that she and her counsel raised in their mediocre fashion were not only constitutional questions of the highest import, they were consecrated by bloody strife for a thousand years of evolution in Anglo-Saxon law.

Madalyn wheeled the big Olds around side streets close to the Supreme Court looking for a metered parking space, as neither she nor Kerpelman had enough cash with them to afford a garage for the day. After securing a spot, they walked to the Supreme Court, its beautiful white façade and cascading steps warmed by a bright but winter-waned February sun. Madalyn wrote, in her description of the day, that just before they took the steps up to the court, Kerpelman suddenly froze and blurted out: "I can't go in. I'm afraid." Madalyn said she was forced to grip her counsel firmly by the arm and walk him through the massive, brass double doors frescoed with portraits of Roman lawgivers into the Great Hall.

Inside, reporters gathered around them. In an impromptu news conference, Kerpelman made a rapid-fire denunciation of atheism, pointedly reminding the media of his Orthodox Jewish faith, as Madalyn shot eye-daggers at him. At the portal to the hearing room, an usher escorted the motley group to the best seats in the house—the front row, directly opposite the elevated bench where Chief Justice Earl Warren, flanked by the eight other justices, would soon listen to and question the lawyers for both sides.

Madalyn was disappointed. She felt that the setting was distinctly inferior to that of the majestic Maryland Court of Appeals. She glanced over at the media section of the gallery. It was packed with reporters. Bill nudged her, nodding over to the public gallery where there were a number of nuns in habit. "See the penguins?" Bill whispered, grinning. Madalyn shushed him. While the hearing room of the Supreme Court of the United States may not have been up to her expectations, it wasn't the place for adolescent humor—even if her son was the reason for her grazing in the highest legal clover there was.

"Oyez, oyez. God save our nation and this honorable court!" The irony of the Supreme Court clerk's cry was not lost on either Madalyn or Bill, and they exchanged knowing smiles as the justices filed in. Madalyn could identify all of them, even if she was somewhat surprised by their gnomish appearance caused by their elevation well above the audience.

In a sonorous and surprisingly friendly voice, Chief Justice Earl Warren invited Kerpelman to the advocate's lectern to present his client's case. Kerpelman, rail thin, was wearing a dark

two-piece, three-button suit with thin lapels and a skinny tie—
the kind of suit you might see a hipster jazz musician wearing for
a 1950s album cover shot. He looked small and scared as he wob-
bled to the podium, which was a sunken pit before the justices.
The justices waited as Kerpelman got himself situated—he was
nervously shuffling a sheaf of apparently prohibited papers.
Attorneys arguing before the Supreme Court were allowed neither to recite memorized statements nor to read from written
tracts. Only notes were allowed.

With a quavering, nasal tone, sugared with obsequiousness,
Kerpelman began, "This Lord's Prayer and Bible reading case
which is before the court today. . . ." As he waxed self-consciously
about "complex subtle systems of religious beliefs" and other
philosophical inquiries into the meaning of life, it seemed that
Kerpelman was reading his statement in direct contravention of
the High Court's basic ground rules.

For about two minutes, with growing confidence in his
voice and increasingly florid prose, Kerpelman droned on. "One
of the standards, of course, set forth in the Constitution and the
Bill of Rights as interpreted by this court, is the principle that
the church and state in this country shall remain separate and
apart, and in fact there shall be a wall of separation between them
which shall be maintained high and impregnable. . . ."

Justice Potter Stewart's rich, smokey baritone interrupted—a potential voice of doom. "I've read the First Amendment. I've never read that language in it. What's the First
Amendment say?" Without hesitation, Kerpelman recited the
appropriate clause from memory and restarted his soliloquy.
Stewart stopped him again, asking for more legal foundation to
his assertions. Quick as a cat, Kerpelman came up with precise
citations, again from memory.

It was an agile performance once Kerpelman got started.
Now, clearly not reading from his notes, he touched on other
points from the brief as the elderly but still irascible and brilliant

southern liberal Hugo Black and the grudging Potter Stewart alternately questioned, lectured, and skirmished between themselves, with Kerpelman becoming judiciously quiescent as the big dogs bayed.

Regardless of how much and how long Stewart tried to grill Kerpelman into making an elementary error of reason, he couldn't—nor would he be allowed to. If Kerpelman hesitated, Black or one of the other justices would jump in to counter Stewart by making a statement in the form of a blatantly leading question to Kerpelman. So, outnumbered and outgunned, Stewart withdrew to sotto voce mutterings and throwing a few procedural questions at Kerpelman, who was now probably feeling more and more like a legal version of Cassius Clay.

After Kerpelman, it was the turn of the attorney for the City of Baltimore, Francis B. Burch. It was probably a combination of his pomposity and the vacuity of his legal arguments that led him into early trouble. He started by telling the justices that "separation of church and state" was essentially a "matter of degree"—a dangerous approach flying against much First Amendment law. Then he implied that school prayer in Maryland was a settled matter and *must* be acceptable since they'd been doing it since 1839.

Justice William O. Douglas, the renowned civil libertarian, wasn't buying. He asked if the school board would allow a reading from the Koran rather than the Bible. Burch stumbled, first seeming to say no, then saying yes, of course. Chief Justice Warren chimed in, asking how the rules would allow for a reading of the Koran. Burch danced a bit before acknowledging that there didn't seem to be provision for such a possibility.

Proceeding stridently, as lawyers are wont to do with frail positions, Burch then proclaimed to the justices—already alerted like lounging pickerel to a crippled minnow swimming by—that the school's required Bible reading and prayer weren't religious exercises at all. They actually were in place because "Dr. Brain, the superintendent of schools, believed that these exercises had an extremely salutary effect" on the students by starting the school day with a "sobering influence"—a sort of calming effect on the overamped little buggers. Even Potter Stewart, Burch's best ally on the bench that day, couldn't let this bit of ludicrousness go by. He cut Burch off and said, "They could just give them tranquilizers, couldn't they?" A harmonic belly laugh rolled through the spectators.

Burch gamely blustered on, outlining more of the educational philosophy of "Dr. Brain" regarding prayer, until the chief justice stopped him. Warren pointed out that Hawaii might have school districts that had a majority of Buddhist students. He inquired if it would be proper for Christian students to have to conform to Buddhist ceremonies every morning. Burch, in a tone brimming with confidence, responded that it would indeed be all right—if the ceremonies "weren't done for religious reasons."

Hearing this, Hugo Black moved in for the kill. With his honeysuckle drawl dripping incredulity, the justice inquired if it was perhaps Mr. Burch's position that Bible reading and recitation of the Lord's Prayer were not religious ceremonies. And if they were, would they not espouse a specific religion? Burch knew these questions had been coming all along. The problem was that there was no good answer that he'd been able to come up with.

The cornered lawyer had to smell his own dung—the dung that he must have known was hidden in all the lower court victories. Burch was forced to say that, no, his position was that having the children saying prayers and reading verses from the Bible were not ceremonies of a religious nature—well, ah, not exactly, at least.

On Tuesday, June 17, 1963, just after public schools went on summer vacation, the U.S. Supreme Court issued its ruling on Madalyn's case along with Schempp's. *The New York Times* ran it

as one of the big stories of the year. It got the right column,
front-page headline and a "double truck" inside—two full pages
with eight columns of text, and not a single advertisement. Not
only did they publish half a dozen sidebar stories, along with
Anthony Lewis's dissecting the complex subject in an analysis
piece, they published the entire court decision and dissenting
opinion—complete with all the arcane legal footnotes the justices had written.

The New York Times also ran a three-column picture of Madalyn, Jon Garth, and Madalyn's mother, Lena, with the Supreme
Court looming behind them. (Bill was conspicuously and mysteriously absent.) They were all in summer outfits: Madalyn wearing a loud shapeless dress with some sort of black-and-white
asymmetric stripes, white gloves and a pillbox hat; Lena echoing
her daughter with her own straw pillbox number, adorned with
fruit and bows. Eight-year-old Jon Garth was togged out like a
miniature Leonard Kerpelman in a dark suit with thin lapels and
a skinny tie. He also wore a Tyrolean hat which, along with his
sad, dark, Italian eyes, gave him the appearance of a stunted
Mafia don. The fill-flashed photo was to catch him in a magnifi-
cently sullen glare, in contrast to the forced toothy grins of his
grandmother and Madalyn.

Madalyn had reason to celebrate. The High Court had ruled
eight to one in her favor, and not only that, the Schempps had
disappeared into the woodwork, allowing her to bask in the full
panoply of media attention. What a day it was. Justice Tom
Campbell Clark had written a lengthy and thoughtful opinion,
and there were concurring opinions by the others, including a
seventy-seven-page tome by Justice William J. Brennan.

There was one dissent—from Potter Stewart—and it was
not strong-hearted. Stewart thought the case should be sent back
because there wasn't enough information to make a sound decision. In other words, because of the school board's filing a demurrer—accepting Madalyn's facts and essentially telling the court

that the case was worthless—Stewart had no purchase and couldn't mount even a weak factual refutation.

It wasn't that the Kerpelman-Murray presentation was so compelling, since their work never got beyond a journeyman effort. No, the position of Baltimore was rendered untenable because the Supreme Court had overwhelming legal and historical precedent to rule against the Board of Education and, because of the demurrer, there were no arguments from Baltimore on the specifics of the case that could be damaging to Madalyn's position.

In actuality, the historical principles supporting her petition went back into the most sacred crannies of American judicial philosophy. It was Thomas Jefferson himself, badly scarred as a young boy by a harsh religious schooling experience including regular corporal punishment, who wrote of the absolute need of "a Wall of Separation between the Church and the State." In his majority opinion favoring Madalyn, Justice Clark prominently cited Jefferson's "admonition against putting the Bible and Testament into the hands of the children at an age when their judgments are not sufficiently matured for religious inquiries."

Not only was there a heavy load of precedents favoring Madalyn's position, but the Baltimore school board had made a crucial error—beyond the filing of a demurrer—a mistake that allowed Justice Tom Clark to destroy the board's arguments with a crafty legal rationale.

Shortly after Madalyn had filed the first local suit against the school board, officials there apparently got nervous about having the Protestant King James Bible Version as the only one available for the reading of prayers. They passed a supplementary rule that gave students the choice of reading either the Catholic Douay Version of the Bible or the King James Version. And equally important, they gave the children the option of leaving the room altogether—on the recommendation of C. Ferdinand Sybert, the Maryland attorney general, in his sop to Madalyn.

Clark deftly turned this waffling into a legal cudgel and rapped them squarely on the head with it. He wrote that if the prayers in question were not religious, then why give students the choice of which Bible to read? Why allow them to leave the room altogether per the attorney general's recommendation, if they didn't think that the prayers had any religious overtones?

Baltimore had also defended the mandatory school prayers as relatively minor encroachments on the First Amendment. Clark scoffed at, then blasted their assertions. "The breach of neutrality that is today a trickling stream may all too soon become a raging torrent and, in the words of Madison, It is proper to take alarm at the first experiment on our liberties."

Clark, dashing and smiting Baltimore's porous arguments, concluded the opinion with resounding words:

> The place of religion in our society is an exalted one, achieved through a long tradition of reliance on the home, the church, and the inviolable citadel of the individual heart and mind. We have come to recognize through bitter experience that it is not within the power of government to invade that citadel, whether its purpose or effect be to aid or oppose, to advance or retard. In the relationship between man and religion, the State is firmly committed to a position of neutrality. Though the application of that rule requires interpretation of a delicate sort, the rule itself is clearly and concisely stated in the words of the First Amendment.

Madalyn's victory was to have huge impact, affecting tens of millions of school children. More than 40 percent of the school districts in the nation were in violation of the Supreme Court's interpretation of the Constitution by either promoting or allowing devotional reading from the Bible. Thirty-six states and the District of Columbia allowed and encouraged religious exercises including Bible reading. Thirteen of them—Alabama, Arkansas,

Delaware, the District of Columbia, Florida, Georgia, Idaho, Kentucky, Maine, Massachusetts, New Jersey, Pennsylvania, and Tennessee—*required* Christian devotional practices of their students. Almost 80 percent of the public schools in the South and nearly 70 percent in the East had ongoing Bible and Christian prayer practices as part of their mandatory curriculum. And the Supreme Court of the United States, at the request of Madalyn Murray, ruled that they had all been breaking the law.

Not just any law, but perhaps the most fundamentally American law framed by the Constitution—that granting the right of religious freedom. Madalyn, via her son Bill, had given the justices a perfect venue for a ringing reaffirmation of the principle that had been a beacon for so many who had come to the shores of the new land. She was central to an event of grandly historic proportions that doubtless would have gotten happy approval from most of the Founding Fathers, obsessed as they were with all aspects of codifying freedom.

As expected, there were voices of dismay and outrage at the ruling. "A great tragedy," was how Roman Catholic cardinal Richard Cushing of Boston characterized Madalyn's resounding High Court victory. "The communists will enjoy this day," he said. The Cardinal of Los Angeles, James F. McIntyre, concurred, saying that the decision "can only mean that our American heritage and freedom are being abandoned in imitation of Soviet materialism and regimented liberty." Their powerful colleague in New York, Francis Cardinal Spellman, came on even stronger, stating, "I think the decision will do great harm to our country, and there is nothing we can do but bear it." Spellman continued, "No one who believes in God can approve such a decision."

But Spellman's charges, while a direct personal attack on the eight justices who voted to ban prayer in schools, were not factually correct. Seven of the justices were practicing Christians; the eighth, Justice Arthur J. Goldberg, was a Reform Jew. In fact, Justice Clark, the drafter of the majority opinion, was a devout Christian who wrote articles in the lay press regarding the importance of religious piety and prayer itself. (Prior to the decision, Madalyn had dismissed Justice Clark as a brainwashed fool after reading some of his writings on prayer, and she was convinced he'd be a sure vote against her.)

There was other strident but factually wobbly criticism of the Supreme Court from evangelist Billy Graham, who was in Stuttgart on one of his global crusades. "I am shocked," he stated in a press release. "Prayers and Bible reading have been part of American public school life since the Pilgrims landed at Plymouth Rock." Graham continued, with more vehemence than real history in hand, "Now a Supreme Court in 1963 says our fathers were wrong all these years? In my opinion, it is the Supreme Court that is wrong."

There was even the specter, raised by the ruling, of another Secession in South Carolina. There, the state superintendent of education—one Jesse Anderson—said he would defy the Court's ban on prayer. The schools in his state would continue to have prayers recited in classrooms despite the Supreme Court's kowtowing to the ungodly rabble-rousers. The South Carolinian expressed regret "that the issue would even come up" but said they weren't going to listen to the Supreme Court.

Yet there were positive surprises in store for Madalyn from powerful Christian leaders. She found herself having quite unexpected allies besides Justice Clark. Some Protestant church groups hailed the Supreme Court ruling, as did a good number of Jewish religious leaders. The National Council of Churches, a federation of most major Protestant denominations, felt the ruling served as a welcomed reminder that "the teaching of religious commitment is the responsibility of the home and the community rather than the public schools." And the council went further, seemingly to directly support Madalyn's position: "Neither the church nor the state should use the public school to compel acceptance of any creed or conformity to any specific religious practice."

Regardless of the whirlwinds of controversy, the Supreme Court ruling was quite a triumph for all directly involved—the winners and the vanquished as well. It certainly didn't hurt Leonard Kerpelman's law practice. Francis Burch, his losing opponent, started a national lobbying organization, the Constitutional Prayer Foundation, whose members were to include Dwight D. Eisenhower, Francis Cardinal Spellman, hotel magnate Conrad Hilton, publisher William Randolph Hearst, and a number of governors.

For Bill Murray, the decision was total vindication. The highest court in the land essentially ruled that the entire school administration—from Superintendent Brain to Bill's spiteful principal, down to the teachers who had harassed him even more unmercifully than the students—was wrong. And he, the courageous teenager, had been right. But Bill was far too psychologically battered to feel any sense of victory—to feel anything other than relief that the whole thing was finally over. He had not an inkling that the worst, by far, was yet to come for him.

And his mother? Madalyn was riding high. She had, in actuality, helped change the spiritual habits of the most powerful nation on earth. She had made good on her threats and then some. An avalanche of donations was coming in now, and she was immediately immersed in another saturnalia of media attention. She would soon thrill over her morning coffee as she heard her name and birthday being announced on the *Today* show segment of great-people-born-today.

By force of will, and nothing more, she had made herself into a historical figure. The once dirt-poor daughter of a bootlegger, and the mother of two bastard children, had come a long way, baby.

*D*avid *Waters combed back his "duck's ass" haircut and scanned the street in front of the Colonial Cove Restaurant, hoping that his girlfriend, Linda, would drive by with her mom's car. It was a cold, Midwest December night and even with the whiskey he—along with his three buddies—had been drinking, he probably had to be careful to keep his teeth from chattering and blowing his alpha-dog image.*

When Dave Gibbs pulled up in front of "the Cove," as the teen hangout was known in Peoria of the 1960s, the four boys eyed his mint-condition, lime-over-green, two-tone Chevy coupe. Gibbs rolled down his window and asked if any of the boys had seen his sister, Mary Jo. They said no, but since they didn't have wheels, would Gibbs give them a ride? Gibbs agreed, and the four—Jerry Peddicord, Bob Taylor, Carl Welchman, and David Waters—piled in the Chevy.

Taylor had stolen a bottle of ether from a hospital emergency room where he'd gone to get stitches. Waters, as leader, presumably told Gibbs, in his soft-voiced but commanding way, that they wanted to drive around and get high. Gibbs said that was fine, but the Chevy was getting low on gas. Somebody came up with fifty cents for a couple of gallons' worth, and after gassing up they drove across the Illinois River into rural East Peoria.

After they cruised around for a while, sniffing ether and swigging whiskey, Waters said that he had a girlfriend that he wanted to impress and asked Gibbs if he could borrow the car alone, just for a short while. Gibbs reacted negatively to the movie-star-handsome young hood. Waters didn't press the issue, but there were low-voiced exchanges in the back seat. Welchman, who lived in East Peoria, said he needed a lift home.

Almost as soon as Gibbs turned onto a gravel road at Welchman's direction—Wham—somebody slammed him in the head with their fist. It was his friend, Jerry Peddicord. Then Taylor started slugging Gibbs too. Waters threw some punches as his seal of approval. Only Welchman seemed to have any pity for the stunned victim. He took Gibbs's glasses off between the blows and laid them on the back seat.

With the car stopped, Gibbs was yanked over the front seat into the back. He was starting to bleed now. Waters quickly got behind the wheel and drove the car farther down the dirt road. He parked next to a harvested cornfield. Gibbs was dragged from the car and the beating continued with increased violence. Then, synchronously, they all suddenly stopped. It was as though a single switch controlling the four boys had been thrown at the same time, allowing them the chance to pause and think.

At this point, all the confessions agreed: Gibbs was bleeding profusely, but his wounds were not life-threatening and not worse than what a prizefighter might suffer—a busted lip, cut over the eye, bloody nose. Gibbs was faint but still conscious. If he begged for his life, nobody would say.

The pause ended as Peddicord and Taylor started "toying" with Gibbs. They took turns tearing and ripping his black-and-white flannel shirt. Then they started bouncing him back and forth, giving him a slap or bump with each turn—like two house cats playing with the same woozy mouse. Somebody picked up a large, thick tree limb next to the barbed wire fence along the roadside and jabbed at Gibbs, now prostrate on the frozen ground.

When Peddicord took the limb, the game ended. With powerful, brutal strokes, he brought it smashing down on Gibbs's face and chest. There was silence except for the terrible sound of the club against flesh and bone—and then the gurgling noise of blood bubbling from Gibbs's mouth. Waters went back to the Chevy coupe and vomited. Taylor and Welchman watched, hypnotized by the horror of what was transpiring.

Peddicord, holding the bloody tree limb in front of them, said, "Everybody is taking turns." It was a statement, a threat, and a ques-

tion—and directed mostly at Waters for endorsement. With his cool regained, Waters responded, "I guess, alright." He took the club and gingerly hit the dying boy on the side of his back. The others followed.

It wasn't enough for Peddicord. "Alright. Let's put his head under the car and back over it." Welchman and Waters quickly vetoed the idea. In unison they said, "No, you ain't backing over his head." Welchman had had enough. He said he wasn't going to touch "that boy" again. But Taylor, the youngest of the group, still had blood lust. He dragged Gibbs, twitching with death throes, in front of the car and crossed one of his legs over the other. He explained to Waters that there was a farmhouse nearby and they didn't want Gibbs to walk there and raise the alarm. Waters agreed and ran the Chevy coupe over the dying boy's legs in a precursor of pitilessness that would be replayed more than thirty years later in a Texas motel room.

SEVEN

The Battle of Baltimore

---

*B*ill Murray was feeling good walking home in the mid-spring dusk. He'd just been elected as an officer of his high school radio club. It was the first nonpolitical organization he'd been involved with on his own, and winning an election—even for the minor position of second secretary—felt great. For once he was doing something that wasn't under the soul-suffocating grip of his mother. Wrapping up his senior year at Baltimore Polytechnic Institute, an excellent science-and-engineering college preparatory high school, Bill was enjoying the easy downhill run that the last half of senior year afforded.

His sights were set on the University of Maryland, but he hadn't heard from them yet. Nonetheless, he wasn't worried. His grades were relatively decent—outstanding, if one considered the responsibilities he had of printing and mailing his mother's national atheist magazine. Sure, she was up to her old tricks again—filing a big new suit against the City of Baltimore to end tax-exempt status for churches—but to his great relief, Bill had nothing to do with Madalyn's latest battle.

Yes. He felt fine on this March evening—that is, until he saw his grandmother waiting for him outside their row house. His heart sunk. There was trouble written all over her long face, as Bill would put it in his autobiography. Lena told her grandson there was a problem, and it was down in the basement—the bedroom/printing plant. Rushing there, Bill found his seventeen-year-old girlfriend standing by his bed with suitcases piled on the floor, crying hard.

Susan Abramovitz was plain, bordering on homely. Her figure was angular. Her hair was frizzy and stacked up on her head. With her thick, black-rimmed glasses—of the sort that a mean-spirited librarian might wear—she looked like a character out of *Mad* magazine. Sure, they had talked about love when they boffed in the back seat of Bill's Cutlass, but as far as Bill was concerned, that was required verbal expediency to get in her panties. He'd also covered his bases by discussing their imminent parting in the fall, when he would go to the University of Maryland and she would go off to the University of Michigan in Ann Arbor.

Now here she was, with all her literal and figurative baggage. Susan's father, a successful Orthodox Jewish anesthesiologist from the Baltimore suburbs, had a history of abusive behavior with his daughter, according to Madalyn and Bill. The current crisis between them was her dating Bill. Susan's father didn't care about Bill's atheism, or the publicity surrounding the school prayer lawsuit, but he could not accept a non-Jew as a boyfriend for his daughter.

The crisis facing Bill in his bedroom may have been precipitated by Susan's father's maltreatment of her, but the huge problem he now had was caused by his mother—and he was furious with her. The day before, without any consultation with him, she had invited Susan to move in. It was difficult to plumb her exact motives. She must have felt some sympathy—such as she was capable of—for Susan, given her own mistreatment and neglect by her parents. However, by now Bill was sophisticated enough to realize that Madalyn's largess toward Susan could also be viewed through a darker prism. With Susan moving in, Madalyn would have an additional human being whom she could control.

For two months, it looked as if Madalyn's offer of a haven for

Susan wasn't going to have serious repercussions. Sue and Bill continued to go to high school during the day and frolic in Bill's basement bed in the evenings with Madalyn's full approval. It was to be the calm before the storm. Susan's father was not to be toyed with—not with his money and prestige. On Bill's eighteenth birthday, May 26, 1964, the Baltimore papers reported that Dr. Abramovitz had filed criminal charges against Bill. The father claimed that Bill was holding his daughter against her will and trying to brainwash her into abandoning her religion.

Both Madalyn and Bill were incensed at the charges. According to Madalyn, before Susan left home for the Mays-Murray row house, her father had beaten her so badly that Madalyn wrote that she arrived with a "black eye, a chipped tooth, broken glasses and multiple contusions and bruises." Whatever Susan's condition was, it wasn't good and wouldn't improve. To the contrary, she had jumped from the proverbial frying pan and landed in an active volcano. Soon enough her boyfriend's fists would replace her father's.

But that was the future. Right now both teenagers faced jail. Madalyn had so poisoned the judicial system in Baltimore with her prayer suit and newly filed attack on church tax exemptions that there wasn't much realistic chance that Bill would get a fair hearing. According to Madalyn's analysis, he would get at least six months in jail and Susan would probably be put in a juvenile detention facility for an equal duration. The evening that the story broke on the news, the trio gathered for a conclave in the basement bedroom.

Susan was stricken with fear and begged Madalyn for guidance. In her usual ex cathedra manner, Madalyn suggested a relatively simple but not necessarily beneficial solution: "Get married and fast." Of course Bill's heart dropped like a runaway elevator when he heard his mother's advice, but he also saw the efficacy of such a move in dealing with the calamity that was about to engulf him. While Susan didn't seem averse to the idea, there was a fly in Madalyn's ointment. Susan was only seventeen and couldn't marry without parental permission—and that she would *never* get.

Madalyn said she'd research the situation. She soon came up with what she termed a legal loophole for the teenagers. Marriage requirements in Maryland were not uniform statewide and the age for consent varied. Not far from Baltimore, there was a county where—depending on circumstances and the willingness of a J.P.—a girl could get married at fourteen years old.

While they mulled this possible course of action, there was a court hearing on the complaint against Bill by Susan's father, Dr. Abramovitz. Even though he was the central figure of the court action, Bill never received a summons to appear. Thinking this could be used to their advantage, Madalyn told her son to just lay low and not show up.

There couldn't have been worse advice. The judge, hearing the case without Bill's or Susan's side, granted the father's petition. Now Bill and Susan could be picked up at the whim of the Baltimore police and thrown in jail. As though that were not enough, Bill's bride-to-be had other news. She was pregnant.

Perhaps this was a good thing for Bill. It forced an end to any thought of freedom from Susan and the circumstances. He had to marry her now. He had been a bastard, and he wasn't about to let his own child be one. Depending on different versions, Bill and Susan got married either in Hagerstown, Rockville, or Frederick, Maryland. Susan bypassed the age requirement of eighteen by producing a certificate of pregnancy. With a bailiff as witness—since no family members on either side could or would attend—Bill wed Susan by placing a gold wedding band, purchased a few hours earlier at a pawnshop, on her finger.

With an early "bun in the oven," as Madalyn so empathetically put it, the newlyweds spent their wedding night in Bill's basement bedroom at the row house. Although Madalyn was convinced that the marriage would nullify the court proceedings against Bill, she recommended that they leave at midnight the next day for New York City, just in case the cops might be on the lookout for the errant couple.

Madalyn called her publisher-editor and benevolent mortgage underwriter Paul Krassner in New York and apparently beseeched him successfully to let Bill and Susan stay at his apartment in Greenwich Village. But he was to be a less than enthusiastic host. Krassner and his wife had a new daughter, and he was himself constantly on the precipice of dire legal troubles with the authorities due to the hyperradical content of *The Realist.* Reasonably, Krassner didn't look forward to being arrested for harboring fugitives from Baltimore, and while he couldn't bring himself to tell Madalyn no on the phone, he did turn the newlyweds away when they arrived at his apartment in the Village.

Bill and Susan were forced to take a room in a seedy downtown New York hotel, and before they even checked in Bill had his prized 35-mm camera stolen. He called his mother to explain the Krassner situation and told her that he was rapidly depleting the small funds he'd brought with him. Madalyn said she couldn't help with the finances—and she had bad news of her own for him. Susan's fuming father had somehow discovered that they had fled the State of Maryland and his lawyers had gotten the judge to slap them both with contempt of court citations. Now they really *were* fugitives.

Madalyn asked Bill to hold out in New York as long as possible while she tried to smooth things over with the court. Uncle Irv, on orders from Madalyn, drove Bill's car to New York and then took the bus back to Baltimore by himself—rather than risk being caught driving with his fugitive nephew, since the judge had issued an arrest warrant for Bill.

Madalyn's promised diplomatic efforts on behalf of the

newlyweds hadn't taken place. She never called the judge to inform him that Susan and Bill were married. Madalyn certainly didn't forget. She evidently double-crossed her son because she wanted—*needed*—confrontation. Newspaper headlines made for forceful mailing-list solicitations—pleas for cash contributions in her war against the fascist Baltimore establishment. Undoubtedly, the arrest of her teenage son would make fine copy for *The American Atheist* too.

The fugitive teen couple arrived at the row house around noon without incident. Bill took their luggage down to the basement bedroom, but before he could unpack his mother shouted for him to get topside in a hurry. Three prowl cars had parked in a tight line in front of the house. Bill and Madalyn rushed to the back of the row house, and there they saw two more police cars in the alley. Neighbors—perhaps the ones that Madalyn tortured with her yapping mongrel dogs (named Marx and Engels)—had tipped off the police.

Madalyn girded for battle by locating her teargas pen. She also instructed Bill to get their tape recorder ready in order to make audio documentation of the impending clash. After a few minutes, two older officers emerged from the patrol cars and ambled up the walk to the row house. Madalyn met them at the steps and was told they were there to pick up her new daughter-in-law. "Do you have a warrant?" Madalyn inquired.

The sergeant, a well-paunched Irish-American known as "Old Jelly-Belly" Kelly, admitted that they didn't have any "paperwork," but he said that it was common knowledge that there was a court order out for Susan's arrest. Madalyn bristled righteously and informed him that without a warrant there wasn't a chance in hell of her letting them in the house. Scowling, the officers retreated to the prowl cars to ponder and consult with colleagues.

As they did, Madalyn improvised an escape plan for Susan.

She instructed Bill to "distract" the officers who were in front of the house so that she and Susan could make a run for the "Atheist World Headquarters" she had established in a rundown store-front office a mile or so away. Madalyn thought that if she could spirit Susan to her HQ, she could keep the cops at bay by claiming the office was a religious sanctuary.

If the cops didn't buy it, Madalyn figured the arrest would make great newspaper headlines—"Police Deny Sanctuary to Pregnant Atheist Girl." Naturally, the easiest thing to do was let the police take Susan in, and have her explain to the magistrate that she was now married and therefore the contempt citation wasn't applicable. But then there wouldn't have been any hot newspaper copy, and a great fund-raising opportunity for Madalyn would have been squandered for the sake of prudence and parental responsibility.

Bill went dutifully off on his kamikaze mission, slow-walking as casually as he could toward the row of police cars and the crowd of neighbors who had gathered for what promised to be a Roman circus. Bill stopped in front of Sergeant Kelly and started to engage him in conversation. The old Irish cop grunted that he didn't want to hear any smart-aleck stuff, and eyed Bill suspiciously as the teenager started to explain that he and his girlfriend were now man and wife.

Just then Madalyn and Susan made a dash from the house to Madalyn's car. Kelly, caught by surprise at the audacity of the escape attempt, started for the women, but Bill moved to block him. Kelly warned him to get out of the way. Bill stood fast. The cop took out his billy club and waved it at Bill menacingly. The well-built six-foot-three-inch teenager reacted by shoving Kelly so hard that Kelly, off balance, stumbled backward.

It was a serious mistake. The police officers' ranks—now swelled to more than a dozen officers—swarmed on Bill like angry bees protecting a threatened queen. Kelly's partner tackled

Bill and brought him to the ground. Other brethren-in-blue started viciously pummeling him on his back and behind his knees with their nightsticks.

The police neglected Madalyn and Susan's escape to concentrate on subduing and punishing Bill. As she fled to her car with her daughter-in-law, Madalyn screamed at the scrum of officers grunting and flailing their clubs at her son: "You can't do that. You can't do that. You don't have a warrant!"

As Madalyn made good her getaway, Bill's grandmother entered the fray. Lena came tearing out of the house and slapped the nearest officer she could find on the head. He ignored her, but in a dramatic swoon, Lena fell to the ground in a faint. Uncle Irv finally emerged from the house and, like a loyal fusilier retrieving a wounded officer, hauled Lena's body into the house—where she recovered instantly. (Madalyn would later claim in *The Realist* that seventy-three-year-old Lena was clubbed into unconsciousness by police when she tried to pull a 230-pound neighbor away from battering her grandson.)

After depositing Susan safely at atheist headquarters, Madalyn returned to do battle with the police, but Bill was already in custody and there was little to be done about that. However, "Nazi Storm Troopers" were crawling all over the house and this was an unendurable outrage. Of her return home she wrote that she had "found Mother on the couch, white as a sheet, breathing irregularly, her nostrils pinched, her lips blue. Three policemen were standing there, hands on hips." Madalyn screamed at them to get out. In a paroxysm of rage, she attempted to spray them with her teargas pen—but she couldn't get it to fire. With that, the officers quickly moved to subdue and arrest her.

It wasn't to prove easy. Madalyn clung to furniture, then doors, and doorsills, and even doorknobs—with the police prying her grip loose at each stage of the extraction process. It took twenty minutes to get her to the porch, where she then latched on to the screen door and then the porch rail. Now she was in sight of at least a hundred neighbors and onlookers, many of whom were in full-throated delirium. Like spectators at the Roman Coliseum when Christians were thrown to the lions, they screamed for blood as the police dragged Madalyn—still clutching at bushes in her yard—across forty feet of lawn. "Kick her again!" "Kill her!" "Hit her again!" "Kill the bitch!" they screamed.

Madalyn continued with her defiance in the holding cell where the police placed her while they contemplated what charges to file against her and her son. When she was handed supper through the bars—she later described it as "slop of a neutral color and a paper cup filled with something resembling tepid excrement"—she promptly threw the contents at the opposite wall, where the pay phone for prisoners was positioned. She aimed high, hoping to have the slop dribble down the wall onto the phone. Her trajectory calculations were faultless. The jailhouse-dinner slime oozed down the wall, and stuck on the rotary dial and mouthpiece of the phone.

The infuriated matrons attempted to remove Madalyn from the holding cell and take her for fingerprints and mug shots. When Madalyn ascertained where she was being taken and what for, she went limp and had to be dragged to the fingerprinting room. There she told the sergeant, "If you want to fingerprint me you are going to have to knock me out cold." After apparently many and varied threats, the jailer relented. He then ordered her over to the mug shot area to have her picture taken. Madalyn calmly told him that the mug shots of her would have to be taken in a prone position since they'd have to be holding her down.

For her efforts, the jailers put Madalyn in the "whore tank"—the middle cell of a cell block that held mostly hungover prostitutes picked up on street sweeps. Madalyn settled right in. She took off her shoes and started banging the steel bars with them to accompany her singing, in a "lusty part-baritone," a Christian hymn:

> Jesus loves you, yes I know,
> For the Bible tells me so.
> Little minds to him belong,
> They are weak and he is strong.

Even though Madalyn professed to like prostitutes in a general sense—perhaps feeling some solidarity with them—her yowling and banging quickly began to rile the hungover ladies of the night from their stupors into open anger. They shouted at the matrons to get "that atheist bitch to shut up." And when that got no response, the fallen women started a din of their own that soon reached a crescendo with screaming and head banging. All the while, Madalyn maintained her tattoo of shoes-on-bars with unending choruses of praise to Jesus.

It gave Madalyn the greatest joy. Gawd, how she craved inducing chaos. Gawd, how she loved suffering—her own and others' equally. She was almost unhappy to be released to the custody of her liberator—Leonard Kerpelman. When they went to pick up Bill from the county jail, he limped slowly toward them from the beating he had taken. Driving over to get Susan at another facility, Kerpelman gave Bill and Madalyn a chance to gather themselves before he told them that—so far—ten felony charges had been filed against them in court.

The next day—Sunday—mother and son were to be arraigned and their case bound over to the grand jury. Oddly, what Bill recalled in his autobiography years later was that his grandmother, Lena, made her usual rubbery pancakes for Sunday morning breakfast as though nothing was amiss. The quality of the pancakes was not improved by pouring on massive amounts of the cheap syrup that Lena urged on the breakfasters. As they all fed on the cudlike flapjacks, Madalyn ruminated on their bleak future. "They'll crucify us," she intoned. "The judge can throw us in the clinker for a hundred years on those assault charges."

It wasn't quite that bad—but it was going to be bad. The media had gathered in large numbers to cover any barmy antics at the arraignment for the accused felonious atheist priestess and her acolyte son. They were not to be disappointed. Before the hearing even began Madalyn was at it, hissing curses at the police in the hallway as they went to the courtroom.

After the magistrate heard the police version of events, he quadrupled bail for both mother and son. When Bill heard the amount he turned pale, his knees buckled, and he fell to the floor of the packed courtroom. Poor, long-suffering Bill—the strong-hearted teenager finally cracked and broke down completely. Writhing on the floor, he shouted: "I will not go back to that cell. You coward, you Christian, you Catholic!"

Five bailiffs and police officers descended on the desperate, thrashing teenager. The judge began furiously hammering his gavel and Madalyn immediately jumped into the fray, screaming at the livid jurist, "Leave my son alone, you Catholic bastard!" Four other officers quickly pinned Madalyn's arms behind her back and restrained her. Kerpelman, the defense attorney, recoiled from the feral scene gibbering incoherently to nobody in particular, as Bill and Madalyn were subdued and removed to holding cells.

After a fifteen-minute recess, the defendants were brought back into the courtroom. Without anybody having said a word, the judge started hammering his gavel again—possibly as a prophylactic gesture toward maintaining the fragile decorum he hoped to reestablish. He then issued Bill a contempt citation for his tantrum. The judge also charged him with one count of disorderly conduct—evidently having thought up the new offense during the brief recess. With his gall rising again in his throat, the judge assured Bill that he'd get "thirty years in jail" for "this little episode," and he proceeded to adjust bail upward, once more, for the new set of crimes that the teenager had committed in his courtroom.

Somehow Kerpelman, along with one of Madalyn's atheist supporters, managed to convince a bail bondsman to make bail for the mother-and-son team—twelve thousand dollars cash. It wouldn't prove to be a wise move for the bondsman. His investment—in the persons of Madalyn and Bill—was not destined to be long for Baltimore. In any case, when Madalyn emerged from the courthouse after making bail, she held up her bruised and bandaged arms to the news photographers. They refused to take pictures of either her or Bill. Instead the headlines would trumpet Madalyn's assault on police.

When they got home, Madalyn immediately called for and presided over a family summit conference of the highest urgency. She announced that they had to flee the country. Uncle Irv, who was now working part-time for the Bendix Corporation, was the first to protest. When Madalyn reminded him that if he didn't come along he'd have to cook his own meals and make his own bed, he subsided into meek quietude.

But Bill was more stout. He steadfastly maintained he wouldn't leave the country. Madalyn, ignoring her son's protests, shouted that she had an idea. "Cuba!" She knew somebody who could get them into Cuba. "Cuba?" Bill gasped. After catching his breath, he reminded his mother of her attempt to defect to the Soviet Union five years earlier—when the Soviet immigration officer rejected her application because he thought she'd be a deadbeat. She turned on her son with fury: "Shut up, punk! This is all your fucking fault anyway. Your hot pants got us into all this trouble."

Madalyn broke up the meeting in order to consult with experts. She called a local black militant "freedom fighter," who told Madalyn that it would take time to get to Castro, that he was "very busy" at the moment. She advised Madalyn that instead of Cuba she should go to Hawaii—because it was half Buddhist, and everyone knows Buddhists are "really atheists" deep down. To clinch the plan, the black-radical-turned-travel-adviser offered to "camp out" in the row house to keep an eye on things. Madalyn thought that would be fine—especially since it was sure to flip out her conservative all-white neighbors.

After the consultation, Madalyn hastily regathered the family and announced they were leaving for Hawaii in twenty-four hours—and that everybody should pack their belongings as though they might never return. All hands turned to the task. Bill was to write of this event: "It was interesting to see what items each person chose to take. Mother carefully sealed her mailing list in a large envelope. Susan, of course, had only the clothes she had brought with her the day she moved in. Grandmother made sure the family picture albums were in her suitcase. Uncle Irv packed up his dozen watches and his girlie magazines. I lovingly wrapped up Grandfather's 1908 Luger pistol."

The next morning at first light, with Madalyn at the wheel, the family made their escape toward Dulles International for the long flight to Hawaii. Madalyn later claimed that they were soon being tailed by unmarked police cars, but "in the fanciest driving since I was in the army trying to out-drive an aerial bombardment in a jeep in Southern France, I lost the tail."

After checking in their fifteen suitcases and other baggage, the family cautiously edged toward the departure gate, expecting to see police waiting for them there. Instead, they found only an enterprising newspaper reporter. Madalyn told him they were fleeing to Hawaii because there they would be sheltered by the Buddhist community, who were "absolute atheists."

On the plane, all six were in a state of emotional and physical collapse after the momentous events of the previous forty-eight hours. Strangely, the pregnant Susan and Grandmother Lena seemed to hold up the best. They calmly exchanged quiet snatches of conversation. Bill quickly sank into a depressive daze in an inverse reaction to his mother's manic super-high. Even though exhausted, Madalyn talked incessantly in a nervous high-pitched voice to anybody who cared to listen while repeatedly spilling hot coffee on herself. Ten-year-old Jon Garth likewise blathered in imitative fashion until he got through with his third mini-bottle of whiskey and quieted down.

EIGHT

The Fugitive and Scourge
of the Islands

The Pacific Ocean is a calm, heavenly blue—protecting, almost cuddling the island. Day after day the sun shines, and everywhere is a faint odor of flowers. Calm and undisturbed this island sits.

Madalyn Murray
The Realist, September 1964

*C*alm and undisturbed Hawaii may have sat for millennia—but it wouldn't for long. It was insufferable. People simply *had* to be informed that their world was really a fucked-up cesspool of injustice and ignorance. *Nobody* should be allowed to wallow in the luxury of tropical self-delusion when the incontrovertible facts had to be faced. Hawaii wasn't going to escape from Madalyn. Nor would she use it as an escape from her responsibilities. It was going to be a place to recuperate, to recharge the batteries, and then to regird for her worldwide crusade against God.

Madalyn believed the islands were a good choice for both tactical and strategic reasons. Geographically it made sense to put as much distance as possible between herself and the Baltimore authorities who were understandably inflamed by her flight and already making threatening noises. While she may have mistakenly believed that Buddhists were all atheists, she was correct in surmising that the islanders would have a more relaxed view toward people of radical free-thought persuasion such as herself. Furthermore, the move to the islands—with their unique mix of

Eastern and Western culture—would allow Madalyn to give her battles against God and Religion an international flavor. She could position herself as the true leader of a cross-race, cross-nationality, global crusade. Finally, Hawaii was a great place to convalesce and replenish the reservoirs of personal vitriol necessary for her special kind of jihad.

As soon as Madalyn and her band arrived in Honolulu, a variety of groups, alerted by the media to their arrival, provided comfort. A Unitarian minister, of the same church that Madalyn had violently assailed the Schempps for attending, afforded them housing—loft space in the upper story of his church, no less. Others, mostly of the antiestablishment stripe, provided food and transportation for the family until more permanent digs could be found. It was only a matter of days until Madalyn was able to locate her brood on the first floor of a spacious old Hawaiian wood-frame house near the top of the Punchbowl—the volcanic crater that dominates the backdrop of Waikiki beach and downtown Honolulu.

With this accomplished, Madalyn checked into the Tripler Army Hospital to assess the nerve damage that she received at the hands of Baltimore police. Physical problems were always difficult for Madalyn to deal with. She was caught between the conflicting needs of projecting invincibility and, at the same time, being able to assert martyrdom. This time Madalyn wasn't crying wolf, though. She had in fact martyred herself in the Battle of Baltimore.

X-ray examinations at Tripler indicated that Madalyn had suffered extensive trauma and permanent damage to her spinal column and neck vertebrae in the melee with police. She claimed the injuries came "from the boots of several cops on the back of my neck, the boots that ground my face into the grass of my lawn." Regardless of whether this was accurate, or whether the injuries stemmed from her resistance, the damage did take place and it was severe.

Madalyn had three compressed vertebrae in her neck. The compression of the neck vertebrae in turn affected her right side and the use of her right arm and leg. She would write: "For many months my right eye would not focus and my right hearing was impaired while a sharp knifelike pain skittered constantly up from the back of my neck and over my skull, down to my right eye. My neck refused to turn except creakingly . . . and the pain of those nerves constantly stimulated was excruciating, leaving me with night after night of sleepless experiences while free-floating pain engulfed me."

Thirty years later, Madalyn's skeletal remains, under the examination of Dr. David Glassman, would confirm the damage that was caused by the Baltimore melee—damage that gave rise to the unceasing physical anguish that would end only with her strangling.

But for now, Madalyn was to spend day after day soaking in the healing sun and salt water of the Ala Moana beach. Soon she gained control of her eyes. She could focus them both in the same direction. She could finally walk again without her leg cramping "hard as a ball," and her neck could turn just enough to allow her to hunch over an electric typewriter—even though her right hand would still drag over the keys, firing them at unwanted intervals.

No matter. Madalyn was back in business. Actually she was the toast of the town. Even though Maui's governing council offered to pay her way to the Soviet Union to get rid of her, Madalyn found the Hawaiians to be—initially at least—warm and accepting. She believed that she had made "inroads to their hearts." Her Hawaiian speaking calendar was packed with engagements—chambers of commerce, business groups, high schools, the University of Hawaii, "even churches!" Madalyn bragged. To her surprise, Madalyn wrote, she'd finally found a "niche of toleration" and "security" in Hawaii.

But the toleration and security that Madalyn found weren't the godsend they would be for most normal people. Actually they were a serious problem for Madalyn. Deep down she scorned toleration. She detested security. No, Madalyn needed enmity and conflict. She needed to be able to generate chaos at her will. She needed to be hated to feel content.

Her first assault from her new base of operations would be on her friends—her left-wing allies. Although her good-hearted supporter Paul Krassner had made her monthly mortgage payments on the Baltimore row house, although he had given her a national audience, paid her first fees as a journalist, and made her a radical celebrity, Madalyn excoriated his readers—many of whom had been financial supporters—in *The Realist*.

"Dear Reader," Madalyn wrote. "You gutless bastards have exchanged 'respectability' for human rights. . . . You live a lie and prosper, which is why you are paralyzed and cannot help us who live the truth; for you would be helping your conscience to survival by giving a helping little finger, and you will be more comfortable when your conscience is drowned." She closed out the harangue on her old supporters by having Krassner print her address in Hawaii so that the readers, whom she'd just vilified, could send her donations.

Then, in one of her patented reverse slam dunks, after excoriating the Left, Madalyn went on to sing the praises of right-wing America—whose political values she had vowed she would literally die fighting against. In point of fact, the Right *had* been supportive of her. The Baltimore *Sun*'s editorial page chastised the city power structure for its treatment of her. Henry Luce's conservative *Time* magazine had written a balanced and quite sympathetic story on the police conduct and Madalyn's legal problems. Even the Barry Goldwater camp in Honolulu had sent her money.

After her rank betrayal of past supporters came the attack on her Hawaiian hosts—the very people who had accepted

Madalyn into their hearts. Madalyn somehow retained perhaps the finest trial lawyer in the Hawaiian Islands at the time—the elegant Hyman M. Greenstein—to file suit against the island school system because the phrase "one nation under God" was used in the Pledge of Allegiance. Madalyn claimed that her son, ten-year-old Jon Garth, who was enrolled in a public elementary school, had been forced by the State of Hawaii to practice religious ceremonies that were incompatible with his true atheist convictions.

Yes. These pretty islands needed some rousting. Also on Madalyn's agenda was a public investigation of a school for children of native Hawaiian ancestry. Madalyn felt that this school—funded completely by the estate of the great-granddaughter of Kamehameha I, the king of Hawaii—was involved in discrimination by enrolling only students of Hawaiian descent. However, since no public monies were involved, Madalyn's investigation led nowhere except toward the dawning perception amongst Hawaiians who bothered to follow her capers that their islands had been invaded by an acutely noxious alien species, a human plague—of one.

With Hawaii set upon and the locals assailed, now it was the turn of the federal government. Madalyn had scanned the radio dial and discovered that at least fifteen Honolulu radio stations carried religious programming—Buddhist and Christian. She filed a petition with the Federal Communications Commission in Washington, D.C., requesting that she be granted "free and equal" airtime from the same stations so that she could counterbroadcast the atheist viewpoint. In fact, FCC regulations of the era conformed to the "fairness doctrine," which required that broadcasters give equal time to opposing sides in "controversial issues of public importance." With that statutory clause, Madalyn smelled the chance of acquiring a major fund-raising venue without cost.

Unfortunately, the FCC commissioners sensibly concluded that atheism was not that controversial an issue—even if the petitioner herself may have been—and they ruled for the broadcasters. But it was another first-rate rumble for Madalyn, who firmly believed that publicity—good or bad—was always good.

The family's initial week in Hawaii had Bill seriously contemplating killing both his mother and his pregnant wife, Susan, with his grandfather's Luger. When Susan confronted him as he toyed with the pistol, he got to his feet. Towering over his wife, he struck her to the floor and shouted, "That's for you, you little Jew bitch! Now leave me alone!" The following day he looked for the Luger, and it was gone. Madalyn had taken the heirloom pistol and given it to police at the local station house—and for Bill the last vestige of masculinity had been taken from him by his mother. Still, he accepted her offer to pay for his and Susan's tuition at the University of Hawaii.

And why not? Somehow his mother had gotten thousands of dollars out of different bank accounts in Baltimore before they fled. (She had had no qualms about brazenly lying to her *Playboy* interviewer that the family arrived in Hawaii with fifteen dollars between them.) But for Bill, even allowing his mother to pay for tuition, reasonable as it might have been, had hidden risks. Bill knew from his earlier stint on his mother's payroll—printing her atheist magazine at the expense of doing homework—that *all* transactions with Madalyn were the devil's bargains.

Regardless, it wasn't a bolt out of the blue for either mother or son when the State of Maryland began extradition proceedings against them in connection with the criminal charges stemming from the brawl with the Baltimore police. But, in something of a surprise, the judge who had issued the contempt citation decided to hold a hearing and try the Murrays in absentia.

The six-hour judicial proceeding would resemble a show trial held in the outer reaches of the Soviet Gulag. Neither Bill nor Madalyn was ever served with a warrant by Baltimore authorities. The two had no legal counsel in court to defend them. The defense, since there was none, couldn't present witnesses, nor could it cross-examine witnesses. Further, in a parody of a bad Hollywood script, the judge allowed the prosecutors to dramatically address questions and accusations to two empty chairs.

Naturally, he found Madalyn and Bill guilty of contempt of court—not for their flight to Hawaii, but because of the contact both had with Susan. Even though the judge was well aware of the fact that Susan and Bill were now married, he still found the couple and Madalyn to be in violation of the court order that Dr. Abramovitz's attorneys had earlier rammed through the system. The proceedings were legal foolishness that wouldn't hold up, but the judge was not to be denied. Without deliberation, he passed sentence, giving Madalyn a year in the county jail and Bill six months and a five-hundred-dollar fine.

With the media coverage of the Murrays as sizzling as it was, in all likelihood it was not a coincidence that the State Assembly of Maryland contemporaneously was passing a bill that would require mandatory sentences for assault on a peace officer. Baltimore dailies noted the progress of the legislation and calculated that Bill Murray could get 100 years in prison for his five counts of battery of a police officer. Madalyn could get as much as 160 years on her eight counts. Even Grandma Lena could go to prison for 20 years for her one count of slapping an officer on the head and then feigning to faint.

Back in Hawaii, Madalyn—insulated by the continental United States and the Pacific Ocean from the aftershocks of the Battle of Baltimore—was continuing to busily add to her cache of enemies. The Buddhist community was affronted by her characterization of them as atheistic. They were, in fact, deists who believed in a higher power—just not one in the Judeo-Christian-Muslim image. Not only that, it turned out that Buddhists were *not* the majority in Hawaii as Madalyn had been advised by her black-radical-turned-travel-agent house-sitter.

The hated Roman Catholics, adherents of the religion that destroyed Madalyn's dreams of matrimonial bliss with her dashing bomber pilot, were in the majority. Even the governor of the state, John A. Burns, was a devout Catholic, and it was Governor Burns who would decide whether or not to extradite the Murrays back to Maryland to serve their contempt sentences and face the far more serious matter of the assault charges against the police.

In early August 1964, Governor Burns—not unexpectedly—approved the Murrays' extradition. Madalyn's civil attorney, the urbane and well-connected Hyman Greenstein, had agreed to take her criminal case, and he happened to be in Maryland on a fact-finding mission for his client when the governor signed the extradition papers. Greenstein immediately called back to Hawaii and got assurances from the authorities that the order would not be executed until he got back and had time to appeal. He also told the daily newspaper, *The Honolulu Advertiser,* that, after talking to residents of Baltimore, he had no doubt that his client's life would be in danger if she was forced to return to Maryland. "She is," he said, "a very hated person here."

The next day Greenstein flew home to the islands and then, flanked by three assistant counsels, filed an appeal for Madalyn in Honolulu Circuit Court. At first the judge ruled that Madalyn and Bill would be sent back to Maryland in prompt fashion. However, Greenstein gave his word that he would appeal to the State Supreme Court without delay, if the judge allowed Madalyn and Bill to be released into his custody.

They were bad risks, to be sure, having already jumped a very large cash bond (for those days) in Baltimore; however, based on Greenstein's spotless reputation in Hawaiian legal circles, the judge released the duo to him per his request. It was to prove the biggest mistake in perhaps either of their careers.

Meanwhile, Madalyn schemed. She didn't like the handwriting on the wall. Greenstein was good—but to her it looked like the pope's armies held the high cards. She had to come up with a trump. She got in touch with a well-placed island psychiatrist, Linus Pauling Jr. (the son of the Nobel Laureate chemist), and got him to agree to examine Bill for mental illness. Madalyn's strategy was to have Bill found mentally incapacitated, and thus get the court to rule that because of his mental problems, it wouldn't be in the best interests of justice to deport either mother or son back to the cauldron of Baltimore.

The trouble was getting Bill to see the shrink. With good reason, he was chary of *any* entanglements with his mother's concepts at this point. But Madalyn hit on a tried-and-true technique: Bribery. She offered him fifty dollars per session just to talk with the psychiatrist. Bill, broke and with a wife about to give birth, reluctantly agreed.

It turned out that the psychiatric sessions were benign and, as would be expected from anything Madalyn put together, they were a bit weird as well. Bill claimed that he and his examiner mostly talked about high-performance cars. But as Bill was later to write, "getting paid to be crazy" was too much even for the floundering and destitute college student and father-to-be. After a few sessions he quit.

Bill's brief stint at psychoanalysis evidently didn't help his emotional outlook. On February 16, 1965, his daughter Robin was born. Susan did well through the delivery—but the baby was in trouble. The newborn was having difficulty breathing and one lung was filled with fluid. Infant Robin had to be hospitalized in postnatal critical care for a week.

The medical bill staggered Bill. He couldn't pay, and he knew only one person who could help him. Madalyn loaned him the money—but went to the hospital directly to make the payment herself, not trusting Bill to do it. With Susan still frail from childbirth, Bill took out his loathing for what his life had become in an explosion of violence. He had earlier struck Susan for being pregnant and being Jewish, now he beat her for delivering a sickly and expensive child. Robin, born to sickness and violence, was fated to die with the same.

NINE

The Reverend Christos Logos

*H*e was wonderful. Madalyn had never met a man like him and she never would again. Sure, he was too young for her at twenty-nine years old to her forty-six years. And no, the Reverend Keith Rhinehart wasn't her type either—or at least she hadn't thought so. Madalyn liked the he-man kind and the Reverend Rhinehart was decidedly sensitive, delicate—beautiful really—with his long black hair, dark luminous eyes, and lithe build. It wasn't so much his physical appearance that got Madalyn, but his psyche—his persona.

As soon as the Reverend Rhinehart arrived in Hawaii, they were spending eighteen to twenty hours a day together—two peas in a pod. They'd meet on the beach at Waikiki and start talking. They'd bathe, lounge, grab a light lunch, and go back to the beach until sundown, when they'd depart for the nearest hotel bar for tiki cocktails and dinner. The young Reverend would always gracefully pick up the tab—probably surprising the waiters who had him pegged for a cashless mainland gigolo.

To spellbind Madalyn was a miracle. She was a woman who lived by unbridled skepticism. But the Reverend Rhinehart had immediately managed to have her eating out of his manicured hand. She'd never heard a better rap than the Reverend's. "We were clued in on every wavelength," as Madalyn put it. The war in Vietnam, the House Un-American Activities Committee, segregation, the fascist news media, free love, and the whole problem of Capitalism—the Reverend Rhinehart was right on. His political acumen stunned Madalyn. No matter that he was a religious leader—he was an ATHEIST in his soul. She knew it beyond a doubt.

Then there were the Reverend's unsurpassed skills at flattery. Admittedly, Madalyn was an easy touch in this regard. She had always been susceptible to any form of male sycophancy. Even the most flagrant and primitive types of masculine sweet talk would immediately arrest her attention. However, the Reverend Rhinehart presented Madalyn with a new level of adulation that was breathtaking.

He was on a global tour with a documentary crew, a tour underwritten by the "spiritualist" church group he had founded in Seattle, Washington. His mission was to film twelve people whom he considered to be the most important intellectuals in the world. Madalyn was nestled somewhere in between Bertrand Russell and Aldous Huxley's newly widowed wife, Laura Archera Huxley. This was heady stuff for the Baltimore housewife on the lam. The Reverend Rhinehart just *had* to be brilliant to see the big picture as he did, to see Madalyn in true intellectual historical perspective.

Actually there was much evidence to support the thesis that the Reverend Rhinehart was, at the very least, preternaturally shrewd. Born on April Fool's Day in 1936 in Nunn, Colorado, to a railroad man and his wife, Keith always seemed like "a very refined" child to neighbors and friends of the family—a child who liked to "play at spiritualism." But he was more than a precocious kid. He was a prodigy. By the time he was fifteen he had become a medium, conducting neighborhood séances. At sixteen he was driving a big Cadillac around town. That same year, according to newspaper accounts, Rhinehart stayed at a "spiritualist camp" outside of Tacoma, Washington, for the summer; there he met a "homosexual teacher" who took him to "some of the homosexual places in Seattle," Rhinehart related.

Seattle was a good town, liberal, easygoing. Rhinehart liked the scene, and enrolled in the University of Washington in 1955. Through his mediumship and his dynamic personality, Rhinehart acquired enough followers to found a nonprofit organization—his own cosmic, free-form church—in the then rundown Capitol Hill district of Seattle. His spiritual specialty was communicating with the departed relatives of his flock.

Soon enough, it became evident that Rhinehart had extraordinary powers that went well beyond communicating with the dead. Rhinehart's body could synthesize precious gemstones and crystals! The circumstances had to be just right—but *yes*—he was able to extrude the stones through various areas of his body; including his thighs, chest, and eyes. With this amazing ability he became known to his followers and disciples as "Christos Logos Kumara," or "Master Kumara" for short.

The jewels Rhinehart produced from his physical being—mostly semiprecious crystalline stones—had healing powers. At least, those who purchased them believed so—some disciples allegedly paying as much as ten thousand dollars for a single extrusion from the Master's body. In fact, the Reverend Rhinehart's spiritualist church had a strong incoming cash flow along with the outflow of gems from his person.

Things didn't always go that smoothly for the Reverend Christos Logos Kumara though. Sure, sometimes it was great, like the session in upstate New York when, with his psychokinetic powers at full throttle, he got a trumpet to fly around a room, almost dinging a local newspaper publisher on the noggin. But there were many bumpier times for the guru, as when he caused a riot at the University of Windsor, in Ontario.

The Reverend had gone to Detroit to purchase his favorite car—two of them, in fact—white Cadillac Eldorados direct from the factory. He evidently thought he might make a little money to defray his travel expenses by holding a séance and gem extrusion for students at Windsor, just across the Canadian border. At two bucks a head, the Reverend packed an auditorium with five hundred people. After doing his usual netherworldly communications—this time contacting a dead Kennedy—he went on to proclaim that he was in the right frame of mind to perform gemstone extrusions from his body and these precious by-products would be dispensed as gifts to those who wished to come up and receive them.

After filling his mouth with water and getting it taped shut, he had assistants lead him—apparently already entranced—to a tentlike structure on the stage, according to reporters who were present. Approximately a hundred people were allowed to gather around the tent to get their gift extrusions. "Volunteers" had supposedly already checked the Reverend's person and the tent, to make sure that everything was on the up-and-up.

Soon, to the accompaniment of spirit voices of many timbres and pitches, a good volume of small stones began appearing from underneath the tent. The stones were, as promised, distributed to the audience. It was then tactfully suggested that the Reverend could produce larger stones—with commensurately stronger healing powers—if anyone cared to donate to his Seattle church. For an hour, with the Reverend's followers singing hymns and intermittently chanting the Lord's Prayer, he prolifically extruded, until a university student named Leyla Zogbi popped from behind the tent and shouted: "It's a rip-off!"

The student exclaimed that she saw Rhinehart remove the tape from his mouth and use a trumpetlike device to produce the weird voices. "The stones," she charged, were "coming from a pouch on his lap."

Pandemonium ensued. The professor who had set up the session—a friend of the Reverend's who had been relieved of duties at the University of Washington for unspecified reasons—stepped forward and pleaded with the audience to hold tight and let Master Kumara defend himself.

After some delay, according to eyewitness accounts, the Reverend emerged from the tent in a state of dishevelment and agitation—the tape visibly twisted and out of place on his mouth. He removed it completely, spat out some water, pointed dramatically at his student accuser, and thundered: "Liar!" Again chaos reigned. As devout believers and doubting infidels screamed at each other, campus police spirited the Reverend safely away from the bedlam he had conjured.

In Hawaii, things with Madalyn would be different. Reverend Rhinehart was dealing with a sophisticated and knowledgeable woman in her intellectual prime. There would be no talk of his producing gemstones from his body on command. When Madalyn, besotted with Rhinehart but still wary, proposed that he conduct a séance with her "controlling the conditions," Rhinehart enthusiastically agreed. Madalyn went home, lined up participants from her wide-ranging coterie of Hawaiian acquaintances, had four shots of whiskey, and prayed: "*Please* Mr. God, don't let him make a fucking fool out of himself!"

The séance was held in the evening at the beautiful hillside home of a well-to-do, full-blooded descendant of island royalty. The observers, along with Madalyn and the tanned, sleek Reverend Rhinehart, gathered with the lights of Honolulu in the picture window, competing with the decorations of the lovely Christmas tree that dominated the living room.

The Reverend distributed what he called billets—actually just three-by-five cards—to the participants and asked each of them to write at least three questions to "someone in the spirit world." Madalyn felt like a fool and couldn't come up with anything to write so she just stared at the white card. Finally, with everyone around her joking and giving the Reverend a hard time, Madalyn scribbled a silly query to a departed aunt: "Why in hell did you dislike my mother so much?" The billets were all placed in a basket. Rhinehart had his eyes taped shut and a Turkish towel wrapped around his head.

Soon his body began to jerk and his head started whipping back and forth. Madalyn was mortified at this display, but was

distracted by another woman who motioned for all the participants to change places to try and confuse the blindfolded, spas-
modically gyrating Reverend. As they were doing this, a new
voice burst forth from Rhinehart—a resonant, commanding baritone—totally unlike his usually dulcet tones.

Madalyn got chills. The voice coming from Rhinehart was
so different in quality and intonation that it could *only* be the
voice of a different person. Still blindfolded, Rhinehart—or the
spirit now inhabiting him—took cards from the wicker basket
and proceeded to identify each billet with the name of the correct
author. Everyone was flabbergasted. Even Bill, who had been
cynically watching the proceedings from a corner of the living
room, was amazed.

When he got to Madalyn's card, the Reverend had her come
up and receive the billet that she'd written, and then go back to
her chair and read her question out loud. After she did so, Rhinehart informed everyone, in yet another new weird voice—he was
now a "Mr. Kensington"—that there was a trio in the room that
nobody could see but who wanted to communicate with Madalyn. Then he said the names: "Laura, Suzanne, and Marie."

Madalyn froze. They were the first names of three women in
her family; in life the women were inseparable spinster sisters.
Madalyn had thought of them just for a moment when she was
trying to come up with the query for the billet.

Rhinehart, or the guide "Mr. Kensington" working inside
him, proceeded to lead Madalyn through some long-forgotten
family happenings. And as she listened, she realized that her
dress was glued to her body with perspiration. When "Mr. Kensington" left to concentrate on the others present, Madalyn saw
the attendees—each in his or her turn—change from humorous
skepticism to incredulity and finally to sheer astonishment as the
Reverend made equally penetrating statements about their pasts.

It was the most incredible performance Madalyn had ever
seen in her life. She couldn't believe it. Nor could her son Bill,

who had helped set the séance up, thinking it was just another money-making scam of his mother's. Even years later, when rationally dissecting the Hawaii experience regarding Rhinehart, Bill couldn't come up with any explanation for what happened. He just called it "spooky."

Of course, Madalyn—being an adherent of dialectical materialism—knew in her mind that *somehow* Rhinehart was conning them, even if her infatuated heart didn't want to believe it. But the question was, how? How in hell was this guy pulling it off? While watching Rhinehart's ninety-minute performance, Madalyn went through every theory she could come up with to explain the mechanics of the scam, and nothing held water.

Finally the séance ended. After a series of closing convulsions, the towel was removed from the Reverend's head. The tape was still covering his eyes so tightly that when it was pulled off, it took some of his eyebrow hairs with it. The Reverend immediately resumed his normal softly ebullient personality. "Mr. Kensington" had apparently left Rhinehart's body for the regions from whence he'd come. Madalyn tore for home and got drunk.

For two days, Madalyn cross-examined Rhinehart unmercifully over tikis. He said he visualized everything—he was not conscious of distance or time—the ideas instantaneously came into his mind. Madalyn thought it was bullshit. But WHERE had he gotten the information about her family? There had been details that he provided that not even her mother or brother would know.

Madalyn asked him if he'd stay in Hawaii for a while. She wanted to set up controlled experiments with him to document his abilities. Rhinehart counterproposed that they put together a string of fee-based public séances. Madalyn jumped. You betcha! She'd love to start such an enterprise. There was money there, and besides, if *she* couldn't figure out how Rhinehart pulled off his scam, it was gawd damn sure that nobody else would be smart enough either. And perhaps the Master could work his magic with some additional cash flow for Madalyn's coffers. Even though she'd culled money from bank accounts in Baltimore, and good donations were coming in from her mailing lists, Madalyn was still crying poverty. She had just written in her magazine that she was "saving used tea bags for 4th go-rounds."

Actually, the Reverend Rhinehart confided, he was a bit strapped too, having blown most of his funds supposedly buying local television time in Seattle to broadcast his series of one-hour documentaries. So they formed a partnership. They'd charge ten dollars a person for a séance and handle thirteen people for each one-hour show. They'd blitz the islands doing two per night, six nights a week, with—as Madalyn put it—"the Lord's day off." According to Madalyn's estimate, the potential gross would be around fifteen hundred "clams" a week.

However, when he got back to his church headquarters in Seattle, the Reverend Rhinehart decided he had too many other commitments, and he sent a young woman whom he had personally trained as a substitute medium for the Hawaii venture. Unfortunately, the Reverend Rhinehart's pinch-hitting séance leader was not nearly so masterful as he. According to Madalyn, who'd set up all the publicity for the first seance, the sub-guru tried hard but her batting average was only about 60 percent— respectable enough for extrasensory work but well under the 95 percent average that Christos Logos Kumara himself batted for in his séances.

The next day, *The Honolulu Advertiser,* whose reporter had been invited to observe the initial show, ran a big story on the séance, trashing it totally. It was really unfair, Madalyn sniffed at the coverage. But worse than the bad review and perhaps because of it, try as she might she couldn't buy a single spot on any island radio or TV station to promote further séances. As well, the newspapers turned down her proffers of hard cash for ads announcing the program. When she tried getting pamphlets printed to pass out on the street, not a printer would take the job. And, just in case Madalyn did find a printer for her promotional flyers, the police warned her not to distribute them. Finally, a Hawaiian all-night radio talk show host, desperate to fill airtime, allowed Madalyn's substitute medium to hold an all-nighter séance "live on the air" across the Pacific. He allegedly lost his contract the next week.

Madalyn hung on, re-dragging acquaintances to the séances, but she knew the business wasn't going to fly. Before giving up, she sent an SOS to the Reverend Rhinehart asking him for help. It was to no avail. In fact, it was the Reverend who needed help. He was in the slammer. Somehow he had become involved with a sixteen-year-old male hustler in downtown Seattle. The young man reported his encounter with the Reverend to police and they promptly arrested and charged Rhinehart with sodomy. The Master was later convicted and sent to prison, perhaps the first and last prisoner in the history of the State of Washington to be incarcerated in the maximum security penitentiary at Walla Walla for committing consensual sodomy. Rhinehart appealed to the State Supreme Court, claiming that the sodomy laws prevented him from following his personal religious dictates, but unfortunately for the Master, the State Supreme Court upheld the conviction, citing bigamy statutes as a precedent.

More than a decade after his release from prison, having regained his ministry and followers, the Reverend returned in triumph to the walls of the Washington State Penitentiary at Walla Walla. Somehow he talked the tough, legendary warden of the prison—B. J. Rhay—into allowing him to put on an extravaganza for the inmates. The six-hour show, including a chorus line of members of his Seattle flock, was documented by *The Seattle Times*. Reverend Rhinehart, as master of ceremonies, cavorted in a "variety of costumes"—one of which was a tight dress with a slit up the side.

With some degree of asperity, a columnist for the Seattle daily noted that the Rhinehart show also included giveaways of money and presents—some thirty-five thousand dollars' worth—

to the inmates. There was even a gift certificate for a lucky felon
that covered the costs of a two-thousand-dollar sex-change operation. Before closing his performance, the Reverend proselytized
the inmates, urging them to remember: "Nobody's straight and
nobody is gay in our religion. They're just plain sexual!"

As it turned out, Madalyn had no time to think about the implo-
sion of the Reverend Rhinehart's ministry. Even with topflight
attorney Hyman Greenstein working overtime on the case,
Madalyn and Bill lost their appeal of the extradition order filed
by the State of Maryland. It was now inevitable that she and her
son would be taken back to Baltimore to face the possibility of
more than two centuries of prison between them. It was time to
look hard at other options before the Baltimore police extradition
team came knocking at the door, with handcuffs at the ready.

Serendipitously, there was an interesting prospect at hand.
In passing, Madalyn had said in one of her many interviews that
she would like to start a university for atheists. A Bay Area
woman had responded with an inquiry, asking if Madalyn might
be interested in joining the faculty of a newly established "experimental" college outside Mexico City in a small mountain resort
known as Valle de Bravo. The woman said the college administration needed guidance through some rocky financial times.

It sounded pretty damn good when Madalyn noodled the
possibilities. Perhaps the most attractive aspect was that she and
Bill wouldn't need to use their passports to get into Mexico. They
could easily get new ID papers and slip into the country anywhere along the loose border. Anyway, even if they were discovered to be fugitives, Mexico had an honorable history of giving
asylum to even the most controversial political figures, and
Madalyn had no doubt that she was right up there with Leon
Trotsky.

She shared the plan to make a run for Mexico with Bill.

There were caveats for him, though. Madalyn was insistent that he not bring along his wife or the newborn Robin. He was to leave them on their own, with no resources, and not a friend within five thousand miles. It was a rotten thing to do, Bill knew, but his mother was adamant. The choice was, abandon his family or face decades in prison.

In early May 1965, the pair took separate flights to San Francisco to lessen the possibility of their being detected. Madalyn traveled in disguise with forged identity papers under the name of Mary Jane O'Connor. At San Francisco International Airport, her contact, Daphne Stange, said she found Madalyn dressed in a nun's habit. Stange took the disguise in stride. She was in her early twenties, a breezy hippie chick with a cool, seen-it-all air about her—recently returned from Paris where she'd been living with her psychiatrist since she was fourteen.

One of Daphne's current boyfriends—a major Bay Area drug dealer—had procured a beat-up 1953 Plymouth sedan for their trip down to Valle de Bravo. He was undoubtedly a better judge of cannabis than of used cars, since the elderly vehicle had a fatal engine seizure just across the border in Mexico. To his happy surprise, Bill was able to sell it to a cabbie outside Tijuana for $250 cash without a title. It was enough for the trio to take the train down to Mexico City in high style—literally and figuratively.

Daphne turned Bill on to her stash of primo, growers-select weed on the platform next to the bar car as the train rolled south. He thought it was great. Even better was when they made love in his sleeping compartment to the rhythm of the tracks. For Daphne it was less pleasant. She told friends, when they reached Valle de Bravo, that Bill beat her up and also his mother.

David Waters picked up his "fiancée"—Marti Budde—at her place of employment in Peoria, a massage parlor by the name of Belinda's Body Shop, at around 6 P.M. As far as Waters was concerned, Marti may have worked as a masseuse doing her daily share of hand jobs, but she carried herself well. She might not have been classy, but she didn't act like a whore or sound like one. He liked her.

They dropped off a coworker of Marti's and then got a nice little high going—Kessler's whiskey, some good weed. David always needed to relax. He was constantly tensed up. Even though he didn't have a job, no boss yelling at him, no family demands, he was still stressed out, and the only way to relieve the tension was to get high. This tension thing went back a long way. As far back as he could remember, there was this anger inside him, deep down, and it could boil over in a flash, like milk heating in a shallow pan.

Dope took the edge off. But then dope, especially weed, would start him remembering things—bad things. That bitch. He wondered if she still had Stevie's ashes sitting on her living room table. The bitch wouldn't bury Stevie. The cops shot him down like a dog, right in front of her. She got her own son killed—but didn't have the decency to even bury him.

Stevie . . . Damn. Little Stevie . . . They were like two abandoned pups—maybe more like two little soldiers together. God, he loved his little brother like nothing else in this world. He missed him so. They could share a word, even a look, and they'd connect with total understanding. The shrinks might call it "trauma bonding." Whatever it was, it was high-level communication. That is, until Stevie started to lose his fucking mind.

OK. It was time to go over to the bitch's apartment. This had to end. Stevie needed to be buried and he'd do it himself if he had to. But hell, he didn't have any money for a decent burial next to Grandma's grave—Grandma who took care of them while the bitch was walking the streets with her whore-wig on.

Waters pounded on the apartment door. When Betty Waters opened it, she knew there was going to be trouble. David had that wild dope-look in his eyes again—just like Steven used to. She knew all about it. She was NOT ready for this. She was feeling so so nice and mellow from the Valium and those other pills that Dr. Feelgood had given her. She just wasn't ready for David, doped up or not. Nevertheless, she invited Marti and David upstairs and offered David a can of Pabst Blue Ribbon, hoping that might cool him out. Waters took the beer and asked for whiskey. Betty said that there wasn't any in the house—she was back on the wagon.

"When are you going to bury him?" David asked, pointing to the urn on the funky living room table.

"When I get my diploma and got me a job," Betty replied, trying to sound unperturbed.

"You bitch. You whore." The words poured out from David Waters. "He'd be alive today if you hadn't been walking the streets." They were statements, evenly delivered without shouting, but with a deadly menacing edge. Then the cadence of curses wavered. His voice started to quaver and crack. He was crying.

He went into the kitchen and came back and hurled a handful of eggs at his mother. Some yolk splattered on the urn containing Steven's ashes. Marti reached over to wipe it off. "Don't touch that!" Waters shouted. He reached into his coat pocket and removed a glove. Putting it on, he tenderly picked up the urn and dabbed away the egg.

Now in uncontrolled fury, he went back to the kitchen. There was a broom in the corner. A broom! He'd beat the fucking witch with her own broom. It would feel so good. He went back to the living room where his mother was curled in a fetal position on the couch and smacked the broom across her shins in a full baseball swing. It broke. The head of the broom went flying, leaving him with a couple of feet of broomstick left in his hands. Whack. It broke too.

It wasn't enough. He wasn't satisfied. He went into her bedroom. There was that fucking whore-wig of hers on a Styrofoam pedestal. He brought it out to the living room. With his lighter, he tried to set the wig on fire, but it wouldn't catch. He went back and got the pedestal for the wig, put the flame to it, and WHOOSH. It caught fire and quickly created a cloud of acrid smoke.

He started to laugh. It was the odd stoned cackle of a man who didn't know how to laugh. He became hysterical with laughter as the flames consumed the burning wig stand as the women watched, both cowering. But now the flames were too big. Waters dropped the burning mass of plastic onto the apartment floor and stopped laughing. Jesus. The whole place might go up. But—there was a handy fire extinguisher. Hah. He'd piss out the flames! And save a little for the bitch whore.

TEN

Mexican Fiasco

What a place Valle de Bravo was in the mid-1960s—a sanctuary for the cognoscenti, as yet undefiled by middle-aged Canadian sightseers on package bus tours. The climate was gorgeous, the air pristine, and the views, especially of the dormant volcanoes, were inspiring even without a dose of the magic mushrooms or mind-blowing weed that could be acquired for a song.

High in the Sierra Madre, but only seventy-eight miles from downtown Mexico City, Valle de Bravo had been settled for more than four hundred years by Europeans and eight hundred years, perhaps far longer, by Amerinds. Timothy Leary's people had visited to drop acid. Old-money hipsters from the Bay Area had also found the environs salutary in climate and culture. Even upper-level cold warriors—the Soviet and U.S. ambassadors to Mexico—came to spend time at the posh country club bordering on the large artificial lake that was part of the alpine setting.

Valle de Bravo—or Valle, as it was known to the locals—was unusually well organized for a town of colonial Mexico. Streets were laid out in a clean grid, cobblestoned centuries ago by slave labor under the Spanish. Also unusual were the two-foot-high curbs that all the roads had. The importance of this feature became readily apparent when the monsoonal spring rains hit and the streets would become troughs for mini-rivers. But such inconveniences were relatively rare. Mostly Valle was touched with nothing more than a soft nighttime pattering in the rainy season. All in all, the weather was nigh on perfect. In fact, so fine was it that monarch butterflies by the millions made their fabled annual Northern Hemispheric migration to the mountains just outside town, choosing the area as their winter redoubt—covering the high pines like psychedelic snow with their jewel-like wings.

Into this setting an eccentric young academic visionary brought his dream. Raymond Peat's scholastic vita would be a reflection of a heady intellectual mishmash. His master's degree in literature and philosophy came from the University of Oregon, where he wrote his thesis on the mystical, oddball English writer and painter William Blake—whose name Peat was to give his experimental college. Peat's dazzling academic potpourri continued with advanced studies in painting in Mexico, linguistics at Ohio State, and finally a doctorate in biology at the University of Oregon. Peat's dissertation was titled "Age-Related Oxidative Changes in the Hamster Uterus."

Between painting studies in Mexico in the late 1950s and early 1960s, Peat taught at newly flowering experimental colleges in the Midwest and California. At twenty-seven years old, with an appropriate overview of experimental higher education under his belt, Peat decided to found his own college in Mexico City. He would aim at recruiting graduating high school students in the United States who were bright but had trouble working within the system. Practically speaking, Peat was looking for kids with parents who had money, but whose grades were so lousy that no stateside college or university would touch them.

The young educational entrepreneur leased a lovely old two-story building in the hip Colonia Roma section of Mexico City for the Blake College "campus" and gathered a young faculty via his contacts in the fine arts community that was thriving in that bursting megalopolis.

The student body was to be approximately a dozen students. They would pay $135 per quarter. (Professors received $8 for each lecture.) It was a bargain, given the quality and energy of the teachers, even if Blake College was strictly nonaccredited. Peat bought four ads in *The Saturday Review of Literature*—a highbrow, egghead New York periodical—for $50 per issue. He filled his student quota quickly and the dream of Blake College—brave experiment in learning—became a reality.

Peat's strategy—and the fit with his underachiever students—was mostly excellent. Blake College, during its brief lifetime—before Madalyn destroyed it—had some remarkable successes with students who started to enjoy the process of learning for the first time, and who were to matriculate to respected conventional universities and attain academic achievements neither they nor their parents had dreamed possible.

Unfortunately, the landlord who owned the Blake College campus in Mexico City saw the group of well-fed gringos as a potential source of serious revenue and decided to raise the rent past the point acceptable to the cash-strapped young college president. But Dr. Peat had an ace up his sleeve. Peter Marin, his young literature professor—a tough-talking but erudite Brooklyn transplant—played in a high-stakes weekly poker game way up in the mountains in a pretty little town called Valle de Bravo. Marin, who would later become a successful author, had seen a good-sized hacienda for rent that would be perfect for Blake College.

Peat was sold on the idea and the campus was moved. The new campus in Valle de Bravo was a gorgeous, enormous fifteen-room Spanish-colonial home that had been turned into a hotel. Built in 1550, it had four-foot-thick adobe walls, high ceilings, and ancient wood floors. Tiled patios on the sides of the structure overlooked the lake and mountains in the distance. Peat took the topmost bedroom as his office-retreat. He shared it with his appealing, slightly zaftig student-lover Daphne Stange—the recruiter of the fatal virus that was to kill the dream.

When Daphne returned to Valle with her fugitive mother-and-son duo, she told Peat some disturbing news. On the train ride down to Mexico City, Madalyn had brashly outlined her plans for taking over Blake College and making it into an atheist institution. Peat didn't take Daphne's warning seriously. Early on he had seen Madalyn in action with the students, who—not surprisingly—had taken an immediate dislike to her overbearing and authoritarian manner. Shortly after Madalyn arrived, one nymph-like student got up on the communal dinner table and danced barefoot through Madalyn's dinner in protest of her behavior. In turn, Madalyn was openly disdainful of what she perceived to be counterculture rabble, and she was angry at their lack of deference toward her.

Peat was also lulled by the fact that Blake College—or any American outfit like it—depended on sure-footed political skill with their Mexican hosts. Madalyn was certainly not a Latin political operative. Peat had no doubt that with her brash, indelicate ways she'd have as hard a time with the Latino culture as she did learning even a few words of rudimentary Spanish.

In fact, Peat—always an easy touch for any underdog—went to bat for Madalyn, pulling strings in Mexico City to help her with applying for political asylum. Even after being told of her plans for Blake College, Peat set up Madalyn and her son Bill with good housing and three squares a day, which the atheist diva partook of heartily. And that wasn't all. Peat actually found her a lover.

Amongst the unusual sociocultural creatures of the American expatriate community in Valle was a particularly peculiar specimen—one Richard O'Hair, a balding, wiry, leprechaun-like man. He claimed to some to be an artist, and to others to be a

CIA operative assigned by the embassy to keep an eye on the drug-infested American community in Valle. O'Hair had been a Marine during World War II, and had entered into some sort of shadowy intelligence career after leaving the Corps. Prior to his Valle "post," O'Hair's last known employment was as a handyman-custodian in the Chicago area, where he spied on left-wing groups for the FBI. Bouncing down to Mexico, he moved from the FBI's payroll to the CIA's—or at least that was what he liked to brag to people. When drunk, he would pull out his CIA papers along with the long-barreled revolver that he carried in an open holster, and wave them about.

Even with no discernible means of support, O'Hair was a regular in the social scene of expatriates in the little Mexican mountain resort town, and he could certainly be an exciting addition to any guest list. For example, O'Hair, always in his cups, was dazzling a hostess with his revolver one evening when it went off—the bullet ricocheting around the room without hitting anybody, to the amazement of the gathering of stoned cocktailers.

O'Hair was also known to clomp around town on a horse that he had purchased from one of the cast of *The Magnificent Seven,* which was filmed in the mountains around Valle. As often as not, his daily bottle of tequila or vodka would impair his equestrian skills considerably and O'Hair would fall from his mount—mostly on his head. There were few days when the sodden spy didn't make the scene with an assortment of nicks, scrapes, and bruises on his bald pate.

Peat brought his parents down from San Diego to Valle to help with the college administration and they soon were making the social scene there as well. After Peat's father, Sidney, told a hostess that he'd lost his wallet, she introduced him to Richard O'Hair, since "Dick" had "connections" at the U.S. embassy. When Sidney Peat went down to the embassy in Mexico City with his problem, new ID was waiting for him. He was told by embassy personnel that "Dick O'Hair" had vouched for him.

Sidney was impressed, especially since he didn't know O'Hair from a hole in the ground. In any case, they became friends. The retired Sidney Peat enjoyed spending sunshine-filled afternoons listening to O'Hair's alcohol-embroidered yarns and swapping some of his own. Soon O'Hair became an accepted hanger-on at the Blake campus.

It was here that he was introduced to Madalyn. Ray Peat, ever the nice guy, had set up a cot for O'Hair at Blake College so that Richard could sleep off his drunks without having to ride anywhere. And it was this kindness that was the beginning of the Madalyn-Richard matchup—though, in all probability, it was not love at first sight.

Yes, Madalyn was alleged to be horny as hell, but it may not have been physical need so much as the need to quench her vanity. Doubtless she desired to assure herself that not only was she an Atheist Amazon of the highest historical significance, but she was still a hot chick too. Regrettably, it had probably been quite a few years since a normal human male had thought so. But O'Hair, whose vision certainly must have been diminished by his drinking habits, seemed to have lust for Madalyn, regardless of the corporeal realities.

However, as it turned out, Richard O'Hair was more motivated by cash and duty-to-country than carnal desire when it came to romancing Madalyn. Although she would have been thrilled to know it, Madalyn didn't realize that FBI headquarters in Washington had been following her every move. Memos on her activities in Mexico were circulated regularly amongst the highest pooh-bahs of the Bureau.

FBI documents of the time show that Clyde Tolson, J. Edgar's confidant and rumored lover; Cartha "Deke" DeLoach, chief assistant and fix-it man; William Sullivan, the later-disgraced Watergater; and, with near certainty, the Boss Hog—

Hoover himself—had all assiduously kept abreast of Madalyn's movements and doings since the early Baltimore days.

The FBI was, in all likelihood, first stimulated by Madalyn's attempts to defect to the Soviet Union, and by her work for a pro-Castro group shortly before JFK's assassination. Years later, Madalyn would claim in her diary that the FBI had turned over a 650-page dossier on her after she filed a Freedom of Information Act request—and that was just the first installment, Madalyn bragged.

In any case, what better way was there for the G-men to keep tabs on a possible atheistic menace to the American Way of Life than to have one of its own guys marry the subversive threat? This may have been the vital mission of Richard O'Hair when he bedded the compliant Madalyn on his rickety cot somewhere in a corner of the Blake College administrative offices in Valle de Bravo.

Soon, Madalyn wanted to improve her surroundings. So when Peat started teaching nutrition pro bono three days a week in a nearby Mexican village, she and her lover–CIA/FBI informant would move into Peat's office-apartment as soon as he departed, to avail themselves of its fine view and elevated status. Madalyn also took the opportunity of Peat's absences to declare to the students that she was now the official registrar of Blake College and they should to start handing over tuition money to her.

She actually collected and cashed a number of tuition checks in Mexico City with Richard's help before Peat discovered the treachery. Dr. Peat took it all innocently in stride. He only told Madalyn to stop sleeping in his apartment when he was gone, still hoping against hope that if he didn't get her too riled she would teach the sociology and law courses she'd promised as part of their deal. But she never did. Instead Madalyn commandeered his apartment again when he left the next week—and this time, she took the opportunity to burn much of his administrative paperwork.

As his mother plotted and connived, Bill Murray spent his last teenage days in high-octaned frivolity. Bill was a young stud now; he stood six foot three or four and had the unforgettable sly, piercing hazel eyes of his mother. All in all, he was an exceptionally fine-looking male specimen—especially compared to the effete hippie types who had gravitated to Valle.

For Bill at nineteen, Dr. Ray Peat's cutting-edge counter-culture educational offerings had zero appeal—his hormones were just pulling too hard. Bright as he was, Bill wasn't ever really interested in education and certainly not at this point in his ragged life. Instead, he spent the balmy Mexico summer days trying to learn to schmooze and hustle at Valle's stylish lakeside country club, or he'd ride his bike in the mountains. Nights were reserved for smoking primo grass during trysts with the soft and lovely Daphne, free-loving roommate of the young college president.

Unfortunately for Bill, the sweet bachelor days were about to end meanly and abruptly once more. He had gotten a letter from Susan, abandoned in Honolulu, with an alluring request. She had a friend who was in a mess. Would he pick her up at the airport in Mexico City and help her out? The young and willing errant husband—perhaps out of a sense of guilt, perhaps sensing the chance to boff a stray damsel-in-distress—complied. Bill rented a car and drove to the airport, where he waited expectantly for the lady he'd pledged to rescue. When he saw Susan heading toward him down the passenger way, with baby Robin in her arms along with an expeditionary load of baby gear, he almost threw up.

Bill was on the spot. If he took his plain-looking wife and their infant daughter back to Valle, his young Romeo-stud image would never recover. He had brought enough cash along to stay at the Hilton in downtown Mexico City—just in case the damsel-in-distress had needed accommodations and personal comforting. But he could only hold out for forty-eight hours before bankrupting himself, so the panicked young tomcat called his mother for help.

Madalyn caught the next bus to Mexico City and checked into a nearby room. According to Bill's autobiographical account, Madalyn was livid with Susan. "You left my little boy there alone with his grandmother? You bitch, why didn't you bring him with you? That fucking old bitch of a mother of mine will ruin him. We have to get him down here with us!"

Actually, Madalyn wasn't really worried about Jon Garth, the son she'd deserted. She was more worried about what Susan's trek to Mexico would mean for her own legal status. Susan could have been followed and, if she had been, there would be an immediate possibility of deportation. As well, now there was no reason not to have Jon Garth with them. Knowledge of his abandonment would only tarnish her international reputation. On Madalyn's command, Uncle Irv put Jon Garth on a plane for Mexico City after flying all the way to Los Angeles with him.

Actually, it was just as well that Susan, Robin, and Jon Garth had gotten out of Hawaii, as there was no going back for Madalyn or Bill. Hawaiian courts had approved Maryland's extradition request and mother and son were now fugitives from two states facing a hundred years or more each in the penitentiary if caught and convicted. Their attorney in Hawaii, Hyman Greenstein, humiliated by Madalyn's flight after he had vouched for her, urged Bill to turn himself in and face justice in Maryland. Greenstein advised that Bill "was too young to be running away from this thing for the rest of his life."

He had no advice for Madalyn. How much Madalyn owed him in attorney's fees before she left for Mexico, he would not say.

It was probably a goodly sum, since his polished services didn't come cheap. But as far as Greenstein was concerned, if Madalyn paid off one hundred times the fees that she owed him, it couldn't remedy what she had done to his reputation.

It's a good bet Madalyn didn't give a thought to attorney Greenstein's feelings back in Hawaii. Things were getting distinctly rocky in Valle de Bravo. Bill had had enough. With courage well beyond his nineteen years, he decided to split the scene and leave his mother's sway forever. He would try and start a new life in the States with the false identity papers he had acquired in California. This time he'd take along his family and make a go of marriage and fatherhood, such as it was. The generous atheist-nudist from Kansas, Carl Brown, had given him six thousand dollars in insurance stock as a birthday present and Bill intended to use this nest egg to try and build a normal existence.

Guardedly he planned the escape from Valle, hiring a taxi to haul them and all the baby gear to Mexico City at dawn before his mother woke up. Nonetheless, the next morning Madalyn heard the cab being loaded and ran out into the street in her bathrobe. Bill remembered the moment clearly in his autobiography. "They have no *dinero*!" she shouted at the cabbie as she ran after the accelerating vehicle. Finally she gave up the chase, but Bill could still hear his mother screaming, "Come back. I want you here!"

What exact plans she had for her son, daughter-in-law, and granddaughter, she never revealed. Bill believed that she simply wanted to have them around to satisfy her need for dominance— a need that was being frustrated by the obstreperous students of Blake. However, Madalyn *did* have a specific plan for her student enemies—and diabolical one it was. Not only would she take over Blake College in a coup d'etat, she would figuratively liqui- date the entire student body—about a dozen American kids.

She'd get them busted for dope and deported. Then Madalyn would enthrone herself at Blake College and recruit promising atheist scholars from across the globe—at much fatter tuition rates, naturally.

The entire scheme was made possible by the departure of Ray Peat in the early fall of 1965. Dr. Peat's personal finances were not in very good shape, and he'd been offered a fine teaching position in linguistics at Montana State. He felt he had to take the job and let proxies administer Blake College for the next nine months or so. The college was a going affair. He had an able group of professors, a decent lease, and willing students. He also thought he had run Madalyn and her entourage off—banning them from the campus. But ridding oneself of Madalyn was never easy. A queen termite needed the most toxic applications of pesticide for eradication, as Peat was to soon understand.

Right after his departure, Madalyn got in touch with the Federales. She had a lurid tale of drug use and debauchery to relate. Of course, the Blake College students were, in fact, doing some illicit drugs—mostly marijuana and hallucinogenic mushrooms. Sure, there was the usual free and easy sex associated with time, place, and human social chronology. But to the eager ears of the Federales, Madalyn painted Blake College as a bacchanalian dope factory. AND she had proof!

A veterinary hypodermic needle, used by one of the students to clear up his dog's ear infection, became the smoking-gun evidence of a heroin shooting gallery. A tape recording of a music teacher and students in a flute recital—admittedly a quite free-form performance—became proof of orgiastic narcotic rites. Vials of vitamins such as niacin—which Peat had used in his nutrition courses—were transformed into illicit drug stockpiles. Even Peat's morning ritual of attempting to get the students on a more healthy diet, by making wheat-germ pancakes for them, was alleged to be the mass ingestion of some organic hallucinogen.

Within days of Peat's departure Madalyn had gotten the entire student body—seventeen students—arrested in a one-day sweep. They were all thrown into a typically hellish jail outside of Mexico City, without necessity for official charges of any kind being brought, as there was no habeas corpus in Mexico. The young Americans were told they would be made an example of, and would be facing long prison sentences for drug usage and manufacture.

Luckily for the incarcerated, terrified Blake College students, Peter Marin, the young literature professor, had some powerful connections. One of the expatriates living in Valle was the daughter of Charles Mayo, cofounder of the Mayo Clinic. Her husband was a successful Mexican engineer who was a friend of the president of Mexico. Through El Presidente's office, he was given access to officials of the Ministry of Justice in whose hands the fate of the Blake students rested. Assurances were given, and perhaps cash money was laid on the appropriate outstretched palms. Whatever the case, the students were now to be deported immediately rather than being imprisoned for the serious crimes they were charged with.

But things weren't to go as planned for Madalyn, the instigator of the coup. Within a day or so of the student deportation, Madalyn was herself deported for entering Mexico under a false name. She was flown to Houston, Texas, and she made her way to San Antonio. There she stayed at a downtown hotel for four nights, before secretly returning to Mexico in a vehicle that she claimed was provided her by the Mexican government.

It was all very mysterious. However Madalyn may have pulled it off, two American reporters from Mexico City, Emmett Murray with *The Mexico City Times* and Terry McGarry of United Press International, found her, on September 19, 1965, ensconced back at the now empty hacienda that used to be Blake College. Dressed in her usual interview ensemble of housecoat-with-greasy-hair, Madalyn replied to the reporters' questions, saying that yes, she personally had engineered the destruction of Blake College and the arrest and deportation of the students. And yes, it was true—she was indeed going to marry Richard O'Hair within a month.

After the reporters left, Madalyn turned to Richard, who'd been silently slugging at a bottle of vodka during the interview, and asked, how in hell did they know about the marriage plans and even the exact wedding date? O'Hair shrugged, and Madalyn was immediately flushed and swollen with indignation and para- noia. The date had never been discussed outside of their bed- room. There could *only* be one explanation: The U.S. embassy had put a bug in their bed!

Madalyn immediately wrote of this new horror to Paul Krassner at *The Realist.* However, she embellished the event by stating that the reporters had told her at the outset that they had received their information from embassy personnel regarding the pending nuptials. Krassner printed Madalyn's claims—but with a rejoinder from UPI's McGarry, who wrote that he'd never told Madalyn that he'd received the information from the embassy. But, he said, Madalyn was correct—the information *did* come from her bed. It seemed that the only bug in Madalyn's bed was her husband-to-be. Richard O'Hair had planted the story of their wedding himself with the Associated Press stringer in Mexico City.

ELEVEN

Texas and Freedom

$\mathscr{A}$s a squatter in the remains of Blake College—the institution she single-handedly destroyed—Madalyn, the fugitive atheist, snitch, and fabricator of bogus drug accusations against more than a dozen compatriots, insolently and shamelessly held court. After her interviews with the American reporters, Madalyn met with Mexican journalists and recounted her jousts with the drug runners of Valle, and what a sly cover for an international drug operation the college had been. She made regular headlines in the Mexico City papers for days after her triumphant return to the scene of her victory over lawlessness and turpitude.

However, if Dr. Ray Peat, the experimental college's president, had underestimated Madalyn, she was even more guilty of underestimating him. Peat may have been young, but he was a cool customer, and he had his own brand of political savoir faire. He knew what levers to pull to rectify his mistaken judgments and revenge his broken dreams—perhaps more effectively than anybody else that Madalyn was to encounter. It was Peat, on his way to teach at Montana State, who had called the Baltimore police after the Blake College bust to let them know of Madalyn's whereabouts and effect her first deportation. Somehow she had avoided being picked up by authorities when she arrived in Houston on the flight from Mexico City by wearing a disguise—in all likelihood her nun's habit from the San Francisco trip.

This time, though, Peat would put a spike through the coffin lid. He would vanquish the vampire with the tried-and-true method—with the Cross. The youthful educator had excellent rapport with a powerful Roman Catholic bishop in Toluca, where Peat had taught nutrition courses gratis to the locals. Peat explained Madalyn's background to the bishop, her hateful attacks on the Catholic Church, and her plans to start an atheist university—the first one in the world—right in downtown Valle de Bravo. The bishop was outraged. It was intolerable. This could not be allowed to happen.

As Madalyn was setting the dinner table a few days after her last press interview, three plainclothes Federales knocked on the door and told Madalyn that they were taking her to Mexico City to get her "papers checked." She asked them what warrants they had. What right did they have to kidnap an American citizen? And what the hell could she do with her new puppy at this time of night? The Federales, armed with visible *pistolas* in their waistbands, weren't going for any nonsense. They told her it was a "routine matter" and to get dressed pronto. She was ordered not to pack anything—just come along with her younger son—she'd be back *mañana*. Richard was allowed to join them for the dangerous nighttime mountain ride to Mexico City. But on arrival there, he was summarily ordered out of the car and told he could see Madalyn the next day at the federal detention center.

Madalyn and nine-year-old Jon Garth soon found themselves in a forbidding, high-walled, barbwired compound on the crumbling outskirts of the huge city. They were placed in separate cells. When Madalyn asked to use the "facilities," she was accompanied by a male guard as escort for her entire *toilette*. Soon after her male-monitored ablutions, Madalyn was taken to the fingerprinting station.

Using her old Baltimore gambit, she refused to be

processed. But this wasn't gonna be like the good ol' U.S. of A. Without so much as a by-your-leave, the jailers grabbed the squirming gringa and forcibly took her prints. Later, from her cell, Madalyn chanted a litany of requests and questions to her silent jailers: What were the charges? When could she see a lawyer? Why couldn't she talk to the U.S. embassy? What about a gawd damn phone call?

Nada. Instead, an officer came to her cell and told Madalyn to sign papers he proffered without explanation. The documents were written in Spanish and she couldn't read them. It didn't make any difference, she told him—she wasn't about to sign *any* documents no matter what gawd damn language they were written in. But sign she did. Madalyn would later relate that she signed under severe duress, because the Federales made a threat against her that she'd never explain.

Richard was allowed to see her to "say goodbye" a few hours later. Madalyn and Jon Garth were then taken under armed guard to the airport and preboarded on a Braniff flight to San Antonio. Madalyn was advised that it wouldn't be a good idea to try and leave the plane before it took off. Federal officers would be waiting by the passenger gangway, and if she tried to escape, they would shoot her dead in front of her son if need be. Madalyn took them very seriously.

After literally leaving his mother in the dust of Valle de Bravo in August 1965, Bill Murray; his wife, Susan; and their daughter, Robin, flew to New York from Mexico City. The resourceful Bill had had to bribe his way out of Mexico by buying an "exit letter" from a Mexican government official for one hundred U.S. silver dollars. It apparently was an excellent investment, since the teenager had no problems reentering the United States, even with the dozen or so warrants out for his arrest in Maryland and Hawaii.

After cashing in the six thousand dollars' worth of stock given him by his atheist–nudist–wheat farmer benefactor, Bill settled himself, Susan, and infant Robin in a small furnished apartment in the Bronx, in New York City. He looked for work, but soon found that any decent job required references, and he had none. Within three weeks, Bill packed up his family and headed for Canada. There he ran into the same problem. Good jobs in Canada, as in the United States, required references. So Bill again hit the road with wife and baby. In a fading, used Volvo he had purchased, Bill drove for Detroit, where he hoped to find a good-paying factory job.

But before they could get out of Canada, the Volvo's engine died and the estimated repair costs exceeded Bill's cash supply. The jig was up. Bill gave Susan a choice. He could forge a check for enough money to fly her and Robin to Honolulu, or she could come with him. When she asked what he was going to do, he replied, "Rob banks." Susan picked Hawaii.

After putting them on a plane the next day, Bill mulled and then finally took the free advice that his sage Hawaiian attorney had given him a half year earlier. Bill was tired of running. At a ripe nineteen years of age, he decided to face the music. Heading back to Baltimore by bus, he called Uncle Irv in Honolulu from a rundown hotel in Wheeling, West Virginia. He asked his uncle to pawn any of his belongings that could bring some money and wire him what cash he could raise.

Either the phone was tapped or Uncle Irv turned in his wayward nephew to the authorities, since within hours of the call, Wheeling police had arrested Bill. The next day they handed him over to the Baltimore detectives who arrived to take him into custody. The young fugitive declined to fight extradition and upon arrival in Baltimore he began immediately serving the six-month sentence for contempt of court stemming from his trial in absentia.

Finally he would get lucky. A hotshot young investigative reporter, Nicholas Horrock, was working for the Baltimore *Sun.* He had some juice with the sheriff's department and was given a no-time-limit exclusive interview with Bill in jail. The article Horrock produced was a masterpiece of understated sympathy— a masterpiece because if Horrock had come on too strong for Bill, it would have backfired. Instead Horrock painted a portrait of an intelligent, strong young man who had been buffeted hard, who was willing to face the music—even if the melody was patently unjust.

The Horrock article stirred the conscience of Baltimore—or at least the conscience of the Maryland Bar Association, whose president got a couple of good criminal defense lawyers to take on Bill's contempt of court case pro bono. Someone at the bar association apparently pulled strings with the prosecutors as well, since Bill received the best present so far in his crazy young life. All the assault charges stemming from the big police fracas were being dropped. The prosecutor pointed to Bill's youth and his mother's causative actions as reasons for the decision. He pointedly added that they were *not* dropping charges against Madalyn.

Bill wasn't free yet, though. His new lawyers, using a writ of habeas corpus, challenged his contempt sentence in absentia before the municipal court judge in Baltimore. After taking the plea under advisement for a few days, the judge issued a lengthy ruling. The decision was as Madalyn had predicted it should have been, when she urged Bill to marry Susan to solve their legal difficulties. The judge found that the court had no right to prevent Bill from seeing Susan, because at the time they were man and wife. Therefore the contempt citation was invalid and the sentence had to be vacated.

The judge then offered Bill a simple apology for what the Baltimore courts had put him through: "We are rather moved by the plea and we feel badly that he spent thirty-one days in jail on charges that were without substance." And with that unusual expression of judicial empathy and culpability, William Joseph Murray III was set free.

In San Antonio, Texas, Madalyn had been arrested by local police immediately after disembarking from the Braniff flight from Mexico. She had somehow retained another excellent attorney, and he was putting on an awesome show of firepower and political muscle. Within a week of springing his client from the Bexar County jail, Maury Maverick Jr. had gotten the secretary of state to agree to hold a public hearing in the state capital, Austin, on Madalyn's plea not be extradited.

It would be a district court judge who would make the actual ruling in Madalyn's case, but Governor John Connally had the ultimate power to decide whether to send Madalyn back to face the charges in Maryland. In any case, Maverick—a plucky, bantam rooster ex-Marine and son of San Antonio's beloved New Deal mayor and congressman—was clearly capable of putting heavy pressure on the judicio-political system for a desperate client facing more than a hundred years in prison.

He and Madalyn made a good team, too. When they appeared at the packed hearing chamber, Madalyn had been well prepared by her media-hip attorney—and she knew how to deliver. Their theme was FREEDOM—and a fine theme it was for the Lone Star State. Madalyn's statement before the hearing was initially soaring—and obviously crafted by Maverick, a well-known wordsmith and later a newspaper columnist. "The Declaration of Independence of the Republic of Texas contains a ringing cry for religious liberty. There is no state in this great United States which can surpass Texas in the area of political dissent and religious liberty," Madalyn avowed to the much impressed media.

Then, moving from the historical, Madalyn went to the psychological—with a major guilt-trip routine. She told the secretary of state that her plight was worse than that of "a Negro being extradited to the state of Mississippi." In a voice quavering with emotion, Madalyn said that she was in mortal fear for her life. "If I go back to Maryland, I will be murdered," she said, on the verge of tears.

When the lawyer for the Texas attorney general's office was called to present that office's view, he said that Madalyn's problems were indeed eloquently presented, and perhaps even meritorious, but they were irrelevant. The issue at hand was simple: Were the Maryland extradition papers in order? And yes, it was his firm opinion that they were completely in order, and that the State of Maryland's request to bring back Madalyn to face criminal charges for assault on police officers was reasonable and should be honored.

The secretary of state adjourned the hearing by saying that he'd pass along his findings to Governor Connally, who would then decide whether or not to send Madalyn back to Maryland. In the meantime, in a fine show of a manners worthy of a true Texan gentleman, he offered the fugitive atheist and her attorney a state police motorcycle escort back to San Antonio, since she'd expressed concern for her safety. But the attorney general needn't have worried about her fate. Madalyn was going to get even luckier than her son had been.

On October 12, 1965, after reviewing the matter, Governor Connally signed papers allowing Madalyn's extradition. Of course, she and her savvy attorney had lots of appellate possibilities before she could be actually shipped out. But things didn't look good even with all the slick fancy-footing Maury Maverick could do. Her case was a run-of-the-mill interstate extradition with the only real wrinkle being her notoriety. However, as her son Bill was later to put it, "an angel" must have been watching over

Madalyn. What was about to happen in Maryland could either have been an act of divine deliverance on an atheist's behalf—or the best blind luck Madalyn would come by in her life.

The Maryland Court of Appeals had just reversed the murder conviction of a Buddhist, because under an ancient Maryland law, all jurors were required to swear to their personal belief in God. Lawyers for the killer Buddhist argued that his religion did not require a direct belief in a "Supreme Being" and that his co-religionists, as well as atheists and agnostics, were not allowed to be impaneled on juries, and therefore—tah tah—their client's constitutional right to a trial by his peers had been denied. The appeals court agreed, and the entire criminal legal system in Maryland was thereby plunged into an unholy mess from which Madalyn was to emerge smelling like a rose.

An estimated twenty-five hundred grand jury indictments across the state of Maryland were voided by the appellate ruling, since grand jurors also were sworn in with the must-believe-in-God oath along with regular jurors. Madalyn was under grand jury indictment for assaulting the police officers, and within days of the ruling, the chairman of the ACLU's state legal panel in Maryland filed a motion with a Baltimore criminal court to have the charges against Madalyn dismissed.

On October 26, 1965, all criminal charges against Madalyn were dropped—more than a hundred years' worth of prison time. The ACLU lawyer didn't even bother to get Madalyn's contempt conviction thrown out because the Maryland state attorney stated that his office planned no further attempts to extradite Madalyn for contempt alone. "As far as we're concerned," he said, "Mrs. O'Hair is a free woman."

TWELVE

The Atheist Empire and Gulag

*A*fter settling in Austin, Texas, to pursue her new freedom, Madalyn soon set to the task of creating an empire from scratch, using her excellent writing skills to craft rousing antireligious tracts for her *American Atheist* magazine—the chosen vehicle for gathering converts and cash. From the late 1960s to the mid-1970s, she worked diligently, if relatively quietly, at the laborious process of movement building, establishing a national network of atheist groups with local chapters, as well as continuing her legal battles with myriad civil suits for keeping religion out of public life.

But Madalyn recognized the beneficial economies of scale that the national limelight brought, and she itched to bathe in it once again. That opportunity was to arise through an initial series of debates broadcast from small stations in the outback of Louisiana and Texas with one Reverend Bob Harrington, the famed "Chaplain of Bourbon Street."

The Reverend Harrington, who often sported matching white plastic belts and shoes, was an old-school, tent-shaking, fire-and-brimstone evangelist who began his career by trying to save debauched New Orleanians who liked to drink and listen to Dixieland jazz. His place of worship was a small unmarked office–print shop located on the far end of Bourbon Street. (He claimed that he had to keep a low profile because city ordinances prohibited the operation of a church on that sinful street.)

The Reverend's office interior was covered with plaques and photographs of him shaking hands with politicians and leaders of all stripes and strata. A successful gospel singer, his gold records were also placed casually but strategically on the dingy walls. All was a testament to his persuasive abilities as a salesman of Jesus par excellence. Of course, like any good salesman, the Reverend Harrington was always searching for new hooks, and Madalyn looked like a humdinger.

After debating with her on the radio, the Reverend Harrington pitched a forceful offer at Madalyn. They'd go on the road together and they'd split the take 55–45, with Harrington getting the bigger cut and taking care of costs. Madalyn, who was in one of her economic funks and having trouble meeting mortgage payments, reluctantly signed on.

Madalyn's outlook toward the new enterprise was even less enthusiastic before their first "revival" in Tennessee when she found the warm-up act consisted of a dwarf and a gospel band, and the debate was billed as a "fight to the finish" between the Chaplain of Bourbon Street and the "demon-directed damsel." However, she quickly became a convert to the Reverend's concept when he handed her a paper sack with five thousand dollars in hundred-dollar bills after the show was over. That night she wrote in her diary, "Baltimore how long ago and far away you are!"

Quickly, Madalyn and Harrington refined their shtick as they toured the Bible Belt. First the gospel band would stir up the crowd with patriotic and Christian hymns. Then Madalyn would give her talk, usually a well-reasoned argument for the separation of church and state that would be continually interrupted with catcalls and boos. Then Harrington would come on, and really turn on the juice with a series of punchy one-liners such as telling the audience that they better get saved fast because, if they didn't, "Guess who you'll be going to hell with."

The Reverend would conclude by asking the audience to recite the Pledge of Allegiance with him. Just as Harrington got to the words "under God," Madalyn would come storming out on cue and try and grab the mic away from him. The crowd would go bonkers and Madalyn would be escorted out by a squad of armed police officers hired by the Reverend for that specific task.

Later, Madalyn would meet Harrington at his huge Double Eagle bus, furnished him by porn magnate Larry Flynt, who himself had momentarily become a Christian convert from atheism (later to be reconverted by Madalyn herself in a kind of reverse slam-dunk epiphany). The Chaplain of Bourbon Street, who celebrated his teetotaling victory over Satan whiskey, would traditionally pour himself a goodly snootch of Jack Daniel's as he divvied up the night's boodle.

Madalyn would average about fifteen hundred dollars an appearance and she loved the cash rolling in, but there was a problem; she was also in fear for her life—a fear that wouldn't be matched until her kidnapping three decades later. "I'm afraid one of these nuts is going to take it into his head to kill me. I worry about it. I have bowel movements over it," she confided in her diary. "'The coward dies 1,000 deaths, the brave but one.' Bullshit! Over and over and over I die. . . . but I'm still 'brave' (foolhardy) enough to try again. I'm afraid of West Virginia. I'll act externally as if I'm not, but I am. . . ."

Even if she was terrified, her wrestling matches with the Reverend were getting national attention. Phil Donahue had her and Harrington do their thing on live TV coast to coast. It was one of the most highly contentious shows Donahue ever broadcast and one of his all-time favorites. *60 Minutes* profiled her. *Good Morning America* had them on. *Newsweek* did a spread on their debates. Madalyn was back on center stage, but the spotlight soon dimmed.

The O'Hair-Harrington carnival started getting bad press.

One editorial writer summed things up: "Rehearsed like a soft-shoe routine, manipulated for money's sake, it is a debasing performance, a mocking of deeply held spiritual beliefs." As the crowds started to thin, Madalyn was having a hard time with her partner, grousing to her diary that Harrington had "ripped us off ten times." But still she wrote with awe of the potential: "If we could get pre-event coverage we could make a quarter of a million dollars a month just in the collection plate." Nevertheless, on October 22, 1977, Madalyn walked off the stage at a debate, never to return. She claimed she threw away "$50,000 or more in the exercise of being a person of integrity."

While a fifteen-hundred-dollars-a-night debate fee wasn't chump change for the atheist diva, some really big but quiet paydays were on the way. Throughout the late 1970s and the 1980s, Madalyn received substantial bequests from all over the United States for the various atheist enterprises she had established in Austin. "I tell you what, she was an expert," said son Bill, who oversaw some of the early transactions. "Over the years she took in fortunes both large and small." Naturally her preferred medium for gifts was cash or stocks, but Madalyn looked no gift horse in the mouth. She'd take anything of value—land, cars, jewelry, stamps, books—anything.

She also must have had an excellent bedside manner with aged patrons about to expire. You'd have to marvel at the sheer evil energy and skill it must have taken for Madalyn to get an elderly atheist to cut family members—children, siblings, kin—out of their wills and give everything to her. Whatever her rap was, it was mightily persuasive. Six-figure bequests came in like trained pigs. Even a few seven-digit bonanzas were made during the heyday of the 1980s.

The hauls were so big that Madalyn, who always played her financial cards close to the vest, couldn't help but brag in her diary about the fortune she was piling up. A typical entry read: "Well Garth got in last night with $630,000 worth of stock. So that makes $811,000 in one day . . . and we already have $614,000 so the total cash we have is $1,424,000. Jesus Christ! What a way to start a New Year."

And that was the swag that had liquidity. It didn't include things like the one-carat diamond that Madalyn insisted be mounted and sent immediately to granddaughter Robin from an Indiana bequest—an estate that was under the cloud of a lawsuit by a young woman who had allegedly been sexually assaulted by the atheist gift-giver. Nor did the bequest figures in Madalyn's diary over the years include things like the value of real estate holdings received, or the worth of the gold coins and jewelry that she put in Swiss and other offshore bank accounts, or the millions of dollars' worth of books and historical materials she was given.

Madalyn became jaded, but her greed was never slaked. She'd whine about the $33,000 earned from a million-dollar bond investment she made. On a $250,000 cash hoard she was sitting on, Madalyn mused, "Even though it is something, it is not enough with which to do anything." After she became an authentic millionaire, she could only gripe: "I suppose everyone in the world has wondered what it would be like to be a millionaire. We [momentarily] will have the million and the astonishing situation is that it really isn't that much money. Even at 8% interest it is NOT going to bring in any more than $80,000 in a year or $6,666 a month, which will not even pay salaries each month."

Life would always be unjust for Madalyn, even when she was richer than she'd ever imagined in her wildest fantasies from the Ohio dirt-floor days. She would bitterly complain that she had to give more than a $100,000 "bribe" to an attorney to settle an estate that would bring her ten times that amount. About a large trust fund that had been set up for her by a southern follower, she groused: "He had constructed a Trust Fund for us, but that is Mississippi and gawd alone knows how that will work out." Or there were terse entries about bequests in Madalyn's diary such as this: "Reinhold died on 12/3/87 and we are about to be fucked out of $813,000."

To be sure, Madalyn was not a believer in the adage of not saying ill about the dead—even one who had just left her a small fortune. She fumed about a benefactor: "with his dying breath, he lied." The lie was that he hadn't told her there was a small lien on his nearly half-million dollar gift to her. In another case, the ice-hearted Madalyn would write, "Kruse killed himself and today we are $300,000 richer, unless of course, the trust is challenged."

Perhaps Madalyn's ugliest behavior toward the people who made her rich was her hidden but strident anti-Semitism. Some of the largest bequests she received were from Jewish-Americans, yet she would rail long and hard against "the Jews" in her late-night diary effluvium. She'd vilify "that Jew" New York jeweler for destroying her watch or the "ambitious, rich, Jew attorney" and the "Jew Judge" who tried to ruin her when she first came to Austin. Or she'd express her scorn for a Jewish-American rally in Washington, of which she wrote: "200,000 Jews assembled in DC to show their power and every politician in America was there to kiss their Jew ass." She seethed with fury at a newspaper editor who had mildly criticized her granddaughter's public behavior in some minor political altercation. "The gawd damn Jew editor of the newspaper here has gone out of his way to attack Robin in an editorial."

Madalyn hid her paternally transmitted anti-Semitism completely from view; in fact, she kept the expression of all her bigotry for the pages of her diary only. Nobody could recall her ever making a public statement of a racist nature; thus her benefactors were left none the wiser, and she was allowed to rake in the estates of rich Jewish adherents—and perhaps take delight in her own hateful hypocrisy at the same time.

But by far the biggest catch of the 1970s and 1980s would have been a gargantuan $300 million tuna that slipped through Madalyn's grasp at the last moment. Porn magnate Larry Flynt had personally interviewed Madalyn in the mid-1970s for his flagship magazine—*Hustler*. The interview made Flynt a lifelong admirer of Madalyn, who he said was the most "brilliant" woman he'd ever met.

In 1983, Flynt ran afoul of federal judge Manuel Real (the very same judge who would save Madalyn's own financial empire years later) during the trial of cocaine–sports car entrepreneur John DeLorean. Real gave the wheelchair-bound Flynt a fifteen-month sentence for contempt of court after Flynt, swaddled in diapers and the American flag, had an obscene tantrum in Real's courtroom. With the long sentence hanging over him, Flynt decided to hand over his entire $300 million empire to Madalyn and her son Jon Garth via power of attorney. Flynt said that he felt it was a good move because Madalyn had the right financial instincts and "she was frugal."

Alas for Madalyn and the coffers of world atheism, it was not to be. Flynt's brother got a Los Angeles judge to block the transfer of power based on Madalyn's reputation and Flynt's well-documented gnarliness, exacerbated by Judge Real's imprisonment of the porn mogul. When Flynt emerged from months of prison at the federal psychiatric facility at Buckner, North Carolina, he decided to keep control of his empire.

Madalyn bitched grievously to her diary about the lost $300 million porn powerhouse. "I can't believe the perfidy over the Larry Flynt deal," she wrote. "The whole gawd damn world is made up of liars, cheats, and swindlers, whose single driving force is greed. Everyone sells out. Everyone can be bought." Nonetheless, the next year, Madalyn signed on as Flynt's speechwriter in his 1984 presidential campaign. Flynt would always maintain that Madalyn had a special role in his life. She would serve as Flynt's most trusted confidante in all matters spiritual, and she was to play foil in his momentary conversion to born-again Christianity.

President Jimmy Carter's sister, the sexy and dynamic faith healer Ruth Carter Stapleton, became close to Flynt in the mid-1970s, and he claimed that it was she who was directly responsible for his rebirth experience. Flying with Stapleton alone on a cross-country trip in his "labia pink" corporate jet, Flynt—totally sober—had a powerful vision that literally brought him to his knees. Not only did a figure that he took to be God come to him visually and acknowledge Flynt's being, he also saw himself in a wheelchair—an incredible foretelling of events that were just months away from becoming a reality in Flynt's life.

After his high-altitude epiphany, Flynt had himself baptized in a creek in Kentucky near his birthplace and began making plans to convert his empire from pornography to the word of God. But before he could make that happen, Flynt was gut-shot by a sniper with a high-powered rifle in front of a Georgia courthouse where he was on trial on trumped-up obscenity charges. Paraplegic and in horrendous pain after the assassination attempt, he turned to Madalyn for advice.

Flynt asked her, "I have a tendency to agree with everything you say, but how do you explain this epiphany I had?" Madalyn's answer was simple and persuasive for Flynt. She opined that his meeting God was "merely a chemical imbalance in his brain," probably due to an iodine deficiency. With those confident words from his atheist spiritual guru, Flynt renounced Christianity—even if neither he nor Madalyn could ever explain how his vision-prophecy of himself in a wheelchair just prior to the assassination attempt could be "merely a chemical imbalance."

Although Flynt may have idolized Madalyn, she never had

reciprocally positive feelings for the unstable porn king. She would write in her diary about her reservations on Flynt and pornography, always somehow rationalizing her relationship with him and his empire: "He is gutsy. He drags his body around determined to keep going. He is trying. His offices are in good taste. He legitimatizes cunt, not porn—cunt. He takes pictures of cunts who are willing to have them made. Then he sells them to people who want to look at them. So why am I in the middle of this? I don't know."

Actually Madalyn knew all too well why she was "in the middle of this." Flynt may have been wacky and a highly unseemly compatriot for a woman who professed to be a dedicated feminist. But he was a genius businessman, a self-created financial wonder from the dank "hollers" of Appalachia, who showered Madalyn with offerings. Not only did Flynt underwrite the operating expenses of Madalyn's organizations at different times during their decades-long friendship, he allegedly gave the atheist leader gifts of solid gold and diamond jewelry.*

Madalyn's last diary entry regarding her thoughts about her porn sugar daddy was an uncanny and chilling forecast of her own end. In the summer of 1987, Madalyn heard the news of the death of Flynt's drug-addicted wife, Althea, who drowned in her bathtub. "I keep on thinking about Althea Flynt. Thirty-three is a very damn young age at which to die. I can visualize Larry with those powerful arms holding her underwater in that bathtub. She was very beautiful once-upon-a-time . . . and so was her sister. It even gets to murder so tangled is the web. Well I guess it is none of my business." (There is, in fact, no indication that Larry Flynt was involved in his wife's drowning death, which was ruled to have been caused by a combination of drugs and illness.)

* It should be noted that Flynt denies giving Madalyn anything of value that could have created tax reporting problems for her, and none of the jewelry—which Madalyn supposedly kept in a safe at American Atheist General Headquarters—has ever been recovered.

• • •

Even with all the munificence of Larry Flynt and the expiring atheists, Madalyn still couldn't stay ahead of the game much of the time. She couldn't discipline her spending habits. As Bill Murray would relate, gobs of cash from the wills was squandered. He remembers Madalyn purchasing Jon Garth a brand-new Cadillac Seville for cash—and then not being able to meet the payroll for the next week.

Madalyn would cut corners wide and short, rational and irrational. Even though she was living in a sumptuous home (paid for with cash, naturally) in a fine neighborhood, Madalyn moaned plaintively about how she had to raid granddaughter Robin's store of two-dollar bills "to go to Fish and Chips to eat a $1.89 dinner"—because her VA check didn't arrive on time. Equally arresting was how a woman with hundreds of thousands of dollars in liquid assets would have to mend and patch her own underwear—which she did apparently by hand on a regular basis.

With a matchless melding of grandiosity and self-pity, Madalyn beefed about the "money" situation that she faced. She wrote: "Michelangelo had a 'patron'—even if it was the Pope. Marx had Engels. Lenin had the German government. Freud and Darwin had family fortunes. We must fight and produce the money to fight—a double burden." She claimed that all she did was scheme for money, and "how we work to obtain it all is indescribable, and all of our digestive problems can be traced right back to the extraordinary pressures that are on us at all times."

While the serious kvetching about money was unending, the fact was, she'd shown real financial acumen. Madalyn had accumulated a varied and robust fortune. By the time that the talk shows were no longer calling regularly (except for *The Phil Donahue Show*) and Madalyn's fame had dimmed, she was a very rich woman. The office building that she'd purchased in the mid-

1980s in Austin, Texas—American Atheist General Headquarters, or AAGHQ, as it was known—was worth $1.75 million according to conservative appraisals. (Madalyn liked to brag that she paid "cash on the barrelhead" for the acquisition.) It housed a library that booksellers estimated to be worth millions. The office equipment (including printing and publishing gear), the video and audio studios, and the posh office furnishings of AAGHQ were perhaps worth another half-million dollars, minimum. Her home, while modestly furnished in remarkably poor taste, was valued at around $300,000 in the early 1990s—with no mortgage. Then there were the offshore accounts, estimated by son Bill at the time of her death to be as high as $10 million in various banking instruments stashed around the globe.

The handsome brick office building housing AAGHQ, deceptively unassuming from the street, was vast inside, housing seventeen thousand square feet of business operations—all for her atheist jihad. Long gone were the days of the A. B. Dick printing press run by a teenage Bill Murray from the damp basement bedroom in the Baltimore row house. Madalyn had assembled a complete, vertically integrated publishing group.

And there was much more. Beyond the physical printing operations, there were direct-mail collation and assembly areas to meet the needs of Madalyn's fifty-thousand-per-month mass mailings—along with the air-conditioned storage areas. An audio and videotape production studio with high-speed duplicating equipment was available for the making and distribution of cassettes and tapes to the dozens of community TV and radio broadcasters around the country carrying Madalyn's weekly atheist cable TV show.

The spacious offices of Madalyn, Jon Garth, and Robin were expensively and (in contrast to their home), discerningly furnished. Jon Garth's was especially lavish, befitting the president of an international organization—which indeed he was. But if there was a crown jewel at AAGHQ, it was the Charles E. Stevens American Atheist Library and Archives. Through bequests and purchases, Madalyn had amassed the largest collection of atheist books and documents in the world—some forty thousand volumes and between 100,000 and 140,000 documents—with an appraised value estimated at over $3 million.

As to personnel for the empire, for almost two decades before her murder, Madalyn had a full staff of hirelings: typesetters, editors, order-fulfillment staff, collators, pasteup specialists, and duplicator/engineer types, as well as the personal secretaries that the atheist trio shared. Madalyn even had a full-blown media coordinator who did nothing but schedule her and Jon Garth's public appearances. Oversight of the office doings was the responsibility of the office manager, who, along with making a few dollars more than other staffers, had to be at Madalyn's beck and call 24/7.

All the other staffers, regardless of seniority, education, or abilities, were making a few pennies above minimum wage—with no benefits. Some hired on as dedicated atheists and freethinkers, attracted to Madalyn's professed ideals. Others were mildly intrigued—but needed a job more than anything else. Since Madalyn didn't suffer fools well, she tried to hire only smart people, and in fact most of her employees were bright and a testimony to Madalyn's abilities at finding and exploiting people.

There can be no doubt that the tangible assets of AAGHQ were nothing less than the fruition of Madalyn's most optimistic dreams. But if the physical plant was a dream come true for Madalyn, the work environment she created for employees was a nightmare. Madalyn despised her staff. Early in what was to be her unending war with AAGHQ personnel, she wrote in her diary, "We have NO one to work in that office but scum, chicken fuckers, fags, masturbators, dumb Niggers, spicks, witless cunts, derelicts, lumpen proletariat, and transvestites, and I'm supposed to whip them into shape and do something with them."

She would also write of her employees with extraordinary hubris commingled with her disdain: "If anyone can take advantage of us they do. We get lied to and stolen from in a continuous way. I think it's like moths around a flame. They are non-entities. Their lives are nothing. It is exciting and interesting to be around us because they think we make magic—so they steal bits and pieces of it." With a mortal, unconscious irony—and a nod to her own cheapness, Madalyn complained: "To save a fucking buck, I lost years of my life trying to deal with them. They were sick, sick, sick, and we were in the same building with them. YUCK."

Madalyn's was not a simple loathing. It was a complex and "macabre dance" with employees, as she would put it herself. While Madalyn might scorn them, she also took pleasure in controlling them. And the tougher the backgrounds they had, the better. It made her feel like a lion tamer in a circus. Often the only job seekers for the low-paying positions at AAGHQ would have criminal records, and surprisingly, they'd frequently be upfront with Madalyn about their past. In her strange but logical Madalyn-reasoning, their admissions would be a plus in their favor. She knew they'd come cheap *and* she'd get the added thrill of having power over hard-core types.

The Marie Antoinette of world atheism would hire and fire whimsically and implacably, telling employees that she let go with a sardonic smirk that they had been "excommunicated." "The fallen heads!" she cried. "Either they work or they go. If they can't do what they were hired to do, if they lack specific needed skills—they are out the door. The place has to operate."

Then again—just to keep them guessing—Madalyn would confer compassion on select and seemingly random staff members. When an older office worker fell and broke her kneecap—

not while working at AAGHQ but on her own time—Madalyn had her transported to the best hospital in Austin. When the woman got home, Jon Garth showed up shortly thereafter with a wheelchair. She was allowed to draw full salary during her convalescence, even though she only been briefly employed at AAGHQ.

At Madalyn's Gulag, aside from job instability and the low pay without benefits, the worst part of the working environment was the abuse. You never knew when she would descend on you with fire in her slitted eyes and fury in her throat. At any moment, she might come to gut you for even minor infractions of her rules.

Everyone was to work with their hearts and souls, minds and bodies, for the "cause." There could be no higher calling. Couldn't they see that she was offering them an opportunity for salvation? Cigarette breaks, socializing, wasting time—it was not to be tolerated from these *Untermenschen*. Nazi discipline was the only way.

THIRTEEN

The Family Dysfunctional

After getting through the Baltimore ordeal, Bill had fluttered back to Madalyn's sphere of influence in Austin, like a moth to a deadly flame. As a reward, Madalyn made him heir apparent to the throne of American atheism. But by his mid-twenties, Bill Murray had become severely alcoholic and had taken again to pummeling and abusing his wife Susan, who had joined him in Austin along with Robin. When Susan could no longer take it, she left him, and Bill got unenthusiastic custody of his daughter.

After the divorce, his relationship with his mother gradually deteriorated to nothing less than pure, coequal interpersonal hatred—as the rest of his life slid downward. Bill detailed the process of his descent into the Inferno with candor and without self-pity in his autobiography, *My Life Without God*.

Once again Bill was to break from the stranglehold. According to his mother, who sued him, he left with a briefcase full of embezzled stocks and Madalyn's prized atheist mailing list. Not long after leaving, Bill remarried; he had another daughter and another extremely problematic relationship with his wife—so problematic that he went on a drunk in Houston, fired a shot at a police officer, and had to be taken down in a full-dress SWAT operation.

Then came the miraculous. "I went to bed and not long

after falling asleep, experienced a consuming nightmare of unmentionable horror," Bill wrote.

> Suddenly, the nightmare was sliced in half by a mighty, gleaming sword of gold and silver. The two halves of the nightmare peeled back as if a black and white photograph had been cut in half. A great winged angel stood with the sword in his hand. The blade of the sword pointed down, making it resemble a cross. On the sword's hilt were inscribed the words "IN HOC SIGNO VINCES." The tip of the sword's blade touched an open Bible. Then I awoke, realizing that my quest for the truth would end within the pages of the Holy Bible, the very book my family had helped ban from devotional use in the public schools of America.

Bill became a man of God—a Christian man of God. And not the simple garden variety either, but one of the most flamboyant types of religious proselytizers that contemporary Western culture can produce—a born-again, Bible-hawking, testifying fundamentalist—and the embodiment of everything that his mother hated. And unlike Larry Flynt, Bill wouldn't revert.

After his dream-vision, Bill promised to dedicate his life to spreading the Gospel. Of course, Bill had a unique—to say the least—background that gave him instant entree to the talk show circuits and religious groups wanting to hear of his conversion. This made it easy for the cynics to dismiss his finding God as a wonderful convenience, a sweet path for doing his own serious fund-raising.

However, Bill's conversion was not to be so easily dismissed, if the experts who studied such happenings were to be believed. Harvard's William James—the famed psychologist who evaluated the reality of hundreds of religious conversions or "grace" experiences—believed that the circumstances and the specific event are not what should be judged, for they are often too strange and personal to be of analytical value.

To the scientists like James, what indicates whether a conversion such as Bill's is genuine or counterfeit are the alterations in behavior that occur in the life of the converted *subsequently.* The two central questions that James believed would answer whether the conversion was real or not were: What changes are manifested by the experiencing of religious grace in the personality of the chosen one? And was the person's transformation maintained over time?

Using the admittedly simplified criteria of subsequent transformation, there couldn't be, and wouldn't be in the future, any doubt as to the authenticity of Bill's rebirth. His alcoholism and drug abuse ended. He became a marathon runner. His physical abuse stopped. His life went from chaos to an ordered and dedicated spreading of faith, albeit of a sort arguably no less rigid than his mother's was—although a polar opposite. The naysayers could mock him, but Bill was, in reality, a new man.

As could be expected, Madalyn's reaction to her son's born-again status and new calling as a traveling evangelist was neither measured nor maternal. She denounced and then renounced her traitorous son as totally as a mother can—possibly as totally as any mother ever has to the mass media. "One could call this a postnatal abortion on the part of a mother, I guess; I repudiate him entirely and completely for now and all times. . . . He is beyond human forgiveness," she said of the episode.

The event was also to display Madalyn's transcendent ability to turn disaster into triumph and financial gain. The heretic high priestess used her son's betrayal to demonstrate to her followers that if somebody raised like *her* son could be "brain-washed" by those "dirty christers," *anybody* could fall prey to them. She proclaimed that it was time for American atheists to step up and fill the coffers and prepare for long-term struggle.

Madalyn would leverage Bill's conversion in other ways as well. Her piercing denunciation of her son, along with her spirited defense of herself, gave Madalyn a reprise for another full round of the national talk shows—where it was estimated that she'd raise an average of forty thousand dollars per appearance.

The hatred that Madalyn reserved for her elder son, Bill, was matched in quality and quantity by the depth of her inordinate expressions of love for Robin, granddaughter-adopted-to-daughter, and her second son, Jon Garth. Madalyn's boozy diary professions of love for both are a constant refrain. Letting herself soar, she'd gush about them: "I love these two way past any measuring the bounds of containment. I nested them when they were kids and nurtured them. Robin and Garth. These were my two. Bill belonged to my mother. . . ."

Without shame, without a shred of self-awareness, Madalyn deleted any memories of her horrendous motherhood—the endless days of leaving Garth in his crib with his head banging the bars like some horrible metronome, her abandonment of him in Hawaii, the pressuring of Bill to leave his wife and newborn Robin penniless and helpless in order to flee with her to Mexico. These thoughts were so deeply suppressed that they were no longer part of history—replaced by syrupy delusions.

The Murray-O'Hairs were to evolve into textbook codependents. They would have nasty squabbles publicly at AAGHQ on a regular basis—screaming/shouting matches followed by heavy door slamming—*but* they were inseparable. Both Robin and Jon Garth lived with Madalyn at their upscale Austin residence. They worked together every day—same office, same business for decades. (Robin had started at AAGHQ when she was in her early teens.) They lunched together every day without exception.

They vacationed together—not usually, but always. The bonds that glued them were as strong as the individual pathologies contained therein.

As with long-married couples, they even started to morph together behaviorally and physically. Robin talked like Madalyn—same voice, same ability to curse and verbally abuse. She dressed exactly like her grandmother, in similar tentlike dresses. And like Madalyn, she wore no makeup. Her beautiful reddish-blond hair she kept in the same lank and unkempt mode as her grandmother. Even their eyeglasses matched.

Jon Garth, while he was a huge-boned, somewhat swarthy, massive man, and visually not similar to the fair-skinned females, was still a cookie-cutter replica in other ways. He, like Robin and Madalyn, would use a pen with the same distinctive light-blue ink to sign all documents. Jon's signature and Madalyn's were stunningly congruent in form and style—right down to the slightly backward slant of the handwriting. In fact, the only discernible difference between his signature and the signature of his mother was the letters in their respective names. (Robin's signature was a carbon copy as well, save only for the more normal rightward pitch of her lettering.)

The most telling yet bizarre blending of the three came out in court testimony during the trial of one of their killers. According to an AAGHQ office manager, Madalyn and her son and granddaughter had taken to the old upper-class British habit of once-a-week bathing, thus allowing for the culturing of pungent individual fragrances—and these disagreeable aromas all smelled exactly the same.

But regardless of what others might think of her adopted daughter/granddaughter, Robin was wonderful to behold for Madalyn. "Robin is beautiful, fragile, lady-like, charming, intelligent and honest," Madalyn wrote in full contravention of the realities. Actually, Robin could have been attractive, perhaps even beautiful, if she'd given the least damn about her appearance. But like her grandmother, she was aggressively unkempt as a mature adult. That anybody who didn't have gravely vitiated perceptual abilities or a severe emotional block could describe Robin as "fragile" and "lady-like" is unlikely. Robin had been a corpulent slob from her early twenties—physically indolent and foulmouthed.

The "charm" of her granddaughter that Madalyn waxed on about somehow was lost on other human beings, at least according to the historical record. Interviews and testimony given in civil and criminal matters surrounding the deaths of the Murray-O'Hairs were uniformly antipathetic toward Robin. While there were rare good words for Madalyn, there were none for her replicant granddaughter.

But Madalyn's praise was accurate in one area: her granddaughter was intelligent—highly intelligent. Robin, by all accounts, was the smartest of a very smart family. She graduated from a demanding private high school in St. Louis, Missouri, as a full National Merit Scholar at sixteen years old. She was accepted at Brown, one of the most prestigious universities in the country. But Madalyn, ever penny-pinching and controlling, made her go to the University of Texas to save tuition and housing money and to maintain dominance by proximity. Regardless, Robin zoomed her way through UT on another full scholarship in less than three years total, graduating a few months after her nineteenth birthday.

As far as Robin's career was concerned, Madalyn decided what it would be. In her early teens, as an initial test—which she was to pass with high marks—Robin had been assigned the task of computerizing and digitally updating the entire American Atheists organization. By the time Robin was sixteen, she was running the day-to-day operations of the AAGHQ, in deed—but without portfolio. Madalyn, for all her professions of solidarity with the women's liberation movement, would always favor Jon

Garth when it came to titles, salary, and trappings—even though Robin was clearly his intellectual superior and many times more productive and valuable to the "cause."

David Waters—the mastermind behind Robin's murder, and a man who reviled her—would nonetheless extol her skills, saying that she was a "dynamo" at work. "When she fell ill with flu-related pneumonia and was out of the office for several weeks, the entire routine began to crumble," Waters wrote. "Jon had to take on additional duties, but his abilities were sadly lacking compared with Robin's. There were daily murmurs of discontent from the staff, and I realized that the entire organization was dependent on Robin's management skills, which were truly remarkable."

Robin's executive proficiencies may have been exceptional—even to her murderer—but they didn't translate into the most rudimentary social aptitude. Robin, until the day she was strangled, never had a boyfriend that anybody could remember. She had crushes but never a documented romance. Madalyn would run off any potential suitors that weren't turned off by Robin's weight and personal hygiene. In fact, Madalyn was so protective of her granddaughter that she fantasized about murdering a wannabe boyfriend who she thought might instigate a "cruel encounter." "I wanted to kill him in my inner heart of hearts," she wrote. "How DARE anyone cause even an iota of anguish for my darling."

Clearly such thoughts were by-products of Madalyn's streak of narcissistic possessiveness—but there may have been more. While she would declare her preference for "well-hung" men and profess disgust for lesbians as "cunt-lappers," Madalyn also would write very brief but telling entries in her diary about the warmth and goodness she felt when she and Robin would share the same bed. Perhaps it was the harmless union of two very lonely women sharing nonsexual but proximate physical intimacy. Perhaps it was something more, as Madalyn cryptically wrote when she described the two of them as being "tortured" by their late-evening "kissy-kissy play."

The only other intimate relationship Robin had was with her two cocker spaniels, Gannon and Shannon. So fiercely did she love these dogs that when she was being held hostage, just days before her murder, crazed with terror, Robin would spend most of the last few precious minutes of conversation with the outside world worrying about the care and health of her "puppies."

Robin knew her grandmother tried hard to supply compensatory rewards and she usually allowed herself to be seduced. Seduction is seduction—and for some women the act itself can be as enjoyable as the dangled rewards, especially for a forlorn woman. If Madalyn wouldn't allow Robin any human relationships, she would allow her to enjoy the riches that were due an atheist princess: the finest dining in Austin, round-the-world travels, a Porsche, clothing of her choice, and diamonds and jewelry from the bequests of rich departed atheists—not to forget the salaries for Robin and Jon Garth from the variety of "nonprofit" corporate shells created by Madalyn, salaries so munificent that Madalyn never would reveal them.

If Robin did well materially by her grandmother's seductions, Jon Garth did even better for the same price—that price being unconditional subservience to Madalyn and renunciation of all normal relationships. Jon Garth was to have only one brief love affair (that may or may not have been consummated) in his life before he gave up the pursuit of women and the possibility of a family and children. A family friend and board member described that one affair. "Jon got a little horny and got a girlfriend and let her move into the home," he recalled, "and that was a big mistake. Madalyn locked horns with her fast, and that was the end of that love affair."

As Madalyn dominated with one hand, she exalted with the other. She had already ramrodded Jon Garth into the presidency of the American Atheists, over the outcries of board members and upper-echelon activists who all thought that he was an incompetent goon. Unlike his niece, who could command grudging respect, Jon Garth was looked on as a "large doofus." Adding to the picture of ineptitude was his heavy lisp—a lisp so bad that, try as he might, it couldn't be disguised. "Robin" would always come out "Wobin." Poor Jon Garth couldn't even negotiate his own last name—which would inevitably be "Muh-wee."

Madalyn deleted the realities. To her, Jon Garth was handsome, brilliant, and extremely determined to carry the banner of international atheism on high. She confided in her diary: "Despite all his blow ups and ostensive histrionics—when the chips are down, he quietly and stubbornly digs in and stays there until it is done. . . . No matter what happens I can trust this one to stay at it to a determined end." How fatally accurate that perception would turn out to be, Madalyn would never know.

In any case, she basked in her son's faithfulness and dedication, even boasting in her diary how, when she broke her leg, Jon Garth would patiently and lovingly wash her hair in the sink. But she would *never, ever* acknowledge Jon Garth's speech impediment or any of his shortcomings.

No, that might reflect on her motherhood and bring back the long repressed visions of the trauma that she created for him. No, Jon Garth was a knight-in-shining-armor wrought from her own superior loins. Jon Garth was a triumph—her triumph. A queen always produces princes. He *should* be treated royally, because he *was* royalty—atheist royalty.

And she did treat him royally. Jon Garth was even more materially indulged than Robin. From his commodious and expensively appointed office suite—befitting an international executive who was actually little more than the leader of a fractious, fringe political group of a few thousand diehard, dues-paying members—Jon Garth would tell author Lawrence Wright in an interview in the early 1990s of his unapologetic take on the good life provided by Mom and Atheism.

"We're accustomed to good food, to eating in dining rooms with tablecloths, good dishes, a good bottle of wine," Jon Garth related. "Even when we go out for lunch, we go someplace nice. You'd never see us at McDonald's or Burger King—that's just not our lifestyle. All of us have nice clothes. My suits cost a minimum of five, six hundred dollars. My shirts are custom made; my ties are all silk. We have a nice house in Northwest Hills. We've been around the world three times." His only complaint was given with a take-it-in-stride attitude: "We get a tremendous amount of flak over the fact that I drive a Mercedes, Madalyn drives a Mercedes, and Robin drives a Porsche."

If Jon Garth enjoyed the fruits of office, he still had a hard time with some of the trappings—cars being one example. Madalyn would ruefully note her youngest son's constant problems with all things automotive in her diary. His first big Mercedes sedan was a lemon that Madalyn would rage against with a spleen usually reserved for "christers" or her son Bill. Ever after, she went along to supervise the purchase of all new vehicles, since she didn't trust her nearly middle-aged son to make the deal by himself—even as crowned king of global atheism.

Her prudence was well-founded. Jon Garth had a serious judgmental flaw: He was a patsy for even the most outlandish and elementary con games. Once Jon Garth announced with pride to older brother Bill that he had twenty thousand dollars in the trunk of his car—and he only had to put up two thousand dollars to get it! Jon Garth excitedly told Bill that "it was part of a dead old man's insurance settlement" as he rushed to show off his take. Not surprisingly for Bill, when Jon Garth opened the trunk—there was no money. He had been the victim of roving bunko artists in Austin, a relatively sophisticated town not exactly overrun with that type of crime. Jon Garth never would tell his mother the true story of the con. In an ungodly, unconscious foretelling of future events, he told her that somebody had taken him to the bank with a gun and forced him to withdraw the money.

Infected with his mother's mind-set, Jon Garth was of the opinion that the American Atheists organization was a fiefdom of the Murray-O'Hair clan, and he treated the staff as his mother did—like indentured serfs. Jon Garth's callousness may have exceeded his mother's. A Houston atheist member who was in the throes of dying from AIDS while still working heroically for the "cause" was a typical recipient of Jon Garth's pitiless exploitation. Rather than expressing sympathy and appreciation for his work under the most trying circumstances, Jon Garth once telegrammed the dying man that, "should anything 'life-threatening' happen to you, your files and correspondence would be vulnerable and open to who knows who?" Jon Garth ordered him to secure all his paperwork and report back on his daily progress—with not a word about the terminal illness that he knew the man was about to succumb to.

If Jon Garth was bereft of compassion for the staff and membership, he wasn't beyond tapping them for some personal mirth. According to one account, a long-abused staffer brought in his newborn to show off. Everybody cooed over the baby except for Jon Garth, who smirked and stated to all within earshot, "I'll bet [he] had to fuck his wife a thousand times to make that kid!"

Regardless of the fun and games that Jon Garth could indulge himself in with the suffering staff, life wasn't easy. Public arguments with Robin and his mother were frequent. According to observers, the hulking atheist prince usually got shellacked by the two women when passions were aroused. Even when they weren't tag-teaming him, it was not a picnic for Jon Garth. In fact, living with his mother meant being ready to cope with transient but powerful emotional storms at any moment.

Jon Garth never knew when one of his mother's depressive episodes would enshroud her with all-consuming gloom. Bill wrote of one such occasion: "One morning—Garth called [me] on the telephone. He had been driving with Mother to deliver a tape to the radio station when the two of them had begun to argue. At a traffic light halfway between our office and downtown, Madalyn had suddenly opened her door, stepped from the car, and walked into the woods. I told Garth there wasn't much we could do but wait. Hours later Mother called for a ride home. She insisted, though, that only Garth come to pick her up because 'we know what it's like to be alone.' I had no idea what she meant by that and did not bother to find out." Continuing, Bill recalled that on another occasion, "Mother's car was found with the driver's door open and the engine running. Garth thought she had been kidnapped. We found her later in tears sitting on a bench in a public park. A few days later her spirits had brightened so much that she went on a spending binge."

Some of her despondency must have been caused by her marriage to Richard O'Hair. After getting married in Austin, the CIA/FBI informant continued to drink, but in a somewhat moderated fashion. He never worked—preferring to putter around, mostly tending to a flock of pigeons that he kept in a coop next to their modest bungalow of the time. He did, though, generate enough energy to have an affair with Madalyn's personal secretary—leaving their love letters lying about for Madalyn to run across.

But Madalyn was always pensive, rather than critical, about the dualities of her marriage to Richard—even if she did have him jailed for assaulting her at one point. Writing in her diary when he was dying from cancer, she mused: "How he hated and loved me both . . . and [was] repelled by me and attracted by me. . . . Yet how dependent he was on me. And yet I play this out to the end for him to make him look good to the world." Then with candid admiration she wrote: "I hope that I can face death with as much dignity as does he."

She was far less kind in assessing her brother Irv's death in 1988. "Irv had a massive stroke on December 25th and he is on a machine (I guess) in a hospital somewhere. If I know Bill he checked him into a charity ward somewhere and now he'll hit the media with a story of my cold, cold heart." Continuing, she penned: "Irv apparently is a dead man . . . and I don't give a tinker's damn so long is the road from there to here. He'll die as he lived—a leech on someone as he runs up one helluva hospital bill. I have NOT ONE fond memory of that man at all."

For her mother's passing Madalyn reserved a pathological ambivalence. Sometime after Lena's death, Madalyn would stand over her grave and admit to not feeling a drop of emotion for the woman she reviled in public and private. Then, just a few years later, she would write in her diary with booze-ridden mawkishness: "How I loved her!! And for so many years!!"

But save for her late-night diary broodings, for the most part Madalyn concentrated on the tasks that needed tending. Her highest priority was to maintain American Atheists, the organization that she'd crafted from scratch and that she believed would eventually secure her position in world history. Cultivating and growing American Atheists and the other shell organizations she set up also meant protecting herself as chief, as well as safeguarding her lineage. Those who knew the atheist trio never understood why they would take separate cars when they ate lunch together.

The answer was simple. Over the years, Madalyn received

many death threats—some quite legitimate. Fearing an assassination attempt, Madalyn—like the president of the United States, who never travels with the vice president—didn't want to allow for the chance that she and her bloodline could be obliterated in one act of multiple homicide.

FOURTEEN

The Disastrous Final Offensive

Madalyn's accumulation of a large staff and vast assets was assisted by the governments she loathed. Tax-exempt status for her atheist organizations, granted by the State of Texas and the Internal Revenue Service—two entities that Madalyn did her best to flagellate and dishonor—allowed her to save millions in taxes, as well as giving her contributors a handsome tax write-off. Madalyn's atheist groups might have been officially "nonprofit organizations," but for Madalyn and her children, they were all profit.

However, there were risks, given Madalyn's penchant for pissing off and doing bad things to people. She was a bully and her knowledge of how to manipulate civil judicial systems was keen after years of legal combat. Not only did Madalyn litigate against dozens of people and entities, but they inevitably sued her too. The trouble with defending suits for Madalyn was that she never knew what a "christer" judge or jury was going to do to her.

In fact, Madalyn got tagged with substantial judgments for libel, breach of contract, and other civil misdeeds. But since she was over-the-top secretive when it came to legal issues, especially when she got the short end, nobody knew the extent of the damages or her personal reactions to these defeats. However, her public response was to create a slew of atheist front organizations.

1

*Madalyn Murray's Ashland
College graduation picture
from the 1948 yearbook.
Madalyn graduated second
in her class, and the budding
atheist received glowing letters
of recommendation from the
Christian evangelical college.*

*Madalyn Murray and her sons,
Bill and Jon Garth, in front of
the United States Supreme
Court in February 1963. In a
landmark decision, the court
found in favor of Madalyn's
petition and banned prayer in
all U.S. public schools.*

2

Madalyn on the Phil Donahue Show. *Always holding audiences in thrall, she cursed like a sailor during commercial breaks and resumed a grandmotherly repose as soon as the cameras turned on.*

Eighteen-year-old Bill Murray and his new bride, Susan Abramovitz, a few weeks before the entire Murray family fled to Hawaii after Madalyn and Bill were arrested for assaulting Baltimore police officers in 1964. Bill later admitted beating his teenage wife.

Robin Murray and Jon Garth Murray waiting for a flight at the airport. They and Madalyn always went first class because of both their affinity for luxury and their size. Jon Garth was six foot four and weighed about three hundred pounds at the time of his brutal murder.

5

Jon Garth, circa 1989, holding Gannon, one of his niece, Robin's, beloved cocker spaniels. Note the leather-bound books in the background. Madalyn was a bibliophile who amassed an atheist library worth in excess of $3 million.

6

One of the last known photographs of Madalyn Murray O'Hair and her granddaughter, Robin, before their kidnapping and murder in 1995. The tragic irony of this cemetery photograph is that less than a decade later they would be buried together in an unmarked grave on the outskirts of Austin, Texas.

Wearing one of her trademark flower-print dresses, Madalyn barges through the media after appearing in Washington federal court in an unsuccessful attempt to block Pope John Paul II from celebrating mass in a mall in Washington, D.C. in 1979.

Bill Murray holds up the book he wrote about his life with his mother in 1982. Madalyn denounced her son, saying she considered the episode a "postnatal abortion." Murray went on to become a successful Christian evangelist and fund-raiser for conservative causes.

9

The four teenagers accused of murdering David William Gibbs are "perp walked" by Illinois authorities after their arrest. David Waters is second from the right. Three, including ringleader Waters, were tried as adults, and their guilty pleas allowed them to avoid execution.

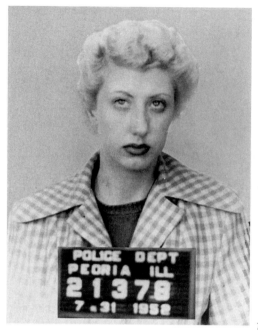

Betty Waters, mother of David Waters, is shown in a mug shot taken after her arrest for child endangerment in Peoria, Illinois, July 31, 1952. Police found four-year-old David and his younger brother sleeping on a sofa during a wild party in which some of the participants were said to be "partially clothed."

11

Ed Martin, IRS special agent, shown at his computer, surrounded by evidentiary documents during the lengthy investigation of the Murray-O'Hair murders. Martin was the lead investigator who put together a brilliant blueprint for arresting their killers.

13

Gerald Carruth, assistant U.S. attorney based in Austin, Texas. A tough veteran federal prosecutor, Carruth led the prosecution team that finally brought justice to the Murray-O'Hair murder case in one of the most complex criminal trials and plea-bargaining deals in Texas history.

Martin, Carruth, and FBI agent Donna Cowling celebrate their victory at an awards ceremony held for them in Austin. Cowling was able to get Waters's terrified girlfriend to turn state's evidence against him.

14

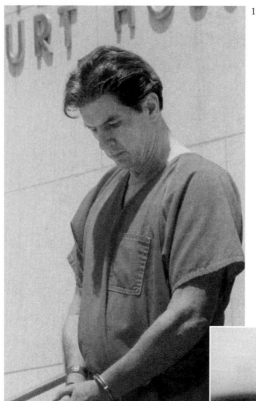

David Waters leaving the federal courthouse after being sentenced for firearms violations, including possession of his beloved Browning automatic.

Gary Karr during a recess at his trial in Austin for kidnapping the Murray-O'Hairs. Karr, a psychosexual sadistic biker, was a prison buddy of David Waters. A female juror at the trial was said to be romantically attracted to him.

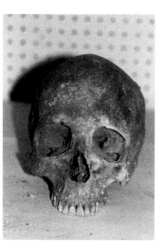

The skull of Madalyn Murray O'Hair during forensic analysis. The study indicated that Madalyn probably spent the last quarter century of her life in unending physical torment from multiple ailments. However, no cause of death could be established from it.

These shell corporations, all controlled by Madalyn and her children, were created and maintained using the most convoluted methods that Madalyn's labyrinthine mind could conceive. The alphabetic maze of organizations she created out of acronyms alone was formidable: SOS—Society of Separationists; UWA—United World Atheists; USA—United Secularists of America; AAP—American Atheist Press; AAGHQ—American Atheist General Headquarters; CESAALA—Charles E. Stevens American Atheist Library and Archives; and the supremely esoteric PALA—Prison Atheists League of America.

After years of questions and confusion by her membership groups, the atheist high priestess was startlingly candid about her thinking in an end-of-the-year newsletter in the late 1980s. Madalyn wrote: "If a person is running a little business and suddenly, fairly or unfairly, gets sued . . . the sensible thing to do is cut back the income of that little business operation. The next day the business owner can always start another brand spanking new identical type . . . at the other end of town."

Not surprisingly, Madalyn's statements and financial activities raised eyebrows high at the Internal Revenue Service. The IRS had been watching her, in all likelihood, as long as the FBI had been. Yet the IRS didn't dispute Madalyn's myriad nonprofit applications. It granted her multiple exemptions for her different shell groups that resulted in a cash saving of even greater magnitude than Madalyn's exemption from ad valorem taxes granted her by the State of Texas. In fact, the IRS had been more than forbearing with Madalyn. Nonetheless, she brashly pushed the envelope of governmental patience, year in and year out.

The problem was—and it wasn't hard to see—that Madalyn, Jon Garth, and Robin commingled their personal assets with those of the shell atheist organizations that had received the tax-free gifts from atheist contributors. "Commingled" isn't exactly descriptive. Essentially the trio, at Madalyn's direction, used the atheist corporate accounts to support themselves in lavish fashion. Their house was paid for with atheist cash. They drove fine cars paid for with the same. The ladies wore silks and satins, and Jon Garth expensive suits and custom-made shirts. When they traveled round the world it was first class. (One secondary reason given by Bill Murray for the first-class travel was that it was essential, since all three were obese and needed the roomiest seating.) They had made substantial and expensive art acquisitions on their extensive overseas jaunts, even if their purchases were trite and insipid. The fact was, they were living high off the hog and declaring comparatively minimal incomes.

The IRS position was simple and reasonable. The atheists' organizations might be paying for the extravagant material lifestyle, but regardless of who paid, it was *income*. It might not be cash income, in the usual form of salary, but it was income nonetheless.

Of course, the supposition was easier stated than proven. Madalyn had arguments, even if they were traditional for tax dodgers: The house? Sorry. I don't have to explain. Statute of limitations is up on that. The cars? We need to have something to get to work. The clothes? We're executives and leaders. We need to dress appropriately. Besides, I mend my own panties when they wear out. Travel? We must oversee an international movement. Art collection? It's not worth much and besides, we do draw some legitimate salary for our efforts and we have a right to spend it on something.

Regardless of her contentions, even the wily Madalyn was aware that big trouble was in the offing—maybe criminal trouble—if her finances got fine-toothed by the revenuers. Even with her ducks lined up as well as possible, Madalyn fretted to her diary: "The IRS form 990 was put to bed at midnight. We did it in two days. Of course it won't hold up if they look at it."

There were lots of little things too, such as keeping undeclared cash donations that would come in after talk show appearances. Or her issuing herself bogus paychecks from American Atheists bank accounts so that she could fatten her social security benefits. Madalyn just hoped that no single transgression would add up to a criminal indictment. Even better, if she was lucky, she could keep the IRS occupied for years just trying to figure out the tortuous highways and byways of all the atheist shell groups she created.

Drained of patience by 1991, the Internal Revenue Service decided to go after Madalyn, Jon Garth, and Robin. But as it turned out, Madalyn was too slick for criminal charges to be brought, so instead the IRS pursued harsh civil penalties on two fronts. First, unless she could convince them otherwise, the IRS was going to revoke Madalyn's tax-exempt nonprofit status. This would cost her millions in income over the long term, destroying her ability to raise funds by stopping donors from taking a charitable deduction. At this late stage in the game, losing tax-exempt status for all her shell groups would mean the end of organized atheism—at least Madalyn's brand of it.

There was more. Equally horrifying for her to contemplate were the IRS's contentions that Jon Garth and Robin owed $750,000 apiece in back taxes dating from the gravy-train days of the 1980s. A $1.5 million back taxes bill! And that wasn't the end of it. That was just *openers* for the IRS. The revenuers told Madalyn that they hadn't even begun to figure out how much she owed the government in back taxes. Gawd damn. It could be $5 million or $10 million.

With the largest and perhaps most powerful civil bureaucracy in the world taking direct aim at all one's assets and livelihood, a normal human being would have been devastated. A normal human being would have been cowed. A normal human being might have started to think of realistic ways to fawn and make amends. Not she. Her response was pure Madalyn. When the IRS agent handling the inquiry sent a normal, run-of-the-mill request to send in some itemized records, Madalyn came back with a two-word reply to the revenuers over her bold signature—"Fuck You."

Alongside her seemingly unending conflicts with the IRS, Madalyn had maintained a burp gun fire of civil legal actions from D.C. to Hawaii and points in between. Beginning with her famous case against the Baltimore school board in the early 1960s, she filed suits for more than three decades, and her filings against enemies large and small would stop only with her murder. Madalyn spent millions on litigation. She sued churches, municipalities, states, and the federal government, as well as her own son Bill, staffers, journalists, and numerous corporate entities. One could never argue that Madalyn was motivated *only* by greed, since she could have pocketed the fortunes she spent on legal fees.

While some of Madalyn's court actions against institutions were initiated out of her need to exact vengeance and feed her consuming appetite for spite, many were filed on genuinely philosophical grounds. The issue of church-and-state separation—the basis for almost all her suits against government—was actually one that especially worried the primary architect of the Constitution of the United States, Thomas Jefferson. No matter how much it might make her detractors squirm, Madalyn and Jefferson believed in the same principles regarding keeping the state and religion from conjoining. It was the ghostly hand of Jefferson, his mortaring the foundations of the Constitution with an eye on maintaining the "Separation of Church and State," that aided, if not allowed, Madalyn's victory in the Supreme Court. It was Jefferson's name that was cited in the justices' opinions more than any other.

But after her historic and resounding 1964 Supreme Court

success, Madalyn's legal efforts had spotty results, even if aspects of her philosophy were Jeffersonian. She won no battles in Hawaii with her suit against the FCC or the Hawaiian private school administrators. Madalyn had sued the State of Texas because atheists were systematically excluded from jury duty since they wouldn't swear an oath to God. She won a favorable decision on this issue, but then many of the state district court judges ignored the ruling. So she won—but lost anyway.

There were no locales safe from Madalyn, the legal marauder, not even outer space. She once sued NASA because snippets with astronauts saying prayers on space missions had been broadcast by the agency. The suit was eventually thrown out of federal court, but it did have some "chilling effect." It prevented astronaut Buzz Aldrin from taking televised communion on the moon.

But for the most part Madalyn failed to get even a nod from the courts. Her multiple suits against the federal government to get "In God We Trust" removed from all currency came to naught, as did her efforts to get municipalities and states to tax the property of the Catholic and Mormon churches, even though legal experts have said there may have been real constitutional merit to some of the actions Madalyn brought.

The losses added up, but it didn't matter. Madalyn knew that if anything made her, it was her signal victory at the Supreme Court. That's when she started to haul in serious money. And it was another "Big One"—another mother lode—that Madalyn sought ever after. That hunt would give rise to her most ravening judicial foray—a foray that would begin Madalyn's descent.

The beginning of the end could actually be traced to her old suit against her son Bill. Madalyn claimed that he had stolen her cherished atheist mailing list and peddled it to an archcompetitor, James Hervey Johnson. Johnson was the dyspeptic and sulfurous racist publisher of the oldest free-thought magazine in the country. The publication had been the central organ of the free-thought movement for nearly a hundred years—regularly printing the work of star freethinkers and atheists like Thomas Paine and Robert Ingersoll.

Unfortunately, the San Diego–based James Hervey Johnson was about as much of a PR blessing for free thought as Madalyn was for atheism. Johnson was a genius investor and a self-made monetary powerhouse—and also a deeply malevolent man. Soon after he bought the magazine, he started publishing racist tirades and tracts. He would sing the praises of South Africa's regime of genocidal apartheid policies and call African-Americans gorillas. Along with his own generally inchoate ravings, Johnson would reprint most of the classics of western racism, such as Henry Ford's *The International Jew,* and the bogus *Protocols of the Elders of Zion.*

Johnson's lifestyle wasn't too wholesome either. The lifelong bachelor went on regular diets consisting of only orange juice and canned milk in his spare Southern California apartment. He was known to fear and despise doctors. As he aged, he contracted skin cancer and refused medical treatment. The cancer ate away his entire left ear and it was said that, in order to hide the disfigurement, he would stuff tissue paper into the hole that was left.

But regardless of his gnarliness, Johnson was a financial whiz. He developed conservative investing techniques involving the analysis of stock dividends that allowed him to amass a fortune—parlaying what was a modest poke into an investment hoard that oscillated in the $15 million to $20 million range by his late middle age. (It was also rumored, but never substantiated, that Johnson had jump-started his assets by augmenting them with illicit gains from his term as tax-assessor/collector in San Diego.)

For the sake of atheistic, free-thought solidarity, Madalyn

professed to make up with Johnson after he used her stolen mailing list, but she never forgave him. Behind his back, with her unique brand of barefaced hypocrisy, she attacked Johnson for being a bigot and nicknamed him "Scurvy." Indulging in her fondness for cloak-and-dagger operations that she'd harbored since her military service in World War II, Madalyn was able to plant a mole inside Johnson's organization, and the informant was to provide Madalyn with a rich vein of financial intelligence, evidently including a copy of Johnson's will.

By the late 1980s, Johnson was slowly dying of cancer— being ravaged by the metastases of his untreated skin carcinoma. Madalyn analyzed the provisions in his will and decided it was time to swoop on the eccentric atheist's hoarded millions. It seemed like a fine opportunity with the old man weakened and fighting for his life and with no family to aid him.

It was to prove a profound misjudgment, as was Madalyn's other strategic concept. Madalyn wanted to use the executor of the estate, banker Lawrence True, as a whipping boy and an excuse for filing the suit, since True was a high-end "christer," a practicing Episcopalian, and for such a man to be allowed to administer an atheist empire was blasphemy. But unfortunately for the warring atheist queen, it would be True who would test her mettle beyond the breaking point.

From her lair in Austin, Madalyn decided on a D Day–like multifront assault covered by a corporate tactical bombing campaign. Her first San Diego legal action against Johnson was filed in 1987. Madalyn's claims were outrageous—even more so given her own conduct. Madalyn charged that Johnson had commingled funds from his atheist organizations with personal investments. She also charged him with the theft of property bequeathed to his organizations by deceased atheists. (Both abuses, of course, Madalyn was clearly guilty of herself for decades.)

There was even some megalomanic reasoning thrown in.

Madalyn contended that since *she* was the preeminent atheist in the world, and since Johnson's estate had been garnered from the wealth and goodness of atheists and freethinkers, she—the acknowledged chief of global free thought/atheism—was the rightful heir to the entire estate.

As the legal bombs were dropped in San Diego, Madalyn went whole hog on the home front in her campaign against Scurvy Johnson. She obtained Johnson's mailing list, probably from her mole again, and with surpassing, breathtaking gall, stole the masthead from his journal and published the purloined periodical herself, using her state-of-the-art printing operation at AAGHQ. It was a coup d'etat of the highest magnitude.

To slam things home, Madalyn announced the election of her own slate of officers to Johnson's organizations, and then shamelessly and brazenly sent the message to Johnson's high-level membership. In a final gut-shot aimed at the dying atheist tycoon, Madalyn had stock certificates printed up and issued under her directions. She claimed that the newly minted stock represented Johnson's assets of approximately $16 million, all of which was now under her control, she claimed.

Sadly for Madalyn, the courts of the United States and the State of California didn't see things her way. Of the three suits she filed, or that she instigated through proxies, all failed—in one case, with ominous words from the bench about the patent lack of merit of the action.

At first Madalyn didn't see her loss as anything that untoward. Sure, the Scurvy Johnson project had cost her a big chunk of change in legal fees and quite a bit of time and energy, but she was a big girl and believed the gamble was well worth the potential return. When Johnson finally died in the summer of 1988, Madalyn figured she'd need to win a miracle appeal to see a dime of his fortune. What she didn't realize was that she'd need a judicial miracle not to lose everything she had.

During the months prior to his death, Johnson, in a last act of will and desperation, assembled a top-notch legal team to countersue Madalyn. Lawrence True, an extremely able executor, was to honcho the effort. The San Diego legal team, fashioned from Johnson's deathbed instructions, filed an elaborate civil action against Madalyn. Their case included carefully drafted claims that Madalyn and her children had violated the civil Racketeer Influenced and Corrupt Organizations (RICO) Act laws.

When she learned of the suit, in one of her last known diary entries, Madalyn did a little whistling past the graveyard—"I have been sued for $1 million (ho hum) again." But bravado aside, the tough old battle-ax must have realized her financial exposure was far greater than $1 million. In fact, all her personal and organizational assets were at risk.

However, the Johnson estate's RICO suit ended in a mistrial. Madalyn and her children had survived, but by only the scantest of margins, and the future looked bad. According to accounts, a single juror had held out on Madalyn's behalf against all entreaties by fellow jurors. The judge was reluctantly forced to declare a mistrial, but the handwriting was on the wall for Madalyn and her children.

Johnson's legal team had done their homework, hiring slick and knowledgeable investigators to look into the many hidden crevices of Madalyn's personal and atheist domains. What was laid out in court must have been scary for Madalyn. Nobody had fine-toothed her like this before. One could almost see her turning to her attorneys during the trial—whispering as Butch Cassidy did to the Sundance Kid, "Who are those guys?" The worst thing about it was that Madalyn would have to face them again. A mistrial meant another full trial, and she knew that a person would have to believe in the tooth fairy to think there might be another intractable holdout juror who would save her bacon.

Madalyn knew that she was in deep water. Not only was she facing the full governmental investigative fury of a stirred-up IRS, but she now had a truly dangerous, powerful civil opponent in the form of Lawrence True and his cadre of lawyers, financed for all intents by the bottomless pockets of Scurvy Johnson's ghost.

If Madalyn lost, and it seemed destined that she would, her exposure was dreadful to contemplate. Except for their home—which in the State of Texas could not be lost to a civil judgment—all her personal and organizational assets were at stake. There was the AAGHQ building and all the printing and communications equipment that Madalyn had accrued over the years. There was the Charles E. Stevens American Atheist Library and Archives. And there were personal bank accounts, business bank accounts, trusts, jewelry, art, automobiles, and a wide variety of stocks, bonds, and real estate sprinkled around the country and the globe. All might be lost.

Madalyn's diaries covering the Scurvy Johnson countersuit phase are missing, so her thoughts can only be surmised. However, it seems clear that she began an uncharacteristically panicky reaction to the near disaster of the hung jury in early December 1993. While hoping to put off the new trial for as long as possible, Madalyn fleshed out radical contingency plans for when the seemingly inevitable judgment was rendered against her and her children.

First, everything had to be done with the tightest security possible. There could be substantial penalties involved—even criminal ones—if Johnson's people got wind of her ways and means. The initial task at hand was to come up with a plan for quick expatriation for her, Jon Garth, and Robin. Madalyn had contacts throughout the world and could relatively easily adopt a new homeland of her choice *and* find followers to help her and her children with the transition.

Except for that gawd damn city named Christchurch, Madalyn had liked the cut of New Zealand's jib ever since Ronald Reagan's election—the last time she seriously contemplated
expatriation. She quickly made the decision to relocate there. Jon
Garth was sent on the appropriate scouting trips, while Madalyn
and Robin started secretly converting assets into transferable
funds.

Within eighteen months, the trio had shifted more than
three-quarters of a million dollars to New Zealand as an initial
nest egg. Madalyn liked the transaction. New Zealand dollars ran
a little less than two to one in the exchange rate at the time. She
and the children were millionaires in New Zealand, with about
$1.2 million sitting in an atheist trust under their sole signa-
tures. She planned on transferring more of her hidden assets
there, in due time.

There were other large logistical problems to solve in order
to prepare for the falling of the guillotine in San Diego. Madalyn's single largest known asset, both in the physical and the
financial sense, was the Charles E. Stevens American Atheist
Library and Archives. It comprised tens of thousands of hard-
bound books and over a hundred thousand documents—including historical pamphlets, leather-bound volumes, early
free-thought publications, and other separationist arcana. The
library even had an X-rated shelf that included a sadomasochistic
section (some of which material her porn-addicted murderer
would steal).

Over the years, Madalyn had gathered the largest collection
of free-thought and atheist writings anywhere in the world, with
a library assembled by a wealthy eccentric in India a distant second. CESAALA had an assessed value in excess of $3 million, and
Madalyn urgently wanted to protect it from plundering by
Scurvy Johnson's minions, or the revenuers who might put a lien
on it and sell it at auction. But how does a physically failing, eld-

erly woman who has never lifted anything heavier than a TV dinner tray move a $3 million, 140,000-item library in secrecy?

Madalyn clearly needed help—and as much as her secretive
nature rebelled at the thought, she had to enlist others in the
process. Working with a Houston-based American Atheists
member who ran a gay-porn enterprise and was dying of AIDS—
the same man to whom Jon Garth had shown so little pity—
Madalyn laid plans to hide the library in a storage facility in
Kansas City, Kansas, where it would be centrally located and safe
from infidel looters.

Madalyn was to be like the presiding priest of some
medieval monastery overseeing the monks' hurried hiding of
priceless manuscripts in a remote cave as the Huns rode unhin-
dered toward the gates of the citadel on a mission of brutal plun-
der. But not all her disciples were to be the faithful trusted
followers she wished them to be. The most rapacious pillager was
to be within—not without.

FIFTEEN

David Waters

*I*n the Texas version of winter, Austin can have a leaden sky that won't go away for days on end. A dank wind from the Gulf of Mexico will mix with the arctic air blustering out of the western High Plains, producing a cold, gunmetal cast of sky that could well remind any Midwesterner of home. On this February 2, 1993, David Waters noted the gloomy weather and a slight arthritic painfulness in his back as he climbed into his rundown red Camaro.

Job interviews. He didn't like job interviews. Yeah, he had his song and dance down, but he could never be sure that he could account for all the years that needed accounting for. He could never be sure that they wouldn't find out—by asking the right questions and checking his references in the right way. Still, this interview had potential. The help-wanted ad in the *Austin American-Statesman* was calling for a typesetter at an "Atheist Press" who knew grammar, could spell, and could type at least sixty words per minute. He could do eighty words a minute, with minimal errors. The last line in the ad made him chuckle— "Religious persons may feel uncomfortable." No. That wasn't a problem.

When he'd called earlier to get directions and more information, Waters learned that the job was at American Atheist General Headquarters and the person looking to hire a typesetter was none other than Madalyn Murray O'Hair. He'd heard of her. Waters had read a copy of her 1965 *Playboy* interview and seen her on television. Prayer in schools certainly wasn't a pressing issue for him, but he did enjoy her iconoclastic rants and was intrigued by the high contrast of her hard-edged views and her benign, grandmotherly appearance.

More importantly, she seemed very intelligent, and if David Waters put a high premium on any character trait, intelligence would be it. Madalyn talked about thoughts, philosophy, ideas. She appeared to be an intellectual, somebody he might be able to match wits with—for Waters knew himself to be an intellectual in the truest sense of the word.

Indeed he was—if the definition of an intellectual is some-body who lives in their mind. Mind-living was how Waters sur-vived the long years in prison, not just the ten years for murder, but the four for forgery and the year for the assault on his mother. His mind was his castle and he tried to explore all its potentiali-ties—mostly by reading.

While prison inmates are often known to craft their bodies into works of art with weights and dietary discipline, it was the muscle of his mind that Waters worked out in prison (although he didn't neglect physical conditioning either). Waters under-stood something that few other inmates did—the mind was a weapon better than any shank. It was the best weapon you could be armed with behind bars—or in the free world, for that matter. But you had to keep it sharp by honing it. So, if Madalyn helped him keep his mind sharpened *and* helped him pay the rent, well, that was doubly good.

As Waters pulled into the parking lot of American Atheist General Headquarters, he was impressed by the Mercedes-Benz sedan and the Porsche 944 near the front entrance. There was no sign on the modern, brick office building, but the address was the right one. As he rang the bell at the front entrance, he tried to look inside; however, the glass doorway and windows were tinted with mirror coating. The atmosphere of secrecy was heightened by the loud clicking of the remote, electromechanical lock releasing the door—which then swung silently inward on its own.

As Waters entered, a chubby thirty-something woman in a tent-sized dress was waiting. She curtly asked, "What do you want?" She was wearing no makeup and had an instantly obvious problem with body odor. When Waters explained that he had an appointment with Robin Murray, she acknowledged that was she, and brusquely explained that he'd have to fill out an application and take a typing test. Waters waited in the well-appointed lobby under the double gaze of his boss-to-be. A large bronze bust of Madalyn looked down at him from a pedestal, as did her oil portrait on the wall.

But he wasn't intimidated. At forty-five years old, David Waters was in his prime. A shade under six feet, he had an athletic build, a fat-free waist, and a head of hair that female barbers liked to dally over—thick and dark brown, with sprinklings of silver—swept boldly back. His nose was straight and well proportioned. Adding character to his face were small scars—a half-inch vertical one just off his left eyebrow and another, slightly longer, over his right lip. He was simply a strikingly handsome man—with one defect, a defect that some women would find fascination with: his peach-pit-brown eyes were ice cold—the eyes of a bird of prey—alert, measuring, pitiless.

Robin beckoned Waters to follow her. She took him to a conference room and seated him at a table in front of a computer. The only decoration on the walls was a poster with two words in all caps—"FUCK AUTHORITY." But before Waters could begin his typing test, Madalyn burst in.

She outdid her granddaughter in slovenliness. Madalyn's hair was almost all white now with a dull sheen of greasiness. Her once shapely calves stuck like spindles from her muumuu, which given her size might have made a fair spinnaker on a small racing sloop.

She too had no makeup on, and she too had a deodorant problem—with aromas identical to her granddaughter's. Ignoring Waters, she started shouting orders at Robin like a drill sergeant—call so-and-so, take names, kick some ass. The barrage transformed the young woman from haughty bitch to cowering lapdog within a few syllables. Madalyn then turned to Waters and fixed a metal-melting, squinty stare on him.

Evidently Madalyn liked what she saw. Waters certainly presented an unusually handsome specimen of the male gender at this point in his life. As well as being impulsive, Madalyn was convinced that she could instantly measure the innate character of any person if she chose to. But more importantly for the problem at hand, the staff at AAGHQ had a turnover rate in excess of what one might expect from a group of itinerant carnie workers. The fact was, she desperately needed a typesetter. Imperiously, she countermanded the typing test Robin had set up, saying, "If you can type and think you can handle all the shit around here, you can start right away. Seven bucks an hour. That okay?" Waters quietly agreed.

We may never know Madalyn's early opinions of the man who would murder her. Her diaries for that period are missing— probably stolen. But there is no doubt that she was taken with him. Madalyn was always gruff with David Waters, as she was with all the hired help, but clearly she held him in high regard. One might even use the word "infatuated" to describe her feelings—infatuated in the sense of what an older, powerful, vain female might feel toward a dynamic and handsome younger man. But Madalyn's judgment toward the opposite sex was historically awful, starting with the uncapturable B-24 pilot who fathered Bill and ending with Richard O'Hair, the alcoholic snitch who married her mainly to stay on the FBI's informant payroll.

Madalyn surely realized that there wasn't going to be any romance between her and her typesetter. However, other staff members, both male and female, had their hopes. Waters was the strong, quiet type—a kind of midwestern Gary Cooper and nearly as good-looking. Not only that, he was charming and deferential, with an air of sophistication and intellect. He had that rare and winning combination of personality traits that can make someone at once formidable and nonthreatening. With few exceptions, he made a fine, often great, impression.

Not only did he win people over with his unassuming and calm outward persona, he was a stable star in the vortex of AAGHQ. Waters was the archetypal quick study, handling everything with an uncanny, underplayed poise. But he was also a ferocious worker, with typesetting capabilities that were both voluminous and high quality. In fact, David Waters was a one-man workforce, and unlike the other employees, he never squeaked—never needed oiling—all for seven bucks an hour.

With the IRS case and the San Diego lawsuit looming as catastrophes, Madalyn made Waters her right-hand man—literally. They worked together for hours alone in the CESAALA library. Madalyn tenderly wrapped the thousands of books, one at a time, in special acid-free paper, preparing them for the move to the secret storage facility. As she readied the books, Waters worked next to her at a computer workstation, cataloging each of them. Madalyn would dictate a title and he'd enter it into the database that he'd created. (Waters was highly computer literate; going under the electronic nom de plume of "Sir Roland," he would eventually even set up a website, called "Madalyn's Attic," where he fenced articles he'd stolen from his murder victims.)

But even for an ex-con in desperate need of a paycheck, the job wasn't good. He and Madalyn worked surrounded by stacks of musty books in a claustrophobic, airtight room. It must have seemed like cleaning the Augean stable and being in prison at the same time. The droning of Madalyn's harsh voice never ceased. The only punctuation in their regimen, which continued for seemingly endless days, would be unpleasant in the extreme: Madalyn, now sickly and without pride, might break wind at any given moment—leaving Waters trapped and gagging in silence. The irony was that Madalyn thought she was according Waters the highest of compliments by allowing him to work in such close proximity to her—the Queen.

Actually, Waters was able to escape briefly to take cigarette breaks. It was a special dispensation that Madalyn granted her favorite. Nobody was allowed to smoke at AAGHQ—with her knowledge, at least—except for David Waters. She did warn him, though, that if he wasn't discreet, the privilege would be withdrawn. But discreet Waters was.

SIXTEEN

The Killer Inside

*M*adalyn decided to fly back to Austin from San Diego for Thanksgiving, where she, Jon Garth, and Robin were being battered in depositions. The lawyers hired by Lawrence True, executor of the James Hervey Johnson estate for the second RICO trial, were dragging the atheist trio over the coals and they badly needed a break. It also seemed a good idea to check up on things back home, since there had been some sort of break-in at the American Atheist General Headquarters.

Both of the trusted atheist officers that Madalyn usually had "baby-sit" whenever she and her children were away on vacation or business had been unavailable. She was forced to leave the entire operation running in the hands of her harried office manager. A week earlier, the office manager had called Madalyn in San Diego to inform her that there had been a "security breach" at AAGHQ—but nothing was taken.

Rather than put things off, when Madalyn arrived in Austin, she and the children had a quickie Thanksgiving dinner and went down to headquarters. The office manager had been wrong. There were things missing. The workstation computer that Waters had been using was gone, along with some peripherals. The computer cost well over four thousand dollars—but that wasn't the worst of it. All the work that Waters and Madalyn had done cataloging the library was missing too. The tape backup had a "glitch" in it, and there were no backups of the months' worth of data that had been so painfully and meticulously collected.

Madalyn called the Austin police. An officer came over and filled out a burglary report. However, the detective handling the matter reviewed the security logs provided by Madalyn's alarm service and concluded that the "security breach" had actually been a false alarm. The officer told Madalyn that his suspicion was that the theft hadn't been a burglary but was an "inside job."

Madalyn rationalized the ill-omened implications. After close to three decades, she was inured to office personnel problems of any kind. Of late, though, there had been a particularly troublesome flux of hassles. A slander suit had been filed against her by an employee. Madalyn had lost the suit but was fighting the judgment on appeal, and she speculated that the ex-staffer/plaintiff might be behind the theft. There also was another suspect.

Madalyn found out during discovery proceedings in San Diego that the Johnson investigators had "turned" one of Madalyn's employees—Scurvy had had his own mole. Madalyn mused that the theft might have been done by this newly identified traitor, especially since the missing library data would be of high value to the Johnson people in proving that she intended to conceal assets.

Historically, Madalyn loved making enemies and she knew she was proficient at it. She also felt confident she could always handle the inherent risks produced by her behavior. And in the past she had, for Madalyn possessed a well-calibrated aptitude for spotting potential foes and homing in on their weaknesses. It was a trait that had contributed not only to her success, but to her very survival. When it came to dealing with threats from people—especially those made from lesser stuff—Madalyn could be a lioness, disemboweling them with a single swipe of a powerful claw.

But the wages of bad living had claimed their toll. Madalyn had never taken care of herself and she wasn't aging well. While her mind was still more than sharp, she no longer had anywhere near the energy needed for maintaining the high-wire act she'd long done. The weight, the lack of physical exercise, the poor diet, the late-night drinking, the never-ending stress—all the chickens were coming home to roost simultaneously, it seemed.

The worst manifestation of her decline was that Madalyn had become a diabetic, a heavily insulin-dependent diabetic, at risk of going into shock or delirium if her blood sugar levels weren't carefully monitored and maintained within tight parameters. Her diabetes was manageable, but managing it took dedication and discipline—psychological resources that Madalyn had to redirect from other critical areas. The most important element of disease management was her weight, which fluctuated around 250 pounds—and she simply didn't have the will to deal with it.

Rounding out the physical hell that Madalyn's life had devolved into were multiple arthritic conditions. The lower part of her backbone had developed bone spurs that must have felt like she was being stuck by the tines of the devil's own pitchfork. Vertebrae in her back and neck had fused as well—the old injuries from the Baltimore police fracas years earlier. Compounding all the problems, Madalyn also suffered from early-onset osteoarthritis, an extremely painful and debilitating bone disease that strikes the elderly. To cope with a deteriorating left hip joint, Madalyn had undergone a replacement—and probably could have qualified for multiple joint replacements, if she'd had the inclination. She didn't. Instead, Madalyn preferred to endure the pain and walk with a walker.

The agonies of Madalyn's physical existence, combined with the pressures of the IRS action and the San Diego suit, made the theft of the computer and data seem trivial to her. But apparently the "inside job" was too much for Madalyn's office manager, a high-strung woman who had developed a corrosive hatred for her boss. She quit, leaving Madalyn in an even more precarious position. The timing couldn't have been worse. Madalyn didn't need to be worrying about AAGHQ. She needed to marshal all possible intellectual resources toward meeting and defeating, or at least temporarily outflanking, the powerful enemies who were vectoring in for the kill.

Luckily there was an answer to the problem at hand—at her right hand, to be precise. She didn't know where Waters came from but he looked like a savior—the reply to all her unsaid prayers. He was the right man at the right time to run the office. He was cheap and probably could be had as office manager for ten dollars an hour if he'd been willing to take seven dollars as a typesetter. He was clearly extremely intelligent—perhaps the smartest man she'd ever employed.

According to Robin's vetting of him, Waters was college-educated in Illinois—which alone put him at the top of the dregs and outcasts that Madalyn felt she could only afford to hire. He was an exceptionally strong worker, got along with everybody, and commanded respect. And for all his strengths, Madalyn found him to be unusually deferential to her. He was discreet, if not just a bit secretive. But then secretiveness was acceptable to Madalyn because she was a devout practitioner herself.

Madalyn had Jon Garth do the formal offer of the office manager's position, and after a little dickering, Waters took the job. Madalyn breathed a sigh of relief. Now she could concentrate on the possible move to New Zealand, getting the library hidden away, and riding herd on her lawyers and accountants to make sure her defenses were in the best condition possible given the gravity of the circumstances.

As far as the "inside job"—the computer theft—was concerned, Waters *couldn't* have had anything to do with that theft—not after all the work he'd put into it. Besides, Robin had carefully checked Waters out, and he didn't have any problems she could find. It made no difference, though. Madalyn trusted her own judgmental abilities, tired as they might be, like a Hill Country dowser believes in his old willow switch.

In fact, Madalyn would go further with her trust of Waters than of any other employee she'd had in the past. She gave him, as office manager, the security codes to the building. However, she also gave him, unlike his two immediate predecessors, passkeys that apparently allowed him the complete run of AAGHQ. Along with the keys to the empire, Madalyn conferred the ultimate imprimatur of confidence: she allowed her new office manager to have the security codes and keys to the Grey-stone Drive house—the Murray-O'Hairs' personal residence—the true sanctum sanctorum.

The second week of January 1994, a week after David Waters officially became office manager of the American Atheist General Headquarters, Jon Garth received a notice from a New York bank that had issued the Murray-O'Hairs seventy thousand dollars' worth of government bearer bonds. The bonds had been "called" and needed to be sent in for redemption. When Jon Garth opened the safe in his office to retrieve them, to his shock he discovered they were gone.

The police were called in, and again they found no security breach in the alarm system. Once more, they declared it an inside job—the second in less than two months.

The Austin Police Department, in what was to begin their virtually lethal pattern, declined to question the AAGHQ staff. Furious at the slacker attitude of the cops, Madalyn interrogated all her staffers herself, without result. However, Madalyn did find that the thief or thieves had dropped one of the twelve bond certificates during the heist. Madalyn called the police again, to see if they could lift a fingerprint from the document. Once more, they refused to become involved.

As final icing on the bitter cake, Madalyn had not a dime's worth of content insurance on anything inside AAGHQ. She claimed that it was because of a "general bias of insurance companies against the proponents of Atheism." In any case, the theft of the bonds was a total loss. Not only were they gone, but the fat annual interest dividend—then between 10 and 13 percent per year—was gone too. The only satisfaction that Madalyn could draw from this latest calamity was that the thief couldn't cash the coupons since they'd require proper ID and the bank had been alerted to the theft.

That there was a serious criminal inside her organization was now apparent. But who was it? And how to deal with him? Madalyn's reaction again seemed to be one of semidenial. When she was asked by organization members what she planned to do, Madalyn shrugged and replied that she couldn't realistically fire everyone in the building, could she?

The last week of March 1994, Madalyn, Jon Garth, and Robin headed out to face manifest execution in San Diego. The federal judge, a jurist known for his ill temper and erratic comportment, was to hear the case himself, rather than have a jury trial. It was this very same judge, Manuel Real, who had sentenced Madalyn's atheist colleague and admirer—the wheelchair-bound porn magnate Larry Flynt—to a year and a half in a federal psychiatric prison for sassing him in court during the DeLorean trial—the outcome of a famous government sting operation that netted the world-renowned sports car entrepreneur in a cocaine bust.

Judge Real didn't make much difference to Madalyn. She thought they were in a heap o' trouble no matter by whom or how the case was heard. A typical, conservative San Diego jury could cause massive financial damage. But having the judge hear the case alone—a judge who seemed to revel in his unpredictability and ugly demeanor—that was scary too. And further, with a judge hearing the case, it meant prolonging the suspense, since it would probably take months for him to render a decision.

Oh gawd, she was weary. If you combined her multiple law-suits against Johnson with his countersuits against her, her legal fees alone were approaching a half-million dollars in San Diego. It was easily the most expensive court battle she'd ever experienced, and it looked like the ramifications would reverberate for years.

That wasn't the worst of it. Actually Madalyn was geared up strictly for offense against Johnson. Her defense, which she never thought she'd have to rely on for survival, was weak, centering around issuance and ownership of stock—and her own self-serving interpretations of the verbal promises and recantings of a nutty, cancer-ridden millionaire.

After the two-week trial in front of Judge Real ended, Madalyn returned home to Texas on an early April evening to await the ruling, lick her wounds, and recharge her drained batteries. It would be the most disastrous homecoming of her life.

What she found at AAGHQ the next day stunned her. When she arrived at the office, she quickly knew something was wrong—very wrong. The parking lot was deserted and the doors were locked. Inside, she immediately saw that none of the employee time cards had been punched. The postage meter was showing a date that was weeks old, and the telephone answering machine overflowed with old messages.

One of them was from her trusted office manager—David Waters. He said that he'd resigned—cryptically adding that he "could no longer tolerate the mystique of the organization." After calling Waters's home phone without result, Madalyn frantically called other staffers, one of whom informed her that, yes, "Mr. Waters had laid off all the employees, by order of a telephone call from Jon Murray from San Diego."

Madalyn roamed further back into the building to assess the

damage. The extent of the disaster continued to unfold. Their long-distance phone service had been terminated. No bills had been paid and "entire sheets of checks" were missing from registers and ledgers. Bank deposits were unmade and no book orders had been filled—evidently from the time they'd left for California.

Since it was Saturday and the banks were closed, it was impossible to get a fully accurate balance on their accounts—but as things turned out, that wouldn't be necessary. When Jon Garth called the automated teller and entered the account numbers, the computerized voice informed him that each corporate account had been liquidated. Jon Garth reported to his mother that "We've been completely wiped out."

SEVENTEEN

From the Brink to the Abyss

---

*J*on Garth tracked down the forged checks on the Monday following. Actually they weren't technically "forged" checks—they were "bad" checks. Waters was so trusted that Jon Garth had left signed, blank checks for him to fill out in order to pay bills while he, Madalyn, and Robin were tending to the trial in San Diego. Using his own name and signature, Waters had bodaciously cashed fifty-five thousand dollars' worth of the checks—and endorsed them using his Texas driver's license number.

Jon Garth located witnesses to the crime. Bank clerks remembered Waters and the transactions. An AAGHQ staff member claimed he had seen Waters readying the checks. He went down to the Austin Police Department and brought along a soft-drink can that Waters had handled. The loyal staffer, one of the few who didn't like Waters's vibes from the beginning, wanted the police to lift fingerprints from the can, and check to see if Waters had a criminal record. According to Madalyn, the Austin police declined to investigate.

Madalyn was furious. When she called her board members to apprise them of the theft, she noted with perhaps good justification, that if that much money had been stolen from another nonprofit organization or a religious institution, there would have been a vigorous investigation and Waters would have been behind bars. Madalyn directed a letter-writing campaign against

the Austin chief of police by the boards of her various atheist
organizations, urging that the police take immediate action. The
chief didn't deign to reply, according to Madalyn. When,
drenched with frustration, she went directly to police headquarters and demanded they do something, she was "stalled off" once
again, she said.

After two weeks had passed, the Austin police finally took
notice—perhaps more than anything else to get the obstreperous
atheist off their backs. A warrant was issued for Waters's arrest—
but with a deferential treatment that might have been accorded
to the son of a Saudi diplomat.

Although they'd issued a warrant, the Austin police would
not put Waters on their fugitive list for immediate pickup, even
though tens of thousands of dollars were involved. Instead, the
previous office manager, with whom Waters had developed a
friendship, was sent as an emissary to talk with him. Waters told
her that he'd be glad to explain his side of things to law enforcement and that he'd see them forthwith. An "appointment" was
set up with police, but Waters never showed.

Still Madalyn continued to hound the Austin PD to arrest
Waters. When she cornered a police captain, Madalyn was
informed that Mr. Waters had been "busy" and that they were
trying to work out a date when he could come in for an "appointment" that was more convenient for him. Didn't she realize that
they needed to consider Mr. Waters's "goodwill" in the community?

With a hotshot, pricey defense counsel at his side, Waters
finally arrived for his tête-à-tête with the amiable Austin police
at the end of April 1994, more than a month after he'd looted the
fifty-five thousand dollars from his employers. His attorney was
smooth, experienced—and obviously far too expensive for a man
who'd been living hand to mouth on a near minimum-wage
salary. It was an easy guess where Waters came up with the large

cash retainer that such high-caliber criminal defense counselors require. When Madalyn asked the Austin police if they'd looked into where Waters got the money for his lawyer, she was told that, no, they hadn't inquired. Didn't she understand that that the "privacy" of Mr. Waters's relationship with his attorney needed to be "protected"?

The late April "interview" with police went well for Mr. Waters—exceedingly well, considering the outcome and the true circumstances. Waters's attorney got the police and the district attorney's office to go along with having his client released on a personal-recognizance bond. Usually such bonds are reserved for long-term residents or citizens with a known and reasonably good reputation. Effectively, it meant that Waters was to be released on his own word that he wouldn't skip town.

Even the most perfunctory criminal background check by Austin police or the district attorney's office would have shown him to be what he was, a violent criminal who had spent a major portion of his adult life in prison doing hard time not only for murder, but for fraud and forgery—the very crimes he was being accused of.

But Waters must have had a soothing rap—so reassuring that both the DA's office and the police felt that even a cursory background check would have been a waste of time. As part of the deal, Waters promised he'd get the law enforcement officials a sworn affidavit with the particulars of *his* allegations against the Murray-O'Hairs within the week.

He was as good as his word, and a wondrous document it was. According to Madalyn, who said she finally received the affidavit months after it was delivered to the authorities, Waters claimed that he'd been told by Jon Garth to steal approximately $100,000 from legitimate atheist organizational accounts using previously signed checks given to him by Jon Garth himself. Some of the money was to be sent to the Murray-O'Hairs in San

Diego, and the rest was to be put in Jon Garth's office safe. Waters, for his services, was to receive a $15,000 commission. According to Waters, Jon Murray wanted the accounts drained because he, his mother, and Robin were going underground to avoid a huge judgment won against them by the Johnson estate. Waters claimed he kept the $15,000 commission, sent a portion of the cash to Jon Garth in California, and put the rest—some forty thousand dollars—in Jon Garth's safe at AAGHQ.

If the Austin police and the DA's office had been anything but somnolent, they could easily have determined that Waters's alibi was nonsense. All it would have taken was a single call to the Federal Courthouse in San Diego to ascertain that there had been no judgment against the Murray-O'Hairs. Further, there wasn't even a timetable for when Judge Real would render his decision.

Perhaps more appalling was the seeming failure of the DA's office to comprehend that Waters's actions could be viewed as a serious felony in their own right. If Jon Murray was stealing tens of thousands of dollars of atheist assets, then Waters was admitting that he was not only an accomplice but a beneficiary of the theft.

The glaring defects in Waters's alibi were not due to his lack of skill or creativity. They were due to circumstance and contingency. To be sure, Waters had carefully been laying the plans for the rip-off for months. He had burrowed deeply into Madalyn's finances with his new authority as office manager. His analysis of the legal situation in San Diego led him to believe, as Madalyn did, that the Murray-O'Hairs were going to lose big-time.

Waters also had gotten his hands on enough documentation to show that the trio were indeed planning to flee the country, in all likelihood to New Zealand, when they lost in San Diego. And finally, most importantly, it was Waters's sly and astute judgment that the Austin police would be lazy and not discover his background—and if they didn't, his credibility would be greater in their eyes than that of the Murray-O'Hairs, who were well known in Austin to be lifelong cop-haters, finaglers, and all-purpose pains-in-the-ass.

How in hell could he have guessed that a federal judge, instead of a jury, would hear the case, delaying the verdict for months. It was this unplanned event that forced him to tear up the script and start improvising; hence his creation of the seemingly self-incriminating affidavit, which investigators wouldn't see as incriminating. He could only hope that the accommodating Austin police would be dumb enough not to see what he'd been forced to do—and if perchance they did, that his slick lawyer would figure out a means for him to slither away.

The Austin police met Waters's expectations. Apparently they never ran a thorough criminal background investigation on the convicted murderer before turning the case over to the Travis County District Attorney's Office at the beginning of May 1994.

The DA's office seemed afflicted with the same stupor as the gendarmerie. According to Madalyn's account, they initially gave strong credence to Waters's affidavit against her, Jon Garth, and Robin, stalling off Madalyn much as the police had. Once more she unleashed a letter-writing offensive by her membership, this time against the district attorney. When she finally got an audience with the DA's deputies who were handling the case, she flogged them for not pushing for fingerprinting of the soft-drink can. In response, she claimed, she was told by the deputy DAs that taking such action was an "extreme measure" not warranted in this case, and that "Mr. Waters's reputation had to be considered."

Madalyn did make some progress, though. She seemed to have finally convinced the DA's office of the absurdity of the Waters affidavit. That they only grudgingly acknowledged how ridiculous the document was, probably was a testament to Mada-

lyn's obnoxious interactions with them. Madalyn not only saw
herself as an international leader and historical figure, but
believed that she was a superior lawyer—either criminal or
civil—and these deputies were just hacks who couldn't cut it in
the private sector. It was frustrating for her to have to educate
them, especially with her expanding realization of the scope of
the damage and the threat that Waters posed.

Whatever the reason, investigators finally ran a thorough
criminal record check on Waters—and what they found sent the
deputy DAs scurrying off to the grand jury. On July 7, 1994,
three months after he had stolen fifty-four thousand dollars,
Waters was indicted. The true bill contained information that
must have made even Madalyn shiver. Waters had a criminal
record that included convictions for murder, forgery, assault, burglary, criminal trespass, drunk driving, and weapons charges.
He'd been first incarcerated in reform school as a teen, and had
spent a decade in the infamous state penitentiary at Joliet, as well
as another half-dozen years of hard time in other Illinois prisons.

Madalyn discovered that she had taken to her very bosom
the most lethal of vipers—an incorrigible, violent sociopath. And
perhaps worse, she'd also pissed on and pissed off the Establishment in Austin to the point where she'd self-destructed the protective shield that law enforcement normally affords its citizens
from the predations of hard-core criminals.

After issuing the indictment for theft, the grand jury pru-
dently recommended that Waters be held on a bond of fifty thousand dollars. It was a moderate figure, given the size of the theft
that he'd been charged with and his criminal history. However,
the DA's office—seemingly snake-charmed by Waters—sided
with his defense attorney and obligingly agreed that the bail
should be lowered to only ten thousand dollars, in opposition to
the grand jury recommendation.

Waters's shrewd analysis, that Madalyn would not get a fair

shake from the justice system in Austin, was turning out to be lethally accurate. There was also some other good fortune for him. Madalyn and the judge who had been assigned Waters's case went way back. As soon as Madalyn found out which court was hearing the Waters matter—Judge Wilford Flowers's 147th District—she filed papers to have the judge recuse himself.

Years earlier, Madalyn had received a notice for jury duty in Flowers's court. She promptly held a news conference and burned the jury summons in front of TV cameras because jurors had to take an oath to God in order to serve. Judge Flowers may or may not have remembered the incident, but regardless, he wouldn't recuse himself.

For David Waters, the mills of justice in Travis County ground neither fine nor fast. Madalyn was to bitterly note in her newsletter the calendar of postponements that Waters's attorney was able to get from Judge Flowers:

> On July 21, the case was set for hearing in the 147th District Court of Travis County: called, then postponed to August 22, called, then reset for September 9, called, then reset to September 15, called, then reset to October 3, called, then reset to October 17, called, then reset to November 7, called, then reset to December 5, called, then reset to January 23, 1995, called, then reset to February 6, called, then reset to March 13, called, then reset to April 10, called, then reset to April 24, called, then reset to May 18, called, then reset to May 22.

On at least two hearing dates, according to Madalyn's court watchers, the attorney for Waters never even showed up, but somehow Waters was granted a continuance by the benevolent Judge Flowers. But by May 22, even Judge Flowers was fed up. When Waters's attorney asked for yet another postponement—

which Waters had been expecting—Judge Flowers refused.

Waters claimed that he was stricken with dread at the thought of a criminal trial, given his background. He said that his instincts told him to fight—fight for justice! He was vehemently opposed to letting Madalyn get away with this gigantic fraud that he been picked as patsy for. If he pled guilty, then the real truth would never come out. Nonetheless, he reluctantly— against what his heart was telling him—allowed his attorney to talk him into a guilty plea.

Whatever Waters's moral and ethical concerns, his lawyer had worked out what surely had to be one of the sweetest plea bargains in Travis County criminal history. In exchange for pleading guilty to theft, to being a habitual criminal, and to three lesser counts, Waters would be given ten years' probation and be required to make restitution. The structure of the sentence, in legal parlance, was known as a "deferred adjudication." It meant that if Waters made his restitution payments on time, and if he stayed out of trouble with the law, after ten years his arrest, his guilty plea, the sentence, his probation—*everything*— would be expunged from the books.

It might have been a wise sentencing arrangement for a remorseful citizen who may have had a single, semiserious lapse of judgment. But with Waters, a "deferred adjudication" was senseless at best. He had no remorse whatsoever, and he already was a convicted murderer and forger. Those convictions could never be expunged. Expunging his present convictions would be a bit like offering underarm deodorant to an angry skunk.

According to Madalyn's account of events, at least a modicum of common sense was briefly interjected in the sentencing proceedings by the Travis County Probation Department. In a special edition of her atheist newsletter, Madalyn told her membership that the probation department would have preferred to see him sent to prison with a long sentence as a habitual offender.

Having pled guilty to being a "habitual criminal," Waters could have been quarantined from society for many years—conceivably for the rest of his life.

If in fact that was the recommendation, usually a judge follows the advice of the professionals, especially when hard-core types like Waters are involved, since it is the probation officers who are most familiar with the day-to-day dangers of recidivism. In any event, Judge Flowers ruled that the remorseless ex-con would receive the tragicomic "deferred adjudication," rather than being sent to the state penitentiary.

Flowers's decision was to be a mortal judgment for the Murray-O'Hairs. Madalyn, the primary victim-to-be, was terrified that Waters was now a free man. Of course, she was far too vain to admit as much publicly. Undoubtedly, she must have confided her alarm about Waters's being free to her children. As well, she would have written extensively about her fear of him in her diary—but the diaries for this period were missing. Madalyn's only public acknowledgment of her fears about her murderer was in respectfully asking Judge Flowers to issue a restraining order against Waters.

Judge Flowers declined. Waters had been instructed that his probation included having no contact with the Murray-O'Hairs. Flowers evidently felt this admonishment was a sufficient protection from the convicted killer for the aging atheist and her children. Madalyn made another request of Judge Flowers, pointing out to the court that the fifty-five thousand dollars in restitution that Waters was required to pay should include interest. Otherwise, Madalyn reasonably argued, it was simply an interest-free loan to a felon. Judge Flowers denied the request.

Back in the old days, Madalyn might would have hatched a plan to get revenge on Judge Flowers. Now she just tried to circle the wagons. Her assessment of the danger that Waters presented to her was clear: She feared for her life. Within weeks, a

seven-foot chain-link fence was erected around AAGHQ. Madalyn wanted a similar one around her residence on Greystone
Drive in West Austin, but zoning restrictions prohibited it in
that fashionable neighborhood. Still, she had all the locks in the
house changed and new security codes put in the alarm system.
At his mother's direction, Jon Garth closed all their bank
accounts—both personal and business—and opened new ones,
since Waters still had many of their checks in his possession.

Madalyn also took another step toward trying to protect
herself and her children from the predator. She decided to write a
tell-all narrative of the Waters situation in a special "members
only" section of *The American Atheist.* Her motive was to explain
the disaster that had befallen them to her followers, and also
establish a semipublic record of events. After the story was published, she felt certain, Waters would be a prime suspect should
anything happen to her and her children. She also wanted to
expose the handling she received at the hands of the criminal justice system in Austin.

Another motive for publishing the Waters story—which
Madalyn may not have admitted, even to herself—was that she
hated the idea of this slimy ex-con being arrogant enough to
think he could get away with what he did to her—a person of her
stature. Since the media weren't interested, and the justice system was clearly favoring this scumbag, she'd set the record
straight herself.

And gawd, she needed the pleasure of retaliation after what
she'd been through. Unfortunately, Madalyn was as incorrigible
in her own way as Waters was in his. She simply could not resist
the temptation of avenging the crimes against her, even if it
meant antagonizing a sociopathic killer who plainly had her in
his sights already.

She did take some precautions, though, fearful as she was of
Waters. She hoped that since her narrative would be sent out only

to her small paying membership of two thousand or so American Atheists, Waters would never see it. But if he did, at least she was going to be careful to be coldly precise in her dissection of him, rather than taking her usual brutally personal attack posture.

Madalyn had good contacts inside law enforcement in Illinois—good enough to give her the specific details of Waters's criminal history, even down to the case numbers. Madalyn laid it all out in the newsletter. There was the murder of Gibbs, the forgery of Caterpillar Tractor paychecks, the arrests for reckless conduct and battery, the burglary charges, and, of course, the maternal-pissing episode. Here Madalyn supplied frosty detail: Waters's confrontation at his mother's apartment, his beating of her with a broom handle, and the final alleged urination.

The most disconcerting passage in the special newsletter came when Madalyn tried to explain how it all happened—how they could have hired such a man to work at AAGHQ. Atheist organization board members had questioned Madalyn's assertions that she and Robin vetted Waters at all, let alone properly. This was an especially bitter accusation for Madalyn.

She explained that Robin had indeed looked carefully at Waters's background before he was hired. She had called past employers. None would say anything against him. His references were in order. His college work was done in the University of Illinois system and Robin was told by the office of the registrar that Waters had definitely completed the credits he'd listed.

After Waters's indictment Madalyn herself checked with the two Illinois colleges where he had received more than fifty credits. It turned out that both educational institutions had neglected to tell Robin that Mr. Waters's credits were earned in the "in penal" classroom instruction program. In other words, he was an inmate in a state penitentiary when he was taking courses— serving time for forgery.

Arguably, Madalyn might have hired him anyway, but never

would she have made him office manager. Never would she have given him the level of trust that she did if she had known he was an ex-con with a lengthy record—especially for forgery. The withholding of the information, that bit of collegial political correctness toward inmate students, may have been as lethal to the Murray-O'Hairs as the Travis County justice system was—and as Madalyn's decision to publish her version of the Waters story would be.

After reading a copy of the newsletter, Waters started having his own revenge fantasies, but they were somewhat more ambitious than Madalyn's. He wanted to first snip off her toes one by one with a bolt cutter and then murder her. Strangling would be good. But before he killed her, he would extort a fortune from her, and her children, so that he and his girlfriend could live in luxury happily ever after.

Life is paradox, the sages say. As Waters began to lay plans for her death, Madalyn won the two greatest personal triumphs in her life against the longest odds. The ill-tempered and erratic federal judge in San Diego, Manuel Real, had taken a shine to Madalyn! Somehow he had convinced himself that Madalyn was indeed a legitimate stockholder with a reasonable interest in the disposition of the James Hervey Johnson estate.

Judge Real's ruling reflected what can only be described as an irrational belief in Madalyn's sincerity. "Despite there being no proof that Madalyn owns stock in the [publication], I choose to believe her when she says she is, in fact, a shareholder." Continuing, the judge explained: "Therefore, on this basis alone, I reject the idea that she is simply a busybody who is trying to horn in on someone else's millions."

With those words of mystifying logic, Judge Real removed the Damoclean sword. Madalyn had beaten the long odds in San Diego.

At the same time, there was great news coming from Washington, D.C., where Madalyn's tax attorney had been negotiating with the IRS. Somehow, possibly due to large-scale political attacks on the IRS, Madalyn's hated revenuers had turned into lambs. They would settle all the claims—$1.5 million combined against Jon Garth and Robin—for somewhat less than $75,000 total. Actually, it was even better than that. The settlement would also secure the IRS's tacit agreement not to initiate another big investigation against Madalyn herself.

Almost certain disaster had been averted by an incredibly providential convergence of events. Madalyn and her children were hanging by their fingernails above the yawning abyss—and then swept up on a magic carpet and transported to safety. It was overwhelming. The million-dollar-plus AAGHQ was safe. The multimillion-dollar library was safe. Her millions in organizational assets and personal trusts and accounts were safe. No need to think about scarpering to New Zealand or other foreign ports of call. The whole thing was a gawd damn miracle!

EIGHTEEN

The Vanishing

The last photograph taken of the world's first high priestess of atheism was snapped on August 11, 1995. Madalyn, wearing a blue print dress, was perched just a bit precariously on a porch swing. Her legs were crossed, old-lady fashion, at midcalf. A cane was resting in her right hand. With a wan smile, she looked into the camera with a cautious squint—a nocturnal rodent's gaze—as if she wasn't used to the soft, summer sunlight filtering through the trees.

The inseparable trio—Madalyn, Jon Garth, and Robin— were vacationing at the home of her favorite atheist board member, Arnold Via. The spry septuagenarian, likened to a gone-to-seed Civil War general with his wild gray beard, had invited Madalyn and her children for a visit to his house sequestered in the northern Virginia hills.

Via was a kindly character, even while being a semihermit who might tramp in the woods on any given day with a .38 revolver. He'd known Madalyn for decades and had watched the children grow up. Besides being a trusted board member, per- haps the most trusted, Via was a friend of the family. Even though Madalyn would grumble in her diary that she didn't think highly of his judgment at times, she was fond of him.

Via reciprocated with a sonlike adoration, even though Madalyn was only a few years his senior. He'd talked the trio into coming out to celebrate after their grueling but glorious victories in San Diego and D.C. Via took them on tours of the nearby Civil War battlefields for relaxation, and Madalyn practiced some home cooking, making a vegetable soup that she liked to bally-hoo. They would also discuss some serious long-term plans.

Madalyn wanted to move the American Atheists' headquarters to Richmond, Virginia. Not only would she get away from the lurking David Waters in Austin, but the move would allow her to return to her Eastern roots to close out her life. She and Via talked about the availability and quality of nursing homes in the area. They even discussed burying her on his property. Via had already established a small cemetery for "atheist prisoners" who died while incarcerated. Even though only one prisoner had taken up Via's offer over the years, Madalyn agreed that it seemed a good burial place for her.

With some of her old gusto, Madalyn nattered about the upcoming "Pope Picket" in New York City. The leader of the Catholic Church had been an object of Madalyn's unwavering hatred for half a century, and she looked forward to protesting the New York visit of the current pontiff, John Paul II, in early October 1995 with the eagerness of an ancient fire-horse whose desire outstripped its old legs. Jon Garth had already set up the logistics and Madalyn was pleased with the plans, which included meeting with her organizational clansmen in the city during the event.

Even though the conversations with Via revolved around issues of mortality and the depressingly nearby eventualities thereof, Madalyn was chipper and upbeat. And why not? She'd just beaten the hell out of her two worst enemies—Scurvy Johnson's ghost and the IRS—and averted financial catastrophe in the process. She had also done everything she could to protect herself and the kids from that shithole ex-con, and moving to Virginia would just add to their security. If her health would hold out, she'd retire to the place of her roots. Then her descendants would carry the atheist torch fueled by the robust monetary reserves that she had accumulated for them. Things were as good as they could be, considering.

· · ·

American Atheists staff members arrived at work on Monday, August 28, 1995 to find a typed message posted on the front door:

> All employees of AAGHQ, Inc. The Murray O'Hair family has been called out of town on an emergency basis. We do not know how long we will be gone at the time of the writing of this memo. Your paychecks for this period of August 16th through August 31st is [sic] enclosed. We do anticipate that we shall return prior to the next payroll period, close date of September 15th.

It had been signed by Jon Garth Murray. Grumbling, the staff congregated at a nearby coffee shop to discuss the Murray-O'Hairs' latest caper. They'd left without notice just a few weeks earlier on a vacation back east to Virginia and—even though payroll had been met—these mysterious departures always reinforced the insecurity and unpredictability of work at the AAGHQ.

The latest incident seemed to be typical of the consistently atypical behavior one could expect from the trio. Why couldn't they just explain what was going on? At least give a hint? No, they were terminally squirrelly, the group concluded. Nothing would change their secretive nature and their high-handed interactions with the hired help.

However, this time their antics might be worth checking into. Spike Tyson, a longtime organization member and now a staffer at AAGHQ, was perplexed. Yes, it was like the Murray-

O'Hairs to keep the staff in the dark about their doings, but they'd usually inform him at least. Tyson had worked with Madalyn for years. A decorated Vietnam veteran, he'd done everything from being Madalyn's bodyguard at public appearances to relatively complex electrical engineering duties required by Madalyn's media enterprises.

Tyson was a trusted member of the inner circle. Madalyn was known to frequently say that Tyson was the son that she wished she had had (at least once paying this compliment in front of Jon Garth, according to witnesses). He was the only staffer/atheist member she provided with keys and codes to the AAGHQ after the Waters debacle—but only a front door key for the residence, not pass codes for the alarm system. In any case, given the semi-odd circumstances surrounding the abrupt exit by the Murray-O'Hairs, Tyson decided to go over to the Greystone Drive house by himself and have a look.

It didn't appear there'd been a break-in, but the doors to the double-car garage were open and the Porsche and Mercedes gone. The house doors were locked and all the windows secure. If they hadn't been, the burglar alarm would have gone off. Madalyn had recently had the house wired with a multiple-entry sensor system, given her fears of David Waters.

More unusual was that Robin's two cocker spaniels, Shannon and Gannon, were in the backyard along with Madalyn's rat terrier, Gallagher. It wasn't out of the ordinary to have the dogs roaming in the back, but it was *very* unusual for Robin to have left them all out together. Gallagher didn't get along with Shannon and Gannon, and Robin made sure that they were separated at all times.

It was strange, but then again, they were a strange family. Tyson, concerned about the dogs' being fed and given water, penned a quick note and left it on the door. He wrote that he'd take care of the dogs and watch the house for the next two weeks or so while the Murray-O'Hairs dealt with their "emergency." When he came back the following afternoon, the dogs were gone—as was his note.

Earlier that day, the receptionist at the office of Madalyn's veterinarian had received a call from Robin Murray. Her voice and demeanor were so out-of-sorts that the receptionist started scribbling a note to file away—something that she rarely did. Robin told her that there was a "family emergency," and that they all had to leave town quickly. The dogs needed to be boarded and could she *please* go and pick them up. It was a routine request, but Robin's tone was frantic, begging—not in context given the circumstances. Yes, the receptionist assured Robin, of course they would board the dogs. Still, Robin persisted in her pleading. It sounded like she was crying at the same time. The receptionist tucked away the note and retrieved the dogs.

A few days later, another uncharacteristic, odd communication emanated from the trio. Jon Garth placed a call to Ellen Johnson, next-in-command of American Atheists after the Murray-O'Hairs. Johnson had met Madalyn at an atheist convention in 1979. She was a young and aggressive ideologue—a bright and pretty blond, who not only seemed to share Madalyn's values but was apparently acceptably intelligent—and, more importantly, perhaps malleable when it came to going along with Madalyn's way of operating.

Ellen Johnson was a go-getter and might have even been an heir to the atheist throne if it weren't for Robin and Jon Garth. Madalyn had moved Johnson up the ranks to vice president of American Atheists by the time that Jon Garth called her in New Jersey with a request. He wanted her to open a bank account to receive funds from a large atheist trust that had been established in New Zealand. They were planning to transfer assets to New Jersey, and they wanted her to open an account at a bank near her home where the funds could be deposited.

Johnson complied with alacrity. It sounded like there would be a large amount of money involved. While she was clearly a trusted member of the inner circle—at least as much so as Tyson—she never had been given quite this much responsibility before, and Johnson welcomed the chance to help out. You never knew exactly what Madalyn had up her sleeve, but there might be positive opportunities presented by the transfer of large sums—and it couldn't hurt her standing with the local bankers, that was for sure.

In the meantime, the otherwise incommunicado Murray-O'Hairs were generating more frustration with their mysterious "emergency." Phil Donahue's producer had been calling, trying to confirm Madalyn's appearance on Donahue's last show. Madalyn had been his very first guest, and had appeared more times on his show than anyone besides Gloria Steinem and Ralph Nader. Even so they'd had their contretemps. Madalyn had boycotted the show for almost a decade after Donahue had chewed her out—on the air—for bad manners. She called him "that shit-head" for years and forwent making appearances with him, even though it probably cost her hundreds of thousands of dollars in donations. But they had kissed and made up a few years earlier, and now Donahue desperately wanted her for the last show blowout, given her historical import—and the fact that she had heroically held fast for Jeffersonian ideals—regardless of her personal raunchiness.

Spike Tyson told Donahue's producer that Madalyn was out of touch, but he guessed it would probably be OK since Madalyn was supposed to be available again in less than two weeks. He said that he'd get in touch with Madalyn and tell her of the request. When he called Jon Garth's cell phone number, Jon Garth answered, sounding completely normal. He told Tyson that they were attending to business, but didn't want to go into details. When Tyson informed him of the *Phil Donahue Show* inquiries, Jon Garth said he'd take it up with his mother. Tyson also took the opportunity to press for his overdue paycheck, and Jon Garth said he would send it along.

A few days later Tyson received his check, some keys, and the rest of the security codes for AAGHQ in a package mailed from San Antonio. By mid-September Tyson and Jon Garth were talking on the phone on an almost daily basis. There was a lot of details to take care of, and Donahue's producer kept on calling. Tyson asked Jon Garth, four times on different occasions, what he should tell her. Jon Garth would always give the same response: Tell her that "they were discussing it."

Ellen Johnson had also contacted the trio via Jon Garth's cell phone number. The first time, Madalyn herself answered but would only talk briefly. Johnson didn't sense any trouble in her voice, even though the conversation was unusually brief.

Nor did Johnson get the impression from Jon Garth that anything was amiss when she spoke with him at length regarding the establishment of the new bank account in New Jersey. But he did make a very strange request. Jon Garth asked that she FedEx two corporate blank checks addressed to him at a commercial post office box in northwest San Antonio as soon as possible. They badly needed money for expenses, he said, but he wasn't sure how much.

This was beyond the pale for even the compliant atheist VP. Johnson balked. "I will not," she said. "I take my job very seriously. I have no idea if there's a gun to your head or not." Jon Garth responded in a strangely placid fashion. "That's OK. That's OK. I understand," he said soothingly. A few days later, Johnson changed her mind and sent the blank corporate checks as well as a personal check of her own for one thousand dollars.

Johnson's concern for the trio would wax and wane. At times she was certain that everything was fine and the eccentric Murray-O'Hairs were just doing their thing—whatever that might be. Her stock was rising, so why rock the boat? On the other hand, everything seemed so borderline. All her interactions with them during their mystery "business trip" could have had either benign or ominous interpretations—save for one.

The last cell phone conversation Johnson had with Robin was beyond chilling. She would never forget the woman's voice. During the trial of one of the men who allegedly sexually assaulted, strangled, and dismembered Robin, Johnson testified to the hidden horror of that last conversation. Although Johnson couldn't remember exactly what they were talking about, she did remember that Robin was clearly not listening. Her voice sounded distraught, constricted with fear. Johnson repeatedly asked her: "What's wrong? What's going on?" Robin would only respond with an almost hoarse "Nothing." Finally Robin said she had to go. "I know you'll do the right thing," she said, and the phone clicked dead.

In the middle of September, a small-time northwest San Antonio jeweler and coin dealer named Corey Ticknor got a promising call from a man who identified himself as Jon Murray. Murray wanted to know if he could purchase approximately $600,000 in gold from Ticknor. He wanted it all in one-ounce coins—specifically, equal amounts of Canadian Maple Leafs, South African Krugerrands, and American Eagles. Ticknor assured him that it would be possible.

But it was a lot of gold—maybe 120 pounds' worth of coins—and Ticknor said he didn't have that large a sum on hand. He'd have to work through a dealer in Dallas and get the gold sent down to San Antonio from there. Before hanging up he took down Murray's driver's license number and told Murray that he required that the money be transferred to his account in advance before placing the order.

A retired ex-Marine MP, Ticknor was security conscious, as

might be expected in his line of business. He'd run a check on Murray and then, if all went as planned and the wire transfer to his account was completed, he'd request shipment from the dealer. Then he'd reconfirm Murray's driver's license number again when the gold was delivered in person.

Ticknor waited for the large wire-transfer. A week after his phone conversation with Jon Murray, $625,000 was transferred from the National Westminster Bank of New Jersey to the coin dealer's personal checking account as per the telephone agreement. The originating party wasn't Jon Murray, though. It was a group called the United Secularists of America.

This wasn't a problem for Ticknor. The important thing was that the money came in. He ordered the gold from Dallas and alerted a San Antonio police officer who moonlighted as a uniformed and armed security guard that his services would be needed for a large delivery/pickup. Ticknor also called a nearby bank to line up a conference room to complete the transaction—the physical counting of the coins with Murray that would close the deal.

Within a few days, $500,000 in 24-karat, one-ounce coins arrived at Ticknor's. On September 28, a Thursday, Ticknor got another call from Jon Murray. He was told that Murray would like to pick up the gold the following afternoon. Ticknor said fine, but explained that the rest of the shipment, $125,000, had been delayed and was to arrive the following week. Murray told him that he still wanted to pick up the half million in gold regardless. Ticknor gave him the bank address and said he'd meet him there.

The next day, Murray wheeled into the bank parking lot in a big Lincoln Town Car, right on time. Ticknor—with his rent-a-cop standing by—shook hands, exchanged pleasantries, and politely asked to see Murray's driver's license. It checked out. Murray opened the trunk of the Lincoln and got out a sturdy, wire-frame roller-dolly—the kind that veteran travelers use to stack their luggage on in airports. The dolly held a black ballistic-nylon suitcase. The asphalt parking lot was baking hot already, and they quickly retired to the air-conditioned quiet of the bottom-floor conference room that Ticknor had lined up at the bank.

As the counting began around a large oval table, Ticknor couldn't help but notice that Murray had a problem with B.O. He was, as Ticknor was to later testify, a "little bit ripe." Adding to the grungy image, Jon Garth was wearing an unpressed shirt that looked like he'd been sleeping in it. Ticknor also noted that he had a "scraggly beard" which magnified the perception that he wasn't shaving or showering regularly. But what-the-hey, rich folks can be very eccentric—especially "gold bugs," as Murray might well have been. Besides, there was no indication to Ticknor that he was under any duress.

The counting proceeded smoothly. The freshly minted gold coins were held in red plastic tubes, which in turn were stacked in six- by six-inch boxes. Ticknor counted the coins one at a time, then passed them on to Jon Garth, who re-counted them one at a time. When they were satisfied with the accuracy of their compared tallies, the coins were returned to the tubes and containers. It took forty minutes of concentrated effort without conversation, other than giving each other the monotonous counts and recounts.

When they finished, the coins were placed in the black nylon suitcase, which was then stacked on the luggage dolly. The three men rolled the one hundred pounds of gold through the bank lobby to the parking lot. After the off-duty officer checked the interior of the Lincoln for any unwanted passengers, all three hefted the gold into the trunk of the car. Both Ticknor and the security guard watched to see if anybody was following Jon Garth as he drove off with his hoard of gold. They saw no one.

As luck would have it, the rest of the gold coins—$100,000

worth (excluding Ticknor's commission)—arrived on the next business day, Monday. Ticknor immediately called Jon Garth's number to give him the good news and arrange the final pickup, but nobody answered his call. For nine straight days, the coin dealer dialed the number over and over again and it just kept ringing.

NINETEEN

The Mystery

When the American Atheists board gathered in New York for the "Pope Picket" in the beginning of October, the meeting was not planned as an emergency confab—but it turned out to be. Madalyn, Jon Garth, and Robin were no-shows, and without explanation. Not only that, they were now completely incommunicado. Spike Tyson, atheist confidant and majordomo to Madalyn, informed the atheist board members that he'd last talked to Jon Garth at the end of September. He related that Phil Donahue's producer needed a definite answer whether Madalyn was going to appear on the last show, and Jon Garth had told him that they were still "thinking about it." Twenty minutes later Tyson called back—on another matter—and there was no answer. He kept on calling the cell phone until it "went dead" a few days later. The board ordered Tyson to begin investigating immediately.

Although Tyson had the front-door key to the Murray-O'Hair Greystone home, he didn't have the security codes. However, he did know the layout of the house intimately—not only from his social visits, but because he'd done extensive electrical wiring for Madalyn. Tyson took a ladder from the still-open garage and entered the house by crawling through the central air-conditioning duct, bypassing the alarm system. What he found left him with a deep sense of unease, if not fear, for Madalyn, Jon Garth, and Robin.

The mail was piled in a mini-mountain next to the mail-drop slot by the front door. All Madalyn's plants—which she was known to talk to and fondle—were dead. While Madalyn could be disorganized about personal effects, Tyson knew Robin and Jon Garth to be "clean freaks to an incredible level." But Robin's room had dog feces on the floor and Jon Garth's bed had the sheets removed. Apparently somebody had slept there on the mattress with a blanket—and Jon Garth would only sleep on sheets, wearing pajamas.

The most sinister discovery was in the kitchen. When Tyson opened the refrigerator, the odor of rotting food was strong. Mold was everywhere. But really what caught Tyson's eye was the medication that Madalyn kept in the fridge. All her insulin was there. As her diabetes had progressed, she had become more and more insulin dependent. By now it could be assumed that she would only go without insulin for a few days, or even hours, before going into diabetic shock.

Given that possibility and knowing that the trio were in San Antonio during September, Tyson drove down to the Alamo City from Austin and checked all the hospitals for a Madalyn Murray O'Hair either as a patient or deceased. In an odd coincidence, Tyson did turn up a person going by the name "M. Bible"—one of Madalyn's favorite aliases—but it wasn't Madalyn. However, Tyson determined, from talking to pharmacy personnel, that prescriptions for Madalyn's heart and high-blood-pressure medications had been filled three times—at the beginning of September, midmonth, and the last week of September.

Since insulin for diabetes is nonprescription, somebody was in all likelihood buying it at the same time they bought her heart medication. The drugstore where the prescriptions were purchased happened to be located in northwest San Antonio—not far from the commercial post office box where Ellen Johnson had sent the checks to Jon Garth.

When Ellen Johnson, now the de facto organizational operating officer for the American Atheists, was told of the situation,
she decided to go to Austin from New Jersey and help with the
investigation. On arrival, Johnson started calling everyone she
personally knew in all the atheist organizations that Madalyn had
founded. She tried to determine phone numbers written on
scratch pads at AAGHQ through pressure indentations from previous pages. Johnson also later claimed to investigators that she
even attempted to decipher the last text written on the family's
office typewriters via their ink ribbons. None of Johnson's amateur detective work helped.

Toward the end of 1995, Robin's veterinarian called Tyson
to let him know that the dogs were still there, the bills were as
yet unpaid, and the vet was going to be forced to put the animals
to sleep unless somebody took them. Tyson picked up the three
dogs and then housed them at AAGHQ. After two weeks, Gannon and Shannon disappeared. A few months later, Gallagher was
gone too.

"Irony" is a word that would do little descriptive justice to the
media reaction to the Murray-O'Hair disappearance. One of the
first articles was by the Associated Press. "I can tell you categori-
cally that Madalyn is alive," an atheist officer reported to the
Associated Press on September 29, 1995. He went on to say that
he didn't know exactly what was happening, but "She's safe, and
that's all I can tell you." The morning that the story hit the state
and regional wires, Madalyn, her son Jon Garth, and her adopted
daughter/granddaughter, Robin, were freshly trussed and await-
ing murder.

While confused and groping for explanations themselves,
members of umbrella atheist organizations mostly assumed a
pose of unconcern for the reporters who intermittently inquired
of the missing trio. Everything was fine, the reporters were

invariably told. Madalyn, Jon Garth, and Robin were tending to urgent business. Everything would be explained in due time.

Actually there was relatively little media reaction to the disappearances. The reporters and editors who had covered Madalyn during her stormy ride across the cultural landscape of the 1960s were mostly gone. In fact, two generations of journalists had passed the baton since Madalyn's glory days. In the fall of 1995, it would be safe to say that the majority of local and state reporters viewed Madalyn as a cranky dinosaur—that is, if they even knew her name.

We will never know, but perhaps Madalyn's long slide into the waters of obscurity suited her. Prior to her abduction, she had become feeble and sickly—imprisoned within a tortured body—while her intellect was as strong as ever. The Reagan-era erosion of public and judicial support for the doctrine of separation of church and state, and Madalyn's own lack of interest in tilting at the windmills of the Establishment, probably rendered relative anonymity a benign state for the old heretic. And Madalyn's ego—like a foie gras goose liver—obscenely engorged by a lifetime of self-initiated force-feeding, must have been satiated for the most part.

Regardless, as the end of 1995 approached with no word from Madalyn, AAGHQ was put up for sale. As one waggish reporter wrote, "God knows where she is." Spike Tyson was the only staffer left, his lone footsteps echoing in the eerily quiet office building. When a reporter for the *Austin American-Statesman* called, researching a brief article on Madalyn's unresolved tax problems, Madalyn's old bodyguard told the reporter that the Murray-O'Hairs were "on an extended vacation" and that he wasn't worried a bit about her.

But if Tyson wasn't worried about Madalyn and her children, the IRS was. Just after their disappearance, the government had further deflated its case against Jon Garth and Robin. It had gone from $1.5 million to $75,000, and now the judgment had been reduced to $29,210 and $7,577 respectively. It was a remarkably generous bargain. However, with the Murray-O'Hairs vanishing mysteriously, IRS officials started to immediately suspect that they'd been made the fool by the sly atheist leader. Soon they began making ugly noises to Madalyn's tax lawyer in Washington. Hey, they'd been acting in good faith, giving Robin and Jon Garth a huge break—and this was their payment for being nice?

TWENTY

Prospects—New and Ominous

*A*ll good reporters are "investigative reporters," even if they don't sport the title. John MacCormack, of the *San Antonio Express-News,* didn't put much stock in titles anyway. He was American iron. Slug away. Get the job done. No frills. No nonsense. He'd done it all—investigative stuff, features, breaking news, rewrites. In his fifties, he'd worked South Texas as a newspaper reporter for two decades—fighting the heat, the floods, covering broad-spectrum mayhem and making deadlines with an unflappable, humorless panache. He looked the part of the grizzled, tough reporter too. Six-foot, broad-shouldered, with a face that was creased with scowl lines. Below his thatch of unkempt hair, MacCormack's bushy eyebrows flared upward, giving him—appropriately enough—a perpetually skeptical gaze that was enhanced by his thick glasses.

It was high-summer doldrums at the *Express-News,* when MacCormack's editor, Fred Bonavita—another old-line newspaperman—suggested a one-year "anniversary" story on the disappearance of Madalyn Murray O'Hair and her children. MacCormack could hardly remember who she was, but getting out of the city and checking the usual traps and circulating around Austin doing some interviews would be diversionary relief from the suffocating San Antonio heat. Besides, over the years of working together, MacCormack had come to respect Bonavita's knack for sniffing a good story.

When MacCormack's "anniversary" article came out in August 1996, it was an excellent piece. The article touched all the bases: Madalyn's faded celebrity, the San Diego lawsuit, the curious events surrounding the family's disappearance, and the problems created for the atheists still trying to run the shop. Other than regenerating interest on Madalyn's disappearance in the other state dailies, the most important event that followed MacCormack's story was the decision by Bill Murray, Madalyn's long-estranged, born-again son, to file a missing persons report with the Austin Police Department.

Bill was now the successful founder and director of an international evangelical organization whose mission it was to bring religion—specifically prayers in schools—back to public life. Based in Washington, D.C., Bill traveled the world spreading the Gospel and raising funds in between high-powered lobbying efforts on Capitol Hill.

He had been a bit harried when, six months earlier, he told reporters from his Washington offices that he was *not* going to file a missing persons report "for people who don't want to be found." But Bill did take time then to mention a perplexing issue that underscored his ambivalence about events back in Texas. He said that he felt it was *extremely* unusual that Madalyn would leave any of the dogs behind.

Things had changed for Bill since that interview. To his increasing amazement over the intervening months, none of Madalyn's atheist compatriots seemed to show any interest in finding her or Jon Garth and Robin. The atheist party line was that everything was just fine. But Bill wasn't so sure of the "good faith" professions from the atheists—who now evidently had access to some, if not conceivably all, of Madalyn's assets. He knew his family too well, even after all the years of estrangement. His gut told him something was awfully wrong and he finally decided to file the missing persons report.

It was a decision that was to provide one of the eerier

moments in his life. "I was in my office in Virginia at the time I made the call to the Austin police," he wrote in the revised edition of his autobiography, *My Life Without God.* Although the disappearance of his family was the object of worldwide speculation, Bill was given a clerk to take the report rather than the detective assigned to the case.

The clerk took the information from him in perfunctory fashion, in all likelihood not even knowing the history of the trio. Bill gave information on dates of birth, physical descriptions, and when and where his half-brother, daughter, and mother were last seen.

Bill's account continued: "Because I kept my phone on my credenza, my back was turned to my office door when I was on the phone. As I finished with the police clerk and hung up I felt a presence near the door and distinctly heard a 'Thank you.'" His heart jumped a beat. When he turned to face the voice from the doorway—nobody was there.

Soon after Bill Murray's filing of the missing persons report, the Austin police made what was to be their first and last major discovery in the case of the missing troika. On October 1—one year and a day after she had been murdered—the police found Robin's red Porsche 944 in long-term parking at Austin's Robert Mueller Municipal Airport. The Austin PD told American Atheists members who made inquiries about the discovery that the car had been impounded and it was being searched for evidence. However, police officials didn't give the impression that they were overly concerned, since the discovery of the car fit precisely into their conviction that the Murray-O'Hairs had absconded.

In fact, the red Porsche was a red herring left to confound the Austin police. It was all part of David Waters's masterful strategy—which was about to receive another, far larger endorsement. In what tabloid aficionados call a "blockbuster," John MacCormack of the *San Antonio Express-News* took the story from a mysterious disappearance by an odd family to a big-time money mystery—just as Waters had hoped.

An atheist tipster told MacCormack to look at the tax statements of one of Madalyn's atheist shell organizations—United Secularists of America. For tax-exempt entities, the IRS requires that the public be allowed to inspect annual tax filings of such organizations and that the paperwork be kept available on site. When MacCormack visited AAGHQ and perused the IRS Form 990, his eyes must have bulged behind his shot-glass lenses. A total of $625,000 was listed as missing in the sworn tax statement. Furthermore, an implication could be drawn from the filing that the money was probably in the possession of Jon Garth Murray.

With MacCormack breaking the news of the missing $625,000, it was beginning to look like a classic, juicy, take-the-money-and-run tale. To make it even more interesting, the IRS loss-filing was a bold-faced contradiction of the statements made to the media by the new atheist president—Ellen Johnson. Before she stopped returning reporters' phone calls, she was quoted as saying that no money was missing and all the books were in order, thank you!

As MacCormack's piece on the missing funds was being absorbed, a quasilegendary Texas print heavyweight broke a story that solved part of the mystery, but heightened the rest of it. In a comprehensive copyrighted article, Evan Moore of the *Houston Chronicle* had determined what happened to Jon Garth's beloved and missing Mercedes-Benz sedan. A San Antonio real estate agent had purchased it back in early September 1995—and one could say that it was quite a steal.

Responding to an ad in the *San Antonio Express-News* for an "88 Benz 300 SEL, $15,000 cash. Firm," Mark Sparrow, an ex-cop turned real estate agent, had apparently stumbled on an unusually good deal. The car was in immaculate condition and at least five thousand dollars under book value. The seller of the car, identifying himself as a Jon Garth Murray, acted nervous, and he was adamant and arrogant. Cash only and—*no*—he would *not* go to the finance office with Sparrow to sign papers. When reporter Moore showed Sparrow some pictures of Jon Garth, Sparrow said there was "no resemblance" to the man who sold the Mercedes. The man who claimed to be Jon Garth Murray was five foot nine, with sandy, graying hair and a gravelly, whiskey-cured voice. Jon Garth was at least six foot three, with dark brown hair and an unmistakable lisp.

Even though Moore knew he was on to something big, he was soon to sour on the O'Hair mystery due to an imbroglio with an editor who thought the story wasn't going anywhere. But his journalistic sortie into the saga established entirely new and obvious possibilities. If the Murray-O'Hairs absconded, why would they have somebody posing as Jon Garth sell his car and risk the attention that such a transaction could bring?

Besides, the Mercedes sedan was Jon Garth's most prized personal possession—a sort of automotive crown for the atheist successor to the throne. It made no sense—this charade by a jumpy, tough-looking low-renter—unless the most obvious conclusion was reached: An impostor had to have done it because Jon Garth would never willingly sell his Mercedes, any more than Robin and Madalyn would leave their dogs.

Two months after the Evans story on the sale of the Mercedes, and more than eighteen months after the disappearance of Madalyn, Jon Garth, and Robin, the Austin police officially addressed the case in the media. A police spokeswoman spelled out the rigid presupposition they'd been feeding to reporters: "Right now this is not a criminal investigation." She went on to explain that it was still a missing persons case. Further, even if the Austin police *did* find the trio, they would not divulge their whereabouts. "If we do locate missing adults," she said, "we respect their wish for privacy."

After the Austin PD's news conference, writer Robert Bryce, of the alternative magazine *The Austin Chronicle,* interviewed Stephen Baker, the detective in charge of the Murray-O'Hair case, regarding his own take on the disappearance. The detective opined that the Murray-O'Hairs had probably been planning the scam for a long time. "That's why I'm of the opinion that they are not dead and that there was no foul play involved."

Detective Baker went on to tell Bryce that he believed Madalyn and her son and granddaughter had gotten new identities while they were in San Antonio, and then had left the country. But when pressed by Bryce, the young, smug detective was forced to admit that he hadn't even interviewed Spike Tyson or Ellen Johnson, the two people with the greatest personal knowledge of the Murray-O'Hairs' everyday habits as well as the facts surrounding their disappearance.

Understandably, Bill Murray was perplexed and angry over the Austin Police Department's blasé attitude—if not downright incompetence. When he heard of Detective Baker's theory about a surreptitious exit by the trio to unknown points on the globe, he thought it was idiotic. Murray said: "And how could Madalyn, Jon, and Robin hide anywhere? You have these three obese people. Robin requires two airline seats wherever she goes. My mother uses the F-word in virtually every sentence that comes out of her mouth."

Bill Murray was tired, beaten down, and preoccupied with running his thriving evangelical organization. He continued: "I don't have any more resources and I don't think the police have any genuine interest. We're at a dead end unless the press finds them." To add weight to his words, he announced that he was withdrawing his application for guardianship of his missing family's extensive assets. He was going to sit things out with the hope that at least his mother might have had an "experience with Jesus Christ" in her final days and hours.

The IRS wasn't so content to take a passive stance. Officials there had waited long enough for Jon Garth and Robin to sign the more-than-sweet offer that would resolve their $1.5 million bill with a pennies-on-the-dollar settlement. Nope, they weren't going to take any more jacking around.

Without warning, in early February of 1997, government vans and trailers lined up at the Greystone Drive residence, where Spike Tyson was encamped, baby-sitting the Murray-O'Hair house. The IRS summarily evicted him, seizing most of the unlucky atheist's meager belongings along with everything else. (Tyson moaned to MacCormack of the *Express-News* that the Feds even took his dirty laundry.)

A trail of government worker ants loaded the Murray-O'Hairs' personal effects for two full days at Greystone, after which the materials were to be inventoried and readied for public auction to settle the IRS lien. All the missing trio's possessions were to be liquidated. The house itself was to be sold to help satisfy the tax debt. The IRS had run out of patience, and now, with Madalyn's property, the Feds were forced into a scorched-earth policy. There wasn't any choice. The IRSers didn't want to be made to look like gullible chumps if Madalyn popped up on some tropical isle—toasting them with F-words and champagne.

TWENTY-ONE

The October 2 Epiphany

With the hard-charging Evan Moore of the *Houston Chronicle* out of the picture, and the Austin media and the other Texas dailies eating his dust, John MacCormack of the *San Antonio Express-News* was about to put even more distance between himself and the competition. After seeing MacCormack's article on the missing $625,000 and the vanished atheists, a young private investigator called the reporter to see if he could donate his skills.

In his mid-twenties, Tim Young looked like his name—young. The fast-talking, skinny Texan could have passed for a teenager. But callow he was not. He declared to MacCormack that in this day and age *nobody* could disappear. If the Murray-O'Hairs were alive—he'd find them. If he didn't find them—they were dead. MacCormack was impressed with the young man's chutzpah and thought his résumé was appropriate. As a private investigator doing "skip traces," Young would track down the location of high-ticket defaulters in arrears on payments for their Lexus or Cadillac—then turn the information over to the repo men for the recovery.

Sometime before MacCormack's article on the missing funds came out, Young had made his biggest catch so far, locating a scam artist who'd decamped with a million plus in investors' money. Young wanted to cement his entry into the big leagues by making a high-profile case, and solving Madalyn's disappearance would be perfect. He told MacCormack that his services would be free of charge until the Murray-O'Hairs were located, if the *Express-News* picked up expenses. It sounded good. MacCormack went to his editors and got the investigator put under a short-term contract.

Young made a good fit with the veteran reporter. MacCormack could take the direct approach, asking for information because of his position as a legitimate journalist. Young could go to the back door and do things that MacCormack couldn't or wouldn't. Actually, MacCormack really didn't want to know how Young did his job. The main thing was that he was energetic, smart, and could shuck-and-jive on the phone like a champ. Besides, MacCormack sensed a great story in the making, but at the same time he was somewhat insecure about his investigative abilities since he'd fed more on breaking news and features over the years. The fact was, having the youthful investigator on board gave MacCormack a feeling of confidence, as well as a regular dose of infectious enthusiasm.

Young proved to be surefooted right out of the chute, and tenacious in the long term. For more than a year, working around their normal job schedules, MacCormack and Young pursued leads through the rabbit warren of financial complexities of the Murray-O'Hairs. It was not an easy task. Honed by a life full of fear that her enemies would materially denude her, Madalyn had become a grand master at fiscal obfuscation, and she had taught her children well too. Using innumerable shells and dummy corporations, the trio had created three lifetimes' worth of convoluted money trails to defeat any would-be pillagers like the Scurvy Johnson people or the gawd damn revenuers.

But Madalyn's talent for large-scale financial deception would ironically contribute directly to her death. David Waters—a man of the utmost cunning himself—had quickly and accurately perceived how easy it would be to use Madalyn's own secretive and devious behavior to cover up his own crimes—and the Murray-O'Hairs' murder. Thus, MacCormack and Young faced seemingly impenetrable smoke screens not only created by a knowledgeable paranoid, but augmented by a genius-level sociopath whose life depended on the opacity of the document trail.

Bravely onward the MacCormack-Young team trudged, soon coming upon a jewel of information that Waters had been unable to hide. From the court-appointed receiver for the estate of Jon Garth, the missing atheist prince, Young obtained a copy of all the calls made to and from his cell phone for the crucial thirty days of September 1995. (It was a prize available to the Austin PD and presumably Detective Baker—but apparently they didn't avail themselves of the crucial information.)

Tracking down more than two hundred calls made to and from the cell phone, Young had proof of what the atheists had seemingly been sitting on all along. Jon Garth himself had purchased and taken delivery of $500,000 in gold coins from a San Antonio coin and jewelry dealer. The phone bills also showed that Jon Garth had been in contact with atheist followers in New Zealand as well as his banker there. It looked like they had indeed absconded.

Or *maybe* not. Young had determined that the Murray-O'Hairs had left Austin in what could only be described as a panic. Food was left on the table at the Greystone Drive house as though they'd been interrupted eating. Young found out that the Murray-O'Hairs had just spent $240 on groceries before they vanished. They'd recently taped multiple TV shows for their cable enterprise. And a day prior to their disappearance, Jon Garth had bought an expensive, large hardbound book—definitely not the kind you'd pack for a trip.

The cell phone records also appeared to show what Young

described as a "frantic" attempt by the Murray-O'Hairs to get cash and medication when they arrived in San Antonio. The majority of evidence pointed away from a planned exit. But then again, Madalyn was just cagey enough to stage it all that way— precisely because it would throw people off.

Once more, there was no reaction from law enforcement when MacCormack ran a big story in the *San Antonio Express-News* on the results of their investigation in early February 1998. The story did, however, catch the eye of an *ABC News* correspondent. Valeri Williams was working for the network out of its Atlanta bureau, but she hailed from Texas and had worked at an Austin TV station during her salad days in news. Williams had interviewed Madalyn back then—and found her repulsively fascinating. With the missing gold, the story was a tantalizing mystery. But there wasn't enough airtime on the evening news to explore the story properly, so Williams started pitching the concept to *Nightline*—ABC's late-evening, in-depth news show.

While juggling her weighty correspondent duties, Williams began to do her own investigation of Madalyn's disappearance. Of course, it couldn't be as thorough as the MacCormack-Young work, but Williams was a gifted, nationally decorated investigative reporter—with an odd twist for the genus: She was a pretty face with a sweet, sincere demeanor to go along with the requisite capacity for ripping open jugulars whenever necessary.

Williams rapidly expanded on a key event that the atheists were loath to discuss: the New Jersey trip by Jon Garth, when he had flown back east in the company of another man, a "Conrad Johnson." Williams not only got the actual flight stubs for that New Jersey trip, she tracked down the bank officer who made the $625,000 transaction. Williams was told by the banker she interviewed that Jon Garth was acting normal, and yes, he was accompanied by another man.

Back in San Antonio, the assiduous TV reporter dug out more good material. Jon Garth had purchased a flawless, one-karat solitaire diamond from a San Antonio gem dealer for $6,660. Williams interviewed the salesman, who remembered the transaction well—not so much because it was a flawless diamond that he had sold, but because of the buyer's behavior. "We sell high-quality diamonds all the time," the salesman told the correspondent. "It's usually a lengthy process of showing customers quality and everything. He had just called on the telephone and said, 'OK, I'll be in.' Came in, and five minutes later he was gone. He didn't want to look at the diamond under a microscope or anything."

It was excellent stuff, but Valeri Williams's biggest coup—which would eventually contribute directly to solving the Murray-O'Hair mystery—was her hiring of a police sketch artist to make a rendering of the man who impersonated Jon Garth during the Mercedes sale. Williams believed, correctly, as events would bear out, that if Jon Garth's impostor could be identified, the case would be solved. It was a long shot at best—that one of the *Nightline* audience might recognize the man in the sketch—but she did have two things in her favor. As luck would have it, Mark Sparrow, the real estate agent who purchased the car, was an ex-cop with an ingrained recall of facial features, and her sketch artist was a talented professional who'd worked extensively with the San Antonio police.

After the national *Nightline* broadcast, Williams took a box full of her investigative leads and documents down to the Austin Police Department. It was somewhat unusual for a network correspondent to do this, but then Williams—as a citizen, if nothing more—wanted the case to be solved and justice done. However, the Austin PD's response to the network correspondent's information was an arrogant yawn.

* *

Phone callers to a working news reporter generally have less than a minute to pique some interest before they're curtly dismissed. It's not because reporters are rude—even though so many are—but because of the pressures of the job. A journalist like John MacCormack of the *Express-News* could have people dancing on his head ten, twelve hours a day if he let them, so he always tried to limit audition time. A few weeks after the *Nightline* show on the Murray-O'Hair disappearance, MacCormack was sitting at his computer terminal when a call came in that immediately broke through the barrier.

"It was a kidnapping," the man blurted. "I have a person's name who organized it. He's from Austin. His name is David. David Walters. Or maybe Waters." MacCormack started pounding on his keyboard, taking notes on the fly as the caller continued. "This David is the one who did all the planning. He infiltrated the organization. The money was the motive. They took them at gunpoint from Austin to San Antonio."

David Waters. David Waters. The name clicked for Mac-Cormack. Waters had been a bit player in the Madalyn mystery. MacCormack knew Waters had gotten into trouble for stealing more than fifty thousand dollars from Madalyn's atheist organizations. But then it couldn't have been *that* serious, considering he was put on probation, and his restitution to the missing Murray-O'Hairs was reduced to a piddling fifteen thousand dollars. Surely the Austin justice system wouldn't allow this to happen if he had *any* serious criminal background.

But the caller—a Bob Fry from Florida—was telling a different story. He'd seen Valeri Williams's *Nightline* show, and the sketch of the man who'd sold Jon Garth's Mercedes was a dead ringer for his younger brother, Danny Fry. Bob Fry went on to say that Danny had been missing since September 1995, after he had gone to Texas to help Waters "set on" some people. According to Fry, these people were "set on" for about a month by his brother and Waters and another man—whose name he didn't know. Danny had called his daughter on her sixteenth birthday, September 30, from David Waters's apartment in Austin and said he was coming home to Florida. He sounded real tense but he promised his daughter that he was going to take her on a "shopping spree" when he got back. But, Bob Fry said, "he never showed up."

Within five weeks of Danny Fry's last telephone call in the fall of 1995, the family had filed two missing persons reports. Danny's daughter gave Florida police a detailed four-page report including David Waters's telephone number in Austin. Bob Fry filed a missing persons report with the police in Austin, since that was the last place that Danny was known to be alive. Unlike the Florida police, who took extensive information, Fry said, the Austin police filled out a short form—not even bothering to take down the physical description of his missing brother.

Bob Fry, a disabled Vietnam vet with serious memory problems, told MacCormack he couldn't remember exact times and dates, but he could get his phone records and those of his niece, Danny's daughter, to prove his contentions. And there was something else. David Waters and another hard-looking man had shown up unexpectedly at his home in Florida. Waters had found out that Danny had sent his brother a letter shortly before he disappeared. Waters got Bob Fry's address through a ruse: He told Bob Fry he wanted to mail him some of his brother's effects. As soon as Waters had the address, he drove down to Florida nonstop and demanded to know what Danny's letter said and where it was.

Bob Fry told Waters that his brother had instructed him to read the letter only if something happened to him, but that Danny had called toward mid-September of 1995 and said that everything was "fine" and he'd be coming home soon—and to please burn the letter. Fry said to Waters that he'd done just as he'd been instructed. However, it took more than two hours to convince a menacing David Waters that the letter was really gone before he'd leave and drive back to Texas.

MacCormack put his investigator, Tim Young, in contact with Fry to check out the details of his story. Everything started to gel. Most of the activity that could be traced to the Murray-O'Hairs formed an irregular arc in northwest San Antonio around a motel-residence called the Warren Inn. The Frost Bank, where the gold was transferred, was located within a few blocks. Corey Ticknor's jewelry and coin shop was nearby, and so was the drug-store where Madalyn's heart medications were purchased. Even the video rental shop where Jon Garth, or at least somebody using his name, rented videos during September 1995 was in the vicinity of the Warren Inn.

The savvy and inventive Tim Young got David Waters's address in Austin and had a "free" calling card sent to him in the mail. Waters took the bait. Young had the company send Waters's bill to him with all the numbers that had been called. Using the phone bill and working his law enforcement contacts, Young came up with a profile for Waters. It wasn't pretty. Young quickly understood what Austin law enforcement couldn't seem to grasp. Not only was Waters capable of a major swindle—he was a man capable of multiple murders.

Again using telephone records, Young compiled a criminal dossier not only on Waters, but on his partner who had accompanied him on his visit to Bob Fry. Although Gary Paul Karr wasn't a known killer like Waters, he was the baddest of badasses. A biker and heavy drug user, Karr had served two decades of hard time in the Illinois prison system for armed robbery, rape, and kidnapping.

Although his convictions were for violent crimes, Karr was not a problem in prison. He served his lengthy sentences quietly, spending as much time as possible partaking of the in-house edu-cational programs provided for prisoners. In fact, he was on camera for the movie *The Blues Brothers,* shot on location at Joliet State Prison. Handsome in a hardened way, and in good shape from lifting weights, Karr was soft-spoken like his buddy David Waters, whom he'd met while in prison. They got along well because they shared similar views on doing time—stay low-key, get buffed lifting, get educated as much as possible, and get out.

As MacCormack and Young reviewed the information that they had amassed, they saw that a classic take-the-money-and-run story had turned into a celebrity murder, quadruple homicide, and big-money heist. And with that realization, the two-man team began to disintegrate.

Young came from a law enforcement background. His father was a cop. When he signed on to help MacCormack and gild his own résumé, Young had no doubt that he was working a missing persons case with absconders. When he realized he'd stumbled on a multiple homicide, his instincts were to go to the police with all the information. Given Waters's history, clearly all their lives were in danger, including Bob Fry's.

To the dour, hyperfocused MacCormack, this was heresy and betrayal. The *Express-News* editors had given the young investigator a shot based on their agreement that the fruits of his work went exclusively to MacCormack and the newspaper. Not only that, MacCormack had gone way beyond tipping his hat to Young's contributions by allowing him costar billing on Valeri Williams's nationally broadcast *Nightline* show. Hired-gun investigators employed by news organizations almost never get a mention—and MacCormack had made Young a momentary celebrity, at the very least.

Young was not to be intimidated or deterred. He would go to the police. And as one would expect from MacCormack, with the defection of his partner he went into damn-the-torpedoes mode. MacCormack was publishing no matter what. Besides, MacCormack predicted to Young that if he went to the Austin police, they'd ignore Young and his theories.

In the meantime, MacCormack was taking his own precautions regarding Waters. He planned to move his sons temporarily out of their San Antonio residence right before the article fingering Waters came out. He also showed the boys pictures of Waters and Karr so that if they saw the "bad guys" they'd tell Dad.

On August 11, 1998, Tim Young sent a memo to Detective Stephen Baker of the Austin Police Department on what he'd discovered. It named names, times, and places. He supplied DOBs, Social Security numbers, addresses—everything a police detective might need to vet a suspect or a victim. In precise detail, Young outlined the disappearance of Danny Fry concurrently with the last known communications from Jon Garth, Robin, and Madalyn. He also pointed out that Danny Fry, a grifter with no known employment in Texas, had sent several thousand dollars home to his girlfriend.

Regarding Waters, Young related the details and timing of events that Bob Fry had provided. He traced Waters's criminal history for Baker—a history that fit the circumstances perfectly—the previous convictions for forgery, weapons violations, assault, and murder. Young also tracked down Waters's purchase of a 1990 Cadillac in San Antonio for thirteen thousand dollars cash during September 1995, even though Waters was supposedly destitute and in arrears on his restitution payments to Madalyn. As well, Young documented that Waters's live-in girlfriend had bought an almost brand-new pickup in Austin for cash—while working as a part-time barmaid in a sleazy cocktail lounge—again during the month of September.

The memo was a summation and solution to a murder mystery for even the most clueless or distracted cop. It had perpetrators, motives, and victims—the whole shebang. Young faxed it to Baker at his Austin PD office. He waited expectantly by the phone for an immediate callback. Nothing. Young called the next day and was dumbfounded by the detective's response. Young got the unmistakable impression that Baker hadn't even read the memo and was skimming it for the first time as they talked on the phone. "Where do you guys get this stuff?" Baker asked. "Looks like it took you awhile to figure this out," he continued insouciantly. "I guess it will probably take us awhile too." Young was incredulous. Even though he was on the outs with MacCormack, he couldn't help calling his ex-comrade to give him Baker's reaction. MacCormack grunted, "I told you so."

Detective Baker had one strong suit, though—consistency. *Austin Chronicle* writer Robert Bryce said that he interviewed Baker after the detective received the Young memo. "He was still dismissive about the entire disappearance," Bryce wrote. "Baker said he had never questioned Waters and knew nothing about the restitution Waters was supposed to pay to the O'Hairs." Regarding the ties between Fry and Waters, Baker told the journalist: "We haven't been able to confirm any connections between the two. . . . We can't dig any more than we already have."

But Tim Young wasn't about to be derailed by Baker's headscratching. No, he'd go right up the ladder to the top rung. He'd call the FBI. Young chose the San Antonio regional office, since he felt that was the general area where the Murray-O'Hairs were held and probably murdered. When Young was finally able to get an FBI agent on the line, he laid out the information he'd compiled in the memo he'd faxed to Detective Baker. The FBI agent listened and then politely took his name and number. Again, Young waited on tenterhooks for the phone to ring—but the FBI never called back either.*

---

* Later, when Waters was in custody, the San Antonio FBI office would deny ever receiving a call from Young on the solution to the Murray-O'Hair mystery. But the youthful private investigator was too smart for them. Young had an audiotape of the original phone conversation between him and the conveniently forgetful FBI agent.

* *

MacCormack broke another blockbuster story—that of the disappearance of Danny Fry during the same period of time as the Murray-O'Hairs'. Except for some loose ends that he'd tie up soon enough, MacCormack actually had published the solution to the entire mystery by pointing to the involvement of the sinister David Waters in the plot. It was superlative journalism—and *another* once-in-a-lifetime story. But the libel lawyer for the *Express-News* supposedly moved down the mention of Waters from the second paragraph to significantly deeper in the story. Apparently the squeamish attorney wanted to mitigate any damages in case Mr. Waters sued the *Express-News* for ruining his good name. It seems a ludicrous notion, given the extensive criminal history of the homicidal ex-con and the importance of the story. In any case, the knee-knocking libel lawyer needn't have worried. Waters was not going to sue.

But he was going to hang tough. It was amazing. Even after MacCormack's story, which all but named him as a quadruple murderer, rather than fleeing to Mexico or *anywhere,* Waters still tried to convince any reporters who would listen that he had the inside scoop on how and why the Murray-O'Hairs disappeared—and *he* didn't have *anything* to do with it.

Waters, jobless and broke, would show up for interviews, flawlessly razor-cut, wearing Armani togs and sporting a Raymond Weil gold watch. It was weird. He'd ask the reporters: Why—if he had stolen all that gold—why was he still living as a down-and-outer, save for the nice clothes on his back? Where was all the gold he was supposed to have stolen? And if he killed them, why didn't he run or at least leave town, especially if he had all that loot? No. He had nothing to hide. And hell no, he wasn't worried about MacCormack's articles. The media-hip Waters said he wasn't bothered by some reporter in San Antonio just trying to make "bleed-and-lead" headlines.

While MacCormack got a reaction from Waters, his story got none from the authorities. It all must have seemed surreal, even for a seen-it-all reporter like John MacCormack. But unbeknownst to him, invisible wheels were turning. Powerful forces were gathering. Tim Young had finally broken through.

Young had gotten in touch with Bill Murray. Bill was not only a prospering evangelical minister, he'd also become a powerful political operator in Washington, D.C. Murray, with his strong right-wing religious camber, had juice with ultraconservatives. While hunkered down somewhat during the Clinton years, the religio-conservative political apparatchiks on Capitol Hill could still vector requests for action in the form of favors from bureaucracies—and Bill Murray knew how to tap in.

To be sure, Murray himself was frustrated and disgusted with how the justice system had handled his estranged mother's disappearance. When he had earlier appealed to his "good friend" Governor George W. Bush, Bush had directed the Texas Rangers (no, not the baseball team) to look into the matter, but the Austin police evidently had convinced the Rangers that it wasn't a murder case—the Murray-O'Hairs had simply absconded and left for regions unknown.

Now, with the new disclosures coming from the MacCormack-Young duo, Bill Murray called another good friend, a fellow ultraconservative and a member of the House leadership, Dick Armey of Texas. He told Armey about Young's findings and things started to happen. All of a sudden Tim Young received a call at his new residence in Arizona. It was from the FBI. They wanted to talk with him *real bad*. The next day the FBI flew the private investigator to San Antonio for a full debriefing.

But regardless of how strong a circumstantial case MacCormack and Young had compiled on Waters and his accomplice Gary Karr, there were some difficult problems with the investigation. Neither man acted like the two had a hoard of gold between them. They were living as one would expect from destitute and unreformed ex-cons—hand to mouth and off girlfriends where possible.

More importantly from an investigative standpoint, there were no bodies. Both the histories and the personalities of the Murray-O'Hairs and Danny Fry could easily account for their mysterious disappearance. No bodies meant that any good defense attorney could take an almost impregnable position behind the ultimate criminal shield—"beyond a reasonable doubt"—if there was no direct evidence that somebody had been murdered. Bodies were needed.

. . .

It was October 2, 1998, a month and a half after John MacCormack had run his big Murray-O'Hair/Fry/Waters–connection story—and three years and two days since Danny Fry had vanished in 1995. As MacCormack put it: "I was sitting there surfing the waves, as we call it, when you pretend to be working but you're really sitting there reading all the wire stories. I hit this story. It was just an AP summary of a *Dallas Morning News* story. It was six to eight graphs and it said police were still baffled by this horrendous crime, this white guy ended up without his head, his clothes, or his hands on this riverbank."

An idea went off in MacCormack's head like a Fourth of July star-burst rocket. As he continued to read the brief story, he thought: Danny Fry? Maybe Danny Fry? The date the body was discovered was the same weekend as Fry's disappearance.

MacCormack called the detective handling the old homicide case in Dallas and asked for a description of the torso. MacCormack knew that Danny Fry was hirsute, with "heavy hair on his chest, even had hair on the top of his feet," according to Fry's fiancée. The body that the police found also was that of a very hairy Caucasian, without major scars or tattoos. Danny Fry was white—with no identifying scars and no tattoos.

MacCormack began to "go back and forth between the cops and the relatives." He talked to all Danny's close family members, "The fiancée, the ex-wife, the daughter, everybody." MacCormack even attempted to get photographs of Fry on the beach or at a swimming pool in order to compare chest-hair patterns with the police photos of the beheaded, handless Dallas corpse. The attempt failed, but, as MacCormack put it, "the punch line was, after about a week of this, I said, why not?" It was the same weekend, and since the head and hands were cut off, it was clear that somebody *definitely* didn't want the corpse identified.

MacCormack flew up to Dallas from San Antonio and met with detectives. Although they couldn't completely follow the intricate web of events that MacCormack described, with that hunch-sense that good, smart cops have, they believed his complex tale, and trusted him as well. Even better, they'd kept genetic materials from the unidentified murder victim.

Since there was no available specimen of Danny Fry's DNA that had been kept prior to his disappearance, the best way to determine if the body was Fry's was by mitochondrial DNA testing—the matching of maternal genetic lineage. Though mitochondrial DNA tests are not as precise as direct DNA matching, the method could still produce strong statistical evidence as to whether the body was Danny Fry's or not. After much negotiation and logistical hassling, MacCormack finally got three of Danny Fry's closest blood kin in Florida—including his brother Bob Fry—to give samples on which he could have the appropriate DNA tests performed.

When the results came back, MacCormack must have felt like he'd pitched back-to-back perfect games in the World Series of Journalism. He had physical proof—incontrovertible evidence that nobody else had gotten—of his earlier solution to one of the most baffling disappearances of the twentieth century. The unidentified, partially butchered corpse buried in a pauper's grave three years earlier in Dallas was that of Danny Fry. The jumble of dots had been connected by MacCormack, and the picture was unmistakable. The Murray-O'Hairs were dead, murdered at the hands of David Waters and his lethal gofer, Gary Karr.

TWENTY-TWO

The Feds

---

*I*t really made no difference if the Murray-O'Hairs were murder victims or absconders—"Uncle" wanted his back-tax money. After a two-year postponement, the IRS sold off the worldly possessions of the vanished atheist triumvirate at an auction barn on the outskirts of Austin. Clothing, books, furniture, and appliances, as well as 160 large boxes of household detritus, both personal and impersonal—everything from toiletries to TV remotes was put on the block.

Because of Madalyn's anal-retentiveness, the auction must have been rewarding for the curiosity seekers, of which there were dozens. However, only a few moments of observation were needed to adjudicate Madalyn as a woman of surpassing tastelessness. Arguably the finest artistic creation up for auction was an owl statuette made of dried sunflower seeds. Madalyn's wardrobe contained no Oleg Cassini originals, to be sure—just her schizoid, garish-to-prim-to-funky clothes, with an emphasis on flower-print dresses, in tent-sized configurations, some hand sewn. The furniture was mostly sturdy (given the family members' bulk) and cheap—typically Naugahyde-covered pseudo–Early American.

An assortment of records and Jon Garth's obsolete video game gear were mounded in cardboard boxes. The family's record collection was dominated by Barry Manilow and Lawrence Welk—favorites of Madalyn's—with a few groups that Robin and Jon Garth liked, such as the Bee Gees and Jethro Tull. Again there was evidence of the contradictions that Madalyn's life embraced. Amongst the videocassettes—along with the complete set of "Godfather" movies—was a copy of *White Christmas,* with Bing Crosby.

Robin's treasured 1985 Porsche 944—one of Madalyn's indulgences or, more aptly, bribes to her granddaughter—sold for the steal-deal price of $2,750. Another relatively high ticket item was a Bible that Madalyn received in 1968—a gift from a girls' Sunday school class at the Winnitka Heights Baptist Church in Tulsa, Oklahoma. The Bible was covered in white leather and looked to be "unsullied by use," a reporter observed. It brought in a surprising $2,000 from an Austin attorney who later said that he might have been a bit "carried away."

Even though Madalyn was a self-professed bookworm, her tastes in literature didn't inspire the auction goers to part with much of their cash. There was *The Atlas of Sex,* along with books on southern cooking featuring lots of fatty, fried foods. There were a few books on history, such as Will and Ariel Durant's *The Story of Civilization,* and some classical philosophy tomes, but none seemed to have been read through. (Madalyn didn't think highly of the Ancients, having once written that the Greek philosophers were a "nutty bunch of homosexuals.")

Madalyn's most personal work, her diaries, did fetch interest from collectors, but not nearly what the IRS had hoped they would. The auctioneers had estimated that the handwritten diaries might bring as much as $100,000. But the Austin attorney who purchased Madalyn's Bible was the high bidder for the diaries too, with an offer of $12,000. Even at that bargain price, the purchase was problematic.

Madalyn had apparently kept a diary faithfully for forty-two years in a strong and surprisingly beautiful hand. Her annual journals ran from January 1953 to August 1995. But there were huge gaps. Decades were missing. There were no entries from 1959 to 1972—easily the most interesting part of her life, spanning her Supreme Court case and the Baltimore criminal and legal conflicts. Even worse, the years directly preceding her disappearance had vanished too.

Missing were all the diaries from 1989 until her death, with the exception of one brief five-page entry in August 1995—the month she was kidnapped. Thus four and a half crucial years were gone—and whoever had these diaries probably had the key to the murder mystery from the very beginning, for Madalyn went into elaborate, often numbing detail regarding the machinations of her atheist organizations and her unending problems with personnel. There could be little doubt that, if investigators had access to these diaries, Madalyn's own words would have pointed directly to David Roland Waters. But they were gone—most likely stolen by somebody who had access to the Greystone Drive residence and who wanted certain years of the diaries suppressed, for his or her own reasons.

According to Bill Murray, the estate had been looted quite efficiently prior to the IRS auction. While his mother may not have been long on taste, she and her children had traveled the world for almost a quarter of a century and never returned from a trip without picking up some expensive, albeit insipid, pieces of art. By sheer volume of acquisitions over the years, there should have been much of value, Bill argued.

Gone was any trace of the gold and diamond jewelry she was rumored to have received from Larry Flynt during his wooing her to take over his empire. Gone were all the valuable acrylic paintings by her friend from Valle de Bravo days—the internationally respected Gus Likan. Even missing was her collection of figurines of different animals copulating. According to son Bill, "The house they lived in had statuettes of mating animals on virtually every piece of furniture." All gone.

Given the apparent plundering of the Murray-O'Hair estate, coupled with the atrocious taste of the trio, the IRS hardly made a dent in the quarter-million-dollar tax lien that the government had instituted after it never got a response on the sweet offer of a reduction from $1.5 million to less than $50,000 to settle the back-tax claims against the Murray-O'Hairs. The auction brought in a total of $25,000.

It was to be the last drops that could be wrung from the Murray-O'Hairs, since no major offshore or domestic personal accounts had been uncovered, even though those familiar with Madalyn's propensities—her surviving son, Bill, and the San Diego lawyers who'd fine-toothed her finances—estimated that she had squirreled away many millions.

The auction, however, did produce some fascinating byplay for the watching eyes of the cognoscenti who followed the unraveling murder mystery. David Waters was at the auction. Neatly groomed as always, and sporting an expensive leather jacket, Waters pranced coolly about the auction barn. As he chatted amiably with journalists, Waters would glance at items being auctioned, sometimes picking things up and turning them over with a smooth, uncallused hand—seemingly without a concern that, a few months earlier, John MacCormack had identified him to the world as a multiple murderer.

San Antonio was a city renowned for its traditional Aztec-like love of violence, blood, and human sacrifice—eagerly fed by an often exploitive press and yapping local TV reporters unable, for the most part, to get beyond habitual ambulance chasing. John Mac-Cormack's banner-headline, front-page, above-the-fold spread on the results of his DNA tests was published on Sunday, January 31, 1999—exactly a week after the IRS auction.

True to the San Antonio media credo of "If it bleeds, it leads," MacCormack's piece in the *Express-News* had the requisite gore. "The corpse minus crudely amputated head and hands. . . . The body was placed chest-up, legs neatly together and arms splayed," MacCormack's copy read. However, his story on the DNA identification of Danny Fry went far beyond the simple prurient satisfaction of the blood lust of San Antonio readers.

MacCormack was publishing proof of the categorical solution to a mystery that ranked with the disappearances of Amelia Earhart and Jimmy Hoffa. His reporting was inspired. To solve such a complex crime and international mystery while at the same time the murderer was wandering blithely around giving media interviews—it was simply mind-boggling. It was also, undeniably, a tour de force in American investigative journalism without parallel in the twentieth century.

One of those most immediately animated by MacCormack's work and his positive identification of Danny Fry was David Waters's ex-girlfriend. And what animated her more—her fear of David Waters or her fear of going to prison for complicity in a multiple murder-extortion-kidnapping—was to be her secret alone.

Patti Jo Steffens was similar in one respect to almost every character in the cast: She was a bagful of contradictions. A tall and large-breasted brunette in her late thirties to early forties, she was a "homey" of Waters's from Peoria who could swing between being stunningly attractive to downright skanky, from svelte to semi-obese, from the Midwestern milk-and-honey girl-next-door to grungy-biker gun moll, and from hetero to bisexual.

Patti Jo had originally dated one of David Waters's half brothers, a mild and meek baker living quietly in Peoria on the right side of the law. The difference in personality between the two half brothers was striking (but not surprising, given their mother's seeming inability to bear two children from the same male suspect). So it was a mystery of the feminine psyche just how Patti Jo could bounce from an early morning, somewhat slow, work-a-day baker to a high-powered, middle-aged Kubrick droogie with a long, wide streak of the old ultraviolence.

When Patti Jo was the star prosecution witness for the federal government at the trial in absentia of her lover, David Waters, she confessed to participation in a range of other criminal activities with Waters—from car theft to helping him dispose of stolen bonds to buying him pistols—even though she knew he was a killer. As well, she had to quietly admit on the witness stand that she was a heroin user.

It was also to come out in the court proceedings that Patti Jo enjoyed "swinging" with Waters, indulging in ménages à trois when the chance presented itself—which may have been quite regularly. Waters was a heavy consumer of pornography and would scour the Internet for any available females in South Texas for himself and Patti Jo to party with. From e-mails discovered on his computer, it was evident that he was successful in pulling off a goodly number of three-ways. Undoubtedly Patti Jo enjoyed the bisexual action. Even though the judge ruled it was irrelevant, her starring role at the trial of Waters's confederate, Gary Karr, would be sorely blemished by a photograph of Patti Jo performing oral sex on another woman at the apartment that she shared with Waters.

Patti Jo may have had some other judicial imperfections. Evidence indicated that she may well have been aware that Waters had committed another murder besides that of David Gibbs. The cold-blooded shooting of a Peoria man in the mid-1980s had remained unsolved until Waters admitted committing the crime almost twenty years later, after receiving immunity during sentencing negotiations with the government. (Waters shot the victim because he had insulted Waters's girlfriend.)

No, Patti Jo Steffens was not an angel, but then again, as all good prosecutors like to say about grimy witnesses who've turned state's evidence and been reconditioned, "Angels don't overhear deals made in Hell."

In actuality, Patti Jo was to make a superb witness for the government. She, like Waters, was exceptionally intelligent. Having majored in literature at the University of Texas, Patti Jo wrote with refinement and spoke with confidence and plausibility. The fact was, without her testimony, Waters could never be prosecuted and the bodies never recovered.

But Patti Jo needed just the right handling, just the right touch. With MacCormack laying out the crime for all to see, Patti Jo was scared—deathly scared. She knew too much. Even though she had broken up with Waters before the MacCormack story identifying Fry's body appeared, she didn't have the least doubt that if she fled, Waters would find her just like he found Danny Fry's brother in Florida—just like he could find anybody he put his mind to. No. She had to go to the cops and see what she could work out.

Patti Jo went to the FBI in Austin. The agent assigned to the Murray-O'Hair case was Special Agent Donna Cowling, and the fit between her and Patti Jo would be one of the sequence of serendipities that danced all along the time line of David Waters's downfall. Cowling was a bright, thirty-ish FBI agent. A graduate of Texas A&M, she had clear blue eyes and an easy manner—a kind of understated charm perhaps stemming from the confidence bred by her background as a star high school athlete. Whatever it was, Cowling had to have the precise personality ingredients necessary not only to quell Patti Jo's fears, but to restructure her, redefine her into a star witness—THE star witness for the prosecution.

It wasn't easy. First, Cowling had to deal with Patti Jo's blustering new boyfriend, who was acting as a combination protector-broker-agent for the frightened woman. When, after a good deal of dickering, Patti Jo finally decided to meet with Cowling face to face at the FBI offices in Austin for the first time, the potential star witness acted as though she was a dead-woman-walking. She seemed scared out of her mind. When Cowling got her calmed down enough for a little conversation, an aggressive detective from a state jurisdiction, who was in on the interview, wanted Patti Jo to sign a sworn statement immediately. She refused and left.

Cowling then visited Patti Jo alone at her Northside Austin apartment—one on one, woman to woman. Cowling didn't talk *at* Patti Jo, she talked with her. She vibed female empathy. She'd had her own difficult marriage relationship. She knew about hopes and dashed dreams. And, of course, she knew criminals and crime. She understood what Waters was about. What he was capable of. She knew the fear and the terror involved. What the stakes were. She also knew a good attorney, well respected by the FBI, who'd help draft an immunity agreement that would guarantee that no matter what Patti Jo had done with Waters, she wouldn't go to prison for the Murray-O'Hair crimes.

As well, Cowling would personally make sure that Patti Jo would be able to start a new life somewhere far away, put everything behind her, maybe even with a cash nest egg provided by the FBI. It worked. Cowling had to touch every button, exactly the right way—and she did. In less than a week, an immunity agreement was drawn up, and Patti Jo started singing like the proverbial canary. But it would still take more—a lot more—to take down David Waters.

In his thirty-year career, IRS Special Agent Ed Martin had busted the spectrum of tax-related crimes: complex Ponzi schemes, large-scale bank and real estate fraud, as well as dozens of tax evasion cases, many of which were of the rich-and-famous variety. Martin was a star operative to be sure, but one with an unusual, paradoxical handicap for an IRS agent and accountant. He was dyslexic. It was hard to imagine. Year after year, page after page, screen after screen of numbers and letters marching in front of Martin's eyes, and every letter and number had to be deciphered and placed in its proper position—each and every one—with not a scintilla of room for error.

The disorder, unusual as it was for his profession, probably contributed to his star billing. He was like a champion marathon runner with a peg leg who beats the pack with pure hellfire determination. Yet it wasn't willpower alone that made Martin so formidable. Although he always had an oversupply of kinetic energy, the IRS special agent could check it when necessary and maintain a reptilian patience during investigations. This patience, coupled with superior abilities at organizing massive chunks of data and an understated New Orleans charm that could lull you into confiding in him, made Martin a dangerous adversary for tax dodgers.

He'd originally been assigned the Murray-O'Hair matter as a relatively simple, celebrity tax-evasion case. His superiors considered (as everyone did except for Bill Murray) that it was a take-the-money-and-run fraud, linked to the atheist trio's long-standing tax problems. Martin's first take on the case was direct. He felt that if he just found Jon Garth Murray, in whose name all the financial transactions were done, he'd have the answers. But as he looked at the facts, rolling them over in his mind, there was too much that didn't fit.

The IRS had agreed to settle the tax case against them for pennies on the dollar, and as well, they were off the hook in San Diego with Judge Real's verdict. There just wasn't any need for them to run. And there were other conundrums. The trio had left their passports behind. If they did flee the country, why didn't they take their passports? The only reason to leave them would be if they were going to take on new identities. But that wasn't necessary. They weren't fugitives. Besides, as Bill Murray said, how could these three huge people—with Madalyn strewing "fuck-yous" around like rice at a wedding—disguise themselves?

The very first time that Martin talked with Tim Young,

Martin immediately took him seriously. He was quickly convinced, after seeing some of Young's work for the *Express-News*,
that he was investigating a multiple homicide—and not a tax-
evasion case. Following MacCormack's first article about Danny
Fry in the summer of 1998, Martin did his bureaucratic thing,
knocking on the appropriate doors of the Austin PD and DA's
office. Neither agency was interested in pursuing murder charges
against Waters. Neither one was evidently impressed with Young
and MacCormack's work—nor even the details that Ed Martin
himself had fleshed out in the meantime.

But Martin wasn't about to spend too much time dealing
with these hopeless lamers. Calling his contacts, he honchoed a
powerful gathering of federal law enforcement agencies, along
with the aggressive Dallas detectives whose lights MacCormack
had originally lit. Now the FBI; the IRS; the Bureau of Alcohol,
Tobacco and Firearms; and the U.S. Attorney were tracking the
case—looking hard at Waters and Gary Karr as probable multiple murderers.

But there was still another problem for Martin—a big one.
Except for some nice clothes he'd wear to interviews, Waters was
clearly living on the margins. Martin took surveillance photos of
Waters, shuffling along, head down, with his hands in his pockets—and even more incongruously, pedaling a beat-up old bike
around his neighborhood. This was *not* a man who had the lion's
share of a half-million dollars in gold. It just didn't add up. Martin was a pro at finding hidden assets—at sniffing out stashed
fortunes. But his intuition told him that Waters wasn't faking.
He really was broke.

Then where in hell was the gold?

TWENTY-THREE

Brought to Bay

W hen Patti Jo Steffens returned to the apartment she shared with David Waters after socializing with some friends, she was fairly drunk. It had been a year since Waters and Gary Karr had killed and butchered the Murray-O'Hairs and Danny Fry. When Waters asked Patti Jo where her pickup truck was, she said that she'd left it at the bar where she'd been drinking. Waters's response was to casually pick up a weight from his weight-lifting set and say with a soft voice that he was going to cause her some serious pain.

When Patti Jo tried to run out of the apartment, Waters quickly blocked the door and came at her. Patti Jo ran toward their bedroom to grab a .357 Magnum revolver from the nightstand drawer. Waters knew what she had in mind, and beat her to the gun. Frustrated, scared, and drunk, Patti Jo started taunting him. "You scumbag," she yelled. Waters turned the large pistol butt toward her face and in a swift motion smashed it into her mouth. Patti Jo spat blood and a tooth at him—and then she spat more. "Is this what happened to the 'O's?"

Now, almost three years later, Patti Jo was lucky to be alive and telling her horror stories to government investigators. Special Agent Donna Cowling of the FBI and Ed Martin of the IRS didn't have to listen to a lot of Patti Jo's tales of domestic life with David Waters to determine that they could build a case using her against both Waters and Karr.

Martin and Cowling made a complementary team, although

there were natural points of friction. Martin, a traditionalist, wasn't that used to working as a coequal with an aggressive woman. Besides, as a senior IRS agent, and a star performer at that, he'd become accustomed to calling the shots. Cowling, on the other hand, was also highly competitive—an ex-athlete who had to shoulder her career through the mostly male corridors of the FBI.

They had opposing MOs too. Cowling worked more on an emotional level. She didn't seem to like the tedium and organizational schlepping that deep investigations required—whereas Martin loved it. An ingrained and prototypical workaholic, Martin liked nothing more than methodically snouting through a forest of records and finding a fat, lovely truffle of crucial datum. They each had strengths, and regardless of whether they wanted to admit it, those strengths melded beautifully together. But it made no difference really. Martin and Cowling were handcuffed to each other for the biggest and most difficult investigation of both their careers.

The Feds had a plan. It was simple in form and complex in execution. With Martin taking the lead, they would gather enough information to get a search warrant issued for the apartment of David Waters. The search warrant would be a de facto blueprint for the entire prosecution. The Feds were betting that they would find something—anything—that could be used to jail both Waters and Karr while they built murder cases against them.

Both men were convicted felons. Both loved guns. Perhaps the Feds would find some sort of weapons violation to hold them on, and then break them down—see if they could get one of the pair, preferably Karr, to flip on the other. If that didn't work, they'd probably have to try them on charges less than murder— unless bodies were found in the meantime.

The best place for Martin to start putting together the search warrant was with Patti Jo Steffens. Cowling now had Patti

Jo's complete confidence, and her debriefing went smoothly considering the horror that lurked between her words. Patti Jo told the investigators that on the last day she saw Danny Fry—September 30, 1995—he'd come back to the apartment in Austin with Waters and Karr. He seemed quiet and out-of-sorts. He also was clearly not on good terms with either of the other two men, who were laughing and kidding with each other.

Patti Jo had clear recall of the last hours of Danny Fry and the events that followed. She had a soft spot in her heart for the alcoholic petty hustler. She remembered that Danny took a nap and when he awoke she packed his bags for his trip back to Florida. She then left to run an errand, and when she got back to the apartment, all three men were gone. The suitcase she'd packed with Fry's belongings had been left behind—empty.

A day later, Karr and Waters returned. Both men were again in good humor. When Patti Jo asked Waters where Danny was, he replied that he'd taken off with some guy. Later that weekend, she looked inside a shopping bag that was placed near the front door of the apartment. She found three pairs of sneakers and a washcloth. All were caked with blood.

The washcloth was her father's that she'd kept after his death, and when she realized what it was, Patti Jo started to cry. Waters jumped up—his "nostrils flaring"—and said, "Get away from there." Steffens, weeping, responded, "My dad's washcloth . . ." Waters grabbed it, washed it off, and handed it back to her—and then walked silently out of the apartment. A few weeks later, she saw him cleaning his glasses with a piece of one of Danny Fry's shirts.

Still, Martin needed a great deal more for the critical search warrant affidavit than the word of a single witness, compelling as she might be. Immersing himself in the financial complexities of the case, using spreadsheets, diagrams, and time lines, Martin determined that in little more than a month, while the Murray-O'Hairs were being held, more than $70,000 was siphoned from their various personal and business accounts. This cash haul by the abductors didn't even include the monies from the sale of Jon Garth's Mercedes-Benz, or the $500,000 in gold coins.

But then—here again was that damn mystery that really bothered Martin. If Waters had stolen all the money, why hadn't he left town to enjoy the loot in Mexico, Europe, or whereever? But that question, disquieting as it was, would have to wait.

Starting with information originally ferreted out by private investigator Tim Young for the *Express-News,* Martin homed in on the motel-residence in northwest San Antonio, the Warren Inn, where the kidnappers appeared to have taken their victims. He and Donna Cowling drove down from Austin and sifted through boxes of old receipts in the manager's office. After a few hours of drilling through the records, they hit the gusher that Martin suspected was there: applications, ledger payments, and registered vehicle logs for cargo and passenger vans—all bearing the names of Karr or Waters.

The federal prosecution team members invariably refer to March 24, 1999 as "the Big Day." Armed with the warrant that Ed Martin had crafted, a multiagency law enforcement squad raided Waters's apartment in Austin on his fiftieth birthday.* The uninvited federal celebrants obviously caught Waters by surprise, yet he maintained his outward cool with them. Nonetheless, he'd made a grave blunder. Federal agents didn't find a gun in his possession—but it wasn't necessary. Waters was keeping a mini ammo dump in his apartment—119 rounds of different-caliber pistol ammunition. There were bullets for a .380 automatic, as well as rounds for a .357 Magnum and a 9-mm automatic.

As the federal agents combed through Waters's belongings, other teams hit different locations in Texas and the Midwest.

* Waters was known to use at least three different dates of birth.

FBI agents arrested the man who had rented the storage unit in Austin where investigators believed the Murray-O'Hairs had been partially dismembered. Gerald Lee "Chico" Osborne, an old running mate of Waters's from Peoria, living in Weatherford, Texas, outside of Dallas, provided an FBI agent with a false Social Security number during questioning—and that was enough to arrest him on federal charges.*

Outside of Chicago, FBI agent Donna Cowling, along with multiagency team members, visited Sidney Karr—Gary Karr's sister. An informant said that Karr had given his sister one of the Murray-O'Hairs' gold Rolexes as a present. When Cowling asked about the watch, Sidney admitted she'd owned a Rolex—but said that she had lost it in a bar. Then she changed her mind, saying that she had misplaced it somewhere in the house. When Cowling, who didn't have a search warrant, asked if they could look around the residence, Sidney Karr sent the agents packing.

But they weren't to be denied. By changing her story, Sidney Karr had given Cowling enough "probable cause" to obtain a search warrant. Cowling came back with the warrant and agents thoroughly searched the premises. No Rolex was to be found. But Sidney Karr didn't fool the clever agents. Looking through family photo albums, they found a picture of her wearing the gold Rolex on a vacation. Also located was a jeweler's receipt for cleaning the watch and appraising it. The agents then found and read Sidney Karr's last will and testament. It contained a bequest to her daughter of a gold Rolex watch.

In Novi, Michigan, outside of Detroit, federal agents descended on Gary Karr just as Cowling's team was rousting his sister. The Michigan task force was led by the IRS's Ed Martin

* His lawyers would later scream "technicality" and "harassment," but Osborne was actually lucky. Federal prosecutors felt that he was a player, but they never could prove his involvement in any of Waters's crimes. Osborne would eventually get probation for providing the false Social Security number.

and Samuel Sykes Houston, a veteran FBI special agent from the Austin office. Joined by other federal agents from Detroit and local police, they found Karr, unshaven, wearing shorts and a tee shirt, shambling up a flight of stairs at the four-plex where he lived. Not having a search warrant, they asked if they could talk with Karr in his apartment, and he agreed.

Inside, the agents had the tough biker sit on a sofa in the center of the living room. They placed chairs facing him in a semicircle and Martin read him his Miranda rights. Karr seemed composed, but he immediately started chain-smoking as Sykes Houston outlined the information that the government had on his stay at the Warren Inn, and on the passenger and cargo vans he rented during the time of the Murray-O'Hair disappearance.

Karr, in an obviously long-planned alibi, admitted to being with the Murray-O'Hairs. He explained that he'd been hired by David Waters to act as a member of a "security" detail that the Murray-O'Hairs themselves requested. Karr told the agents that Madalyn had wanted to "disappear" because she was having legal and tax problems, and that she thought Waters would be the right man to help her and her family quietly flee the country.

When Karr, still acting very nervous, asked to go and relieve himself, one of the Detroit FBI men said they'd need to "secure the area" first. After finishing checking the bathroom for weapons, the agent casually asked Karr if he'd mind if they did a "security sweep" of the apartment. Karr said he had no objection.

When Karr emerged from the bathroom, his fate was literally in the hands of an FBI agent who held up a cheap chrome-plated .22 revolver for him to see. "Whose is this?" the agent asked. "Mine," Karr replied. Given his prior convictions, the discovery of the weapon behind a picture on a night table in his bedroom meant that, with "three-strikes" statutes, Karr could be going to prison for the rest of his natural life. One of the FBI agents immediately told Karr that he was under arrest.

It was a pronouncement that did not please the IRS's Ed Martin. He wanted to milk Karr for everything he could before Karr was officially taken into custody. Martin figured that as soon as Karr was processed at the detention facility—either federal or county—he would be given the chance to talk with an attorney who would surely tell him to shut-the-hell-up. Martin ignored the other agent's declaration and started to talk to Karr with low-keyed empathy, trying to get Karr's mind off being arrested. Martin asked him why he had a gun. Was he afraid of David Waters? Was he worried about his family being hurt? How did he feel about providing security for the Murray-O'Hairs? What were they like as people? What was it like staying at the Warren Inn?

Karr said he'd answer all Martin's questions, but that he was going to follow "the code"—he'd never be a stool pigeon no matter what. However, with his handguns (the agents had found a second one) in the hands of the FBI, and the rest of his life on the line, Karr proceeded to do exactly what he'd just said he'd never do—he gave up David Waters.

Karr related times, places, dates. Martin had such a broad and detailed knowledge of the facts that he knew Karr—chain-smoking even more furiously now—wasn't lying. While he fingered Waters, Karr stoutly maintained that *he* had only provided security. Waters was the mastermind and he was just his water boy. Karr talked for three hours straight under the cautious prodding of Martin.

It was now early afternoon and everybody was getting hungry. A couple of agents volunteered to bring back some lunch. Karr asked for a hamburger. With the touch of an adroit fly fisherman, Martin asked Karr if it would be OK if he used Karr's computer to type up a statement while they ate—just to see if he could get Karr's views down in writing correctly. Karr said that would be fine. As Karr and the other agents ate and made small talk about a pet parrot that the ex-con kept in the apartment, Martin typed.

The eight-page statement the IRS agent had crafted on the fly was a triptych of the kidnapping, extortion, and deaths of Madalyn, Jon Garth, and Robin—all couched to exculpate Karr from any wrongdoing, yet having him admit to firsthand knowledge of how the crimes were committed. With the agents holding their collective breath, Karr signed it.

• • •

It was a fine spring day for flying over the Texas Hill Country, especially so if you appreciated the gorgeous color schemes of God's country. It was like fall in reverse. Instead of reds, oranges, and yellows, the hills were a hallucinatory blending of greens and golds with bands of molten silver where the creeks flowed through the ancient canyons.

Ed Martin enjoyed the view from the FBI airplane, even if he was distracted by both the importance of his mission and the cramped back seat, where he was shoehorned in next to his investigative Siamese twin, FBI agent Donna Cowling.

Gary Karr, during his frenzied attempts to save his skin, had drawn both Ed Martin and Sykes Houston maps of where he claimed the Murray-O'Hairs were buried. Karr had said that he didn't know *anything* about the actual murders, or when the Murray-O'Hairs were buried, but he claimed to know the location because he'd gone out with Waters after flash floods had torn through the area the spring after the killings.

Karr said that Waters was freaked out that one of the Murray-O'Hairs' hands might be reaching up from their shallow grave— just like in the movie *Deliverance*. (It was actually a reasonable concern, given Hill Country's monsoonal rains.) Karr maintained that he had offered to go along for the spooky nighttime ride out to the five-thousand-acre Cooksey Ranch burial site just to provide company for his old prison buddy.

Karr had drawn a map for Ed Martin on the day after his

arrest, but it was a rush job. He drew a second, more legible map on a sheet of lined yellow legal paper for the FBI's Sykes Houston. Now, three days later, Martin and Cowling had that map balanced between them on their adjacent thighs in the tight back seats of the FBI aircraft.

The plane cruised up the Nueces River valley and started to circle a point that Karr had noted on the crude map. The pilot banked from one side to the other, dipping the wings alternately, so that the two investigators could look down on the countryside, each in turn.

In fact, the entire prosecution hinged on Cowling and Martin's locating the secret burial place. If there were no bodies, there still would be a prosecution, but on lesser charges than the most appropriate one—murder. And even with a conviction for lesser crimes, the mystery would linger for years if the bodies were not found. However, if the bodies *were* found, then Karr would receive a reduced sentence for his cooperation. More importantly, David Waters would get charged with three counts of capital murder—with a fair chance that the final chapter of the story would be played out in the federal death chamber at Terre Haute.

The stakes couldn't have been higher as the FBI plane circled over the spring-lush Hill Country. All of a sudden, on one of the lazy banks on his side of the plane—it was all there. What was drawn on the map was before Ed Martin's eyes. *There* were the three gates. *There* was the Y in the road. *There* was the caliche mound. And there was the dry-wash terrace.

The government's ground search for the bodies of the Murray-O'Hairs on Easter weekend of 1999 was supposed to be "hush-hush," but somehow the world seemed to have found out about the operation. Bulky satellite trucks festooned with antennae and dishes, along with an assortment of mostly four-wheel-drive news units, lined the state highway in front of the huge Cooksey

Ranch a few miles south of the little Hill Country town of Camp Wood.

The recovery of the remains was going to be a difficult process and the Feds had decided to bring the full spectrum of gear to bear: everything from ground-penetrating radar to helicopters equipped with state-of-the-art infrared sensor cameras. They would also deploy the lowest-tech of items, but perhaps the most effective—cadaver dogs trained to sniff out the faintest odors emanating from decomposed bodies.

Even though the foliage along the Nueces River valley was refulgent and verdant, deeper in the hills where the Cooksey Ranch spread out, the ground was dry and overgrazed, and as yet unblessed by the early-summer monsoonal rains. Nonetheless, the cadaver dogs worked the bone-dry land valiantly for hours on end. But the area they had been designated to sniff was wide and rocky. What once was good pasture was now little more than desiccated scrubland, holding its deadly secrets far better than its topsoil.

Yet the dogs came close. So close. After the bodies were found nearly two years later, almost precisely where Karr's map had placed them, Ed Martin remembered, with the extraordinary spatial judgment that some dyslexics possess, that one of the animals had sniffed within a bare twenty feet of the hell spot.

TWENTY-FOUR

Trial in Absentia

When the defense attorney for David Waters called the hand of the prosecutor at the hearing on gun charges in Federal District Court, assistant U.S. attorney, Gerald Carruth, laid down what amounted to a legal royal flush. He showed Waters's lawyer photographs that agents had found in the raid on his client's apartment. Waters was shown handling a 9-mm automatic at a firing range—a felony violation of federal law for an ex-con. An additional problem for the attorney was that Waters was wearing a promotional tee shirt for an Austin street festival—with a 1995 date on it.

But even without the inadvertently time-stamped photograph, Carruth had Waters by the short hairs. Not only did the prosecution have all the multicaliber ammunition found in Waters's apartment as evidence, investigators had found his fingerprints on a 9-mm Browning automatic pistol that Waters had sent to his brother in Illinois. It was a federal crime for a felon to transport firearms, or have them transported, interstate.

After seeing what Carruth had against his client, the defense attorney asked the judge if he could be allowed to confer with Waters in private. After a short recess, the lawyer came back to tell the judge that David Waters had decided to plead guilty to all federal charges.

A second defeat would soon follow in the state court of

Judge Wilford Flowers—but it was to be a buffered blow. The judge had originally been kindly enough to grant Waters—even with his lengthy, extremely violent criminal history—probation for the theft of fifty-five thousand dollars from the atheist trio. Then, still amenable to Waters's cause, Judge Flowers had agreed to reduce restitution payments to the Murray-O'Hairs to a mere fifteen thousand dollars. In response to the judge's unusual generosity, Waters took the liberty of kidnapping Madalyn and her children and extorting close to three-quarters of a million dollars before murdering and partially dismembering them.

Given the virtually fatal judgmental mistake that Judge Flowers made granting Waters probation originally, it was assumed that the judge would assess a sentence that would preclude the murderous ex-con from ever being free again. Instead, Judge Flowers still seemed to harbor a strange compassion for Waters, sentencing him to sixty years. It sounded harsh, but the reality was, in the State of Texas at the time—depending on when he would become eligible for parole, and how he served his time—Waters could conceivably serve only around 20 percent of his sentence before being released. More importantly, Judge Flowers's sentence had vested Waters with the most precious commodity a convict can receive—hope—hope of release.

Gerald Carruth, the assistant U.S. attorney directing the criminal cases surrounding the Murray-O'Hair murders, appreciated seeing violent criminals punished to the fullest extent of the law. In his late fifties, Carruth was acknowledged as a top legal gunslinger for the U.S. attorney in the Western District—a large geographic area including much of west Texas and the Hill Country.

His career was distinguished, with many notches on his gun. Just prior to taking the Murray-O'Hair case, he'd defeated the renowned Texas defense attorney Richard "Racehorse" Haynes in the grisly "Slave Ranch" trial—a terrible stew of torture, murder, and cannibalistic rites in the scrubland west of Austin. With his Kojak-shaved head, Carruth sported a jocular, folksy persona that went well with his sprightly portliness. But for the unwary, his collegiality camouflaged a barracuda-like legal mind armed with a prodigious memory for even the minutest details. In a courtroom, his usually merry eyes could turn very hard and cold, while he maintained a charmingly deferential and courtly demeanor.

Carruth was clearly a man blessed not only to love his job, but also to perform it with verve and ability. And as things would turn out, being the chief prosecutor and legal architect of the government's case against Waters, Carruth would—like his friend and colleague, Ed Martin of the IRS—have to put all of his thirty years' experience to the best possible use in order for the United States to prevail over David Roland Waters.

The opening battle of the campaign had gone swimmingly for Carruth, with Waters pleading guilty to the federal gun charges. U.S. District Judge Sam Sparks, who was to hear all the Murray-O'Hair criminal cases, had given Waters an eight-year sentence for the firearms violations, on top of the somewhat misleading sixty years that Waters had received from Judge Flowers's state court (a sentence that could have actually run less that twelve years). In any case, Waters was safely tucked away while Carruth could put together cases against him and his deadly lackey, Gary Karr.

The first trial was to be that of Gary Karr—the not-so-faithful Tonto of Waters—who went along for the big-money score and whatever other opportunities arose that might feed his impulses for sadistic sex and violence. Carruth's strategy for Karr was standard prosecutorial: Get the abettor first—see if you can roll him over and have him plead out in exchange for testimony against the big enchilada. However, even with the meticulous gathering and collating of evidence by the IRS's Ed Martin, and the careful cultivation and grooming of the star witness by Special Agent Donna Cowling of the FBI, Carruth had a difficult case to try against Karr, and Karr knew it.

While he was certain that Karr had helped murder and dismember the Murray-O'Hairs and Danny Fry as well, Carruth was forced to try him on lesser charges—kidnapping and extortion counts. The problem was the no-bodies-found bugaboo. Any smart killer knows that without a body, the prosecutors' case *must* be circumstantial—and circumstantial cases leave the most room for "reasonable doubt" with a jury.

David Waters, a criminal with a superlative grasp of such issues, was well aware of that particular axiom of crime, and he had protected himself and his accomplice by energetically and creatively disposing of the Murray-O'Hairs' remains in the barrens of a lonely Hill Country ranch. Without bodies—*and* with Madalyn, Jon Garth and Robin's secretive and sometimes disreputable behavior—a good defense attorney could easily drizzle enough doubt on the proceedings to cleanly beat a murder rap, and perhaps even get not-guilty verdicts on lesser charges.

Karr's original cooperation with Ed Martin and the investigators had ended after he drew the map. Karr had clammed up and foolishly—as things would turn out—resisted Carruth's offer of a twenty-year sentence in return for his testimony against Waters. He stuck rigidly by the ridiculous alibi that he was only providing "security" for the Murray-O'Hairs while Waters helped them to "disappear" at their own request. But regardless of how preposterous the alibi might be, as long as Karr never took the stand, it probably wouldn't do his defense that much damage either.

Yet the highest hurdle facing Carruth wasn't that legally tangible. The Karr trial was, in fact, the trial of David Waters in absentia. Karr was, in all probability, only a tool in Waters's hands. The entire federal investigation had necessarily focused on

Waters. While the government didn't and couldn't ignore Karr, efforts were always geared toward taking down Waters, not only because he was the mastermind, but because the federal prosecution team knew it would take their best skills and resources to bring a criminal as exceptional as Waters to bay. Luckily for Carruth, Ed Martin had cast a wide net of evidence gathering—sufficiently wide to have caught up Karr's own criminal activities along with those of Waters.

The criminal case was extensive and complex—one of the more intricate ever heard in a federal court in the Southwest. Ed Martin had covered a blackboard on an entire wall of the U.S. Attorney's "war room" in Austin with organizational diagrams of the case, linking evidence, witnesses, and chronology. Carruth had drawn up a list of testimony from 124 witnesses. (He'd eventually call more than 60.) Martin had culled and edited thousands of pages of documentary evidence and data along with lists of the items seized by search warrant. At the start of the trial, some 325 separate items of evidentiary material were to be presented to the federal court jury.

For prosecutor Carruth, the Karr case was like a run around the track to determine the pole position in a stock car race. It was important, yet it wasn't the main event—BUT you could still crash and burn. To be sure, there were many potential pitfalls for Carruth and his team. One of the lesser ones was the federal judge who would be hearing the case. The Honorable Sam Sparks, a West Texan and Reagan appointee, was known for hot-dogging in front of jurors and forcing his mundane humor on his captive audience. As jovial as he was with jurors, he could tear up a witness whose clothing didn't meet his particular standards for the day. He was also renowned for his portentous behavior with attorneys. Younger, attractive female lawyers were known to be prime targets for condescension from his bench.

Although judicial sexism would hardly be a problem for

Gerald Carruth, Sparks was known to make inconsistent evidentiary rulings, and given the prosecution's plans to introduce a
mass of evidence to bolster their circumstantial case against Karr
and, later, Waters, the judge's propensities here could cause serious difficulties for the prosecution.

Karr's court-appointed attorney was also a problem. Tom
Mills was acknowledged to be one of the finer criminal trial
attorneys in the state and a perceptive and vigorous adversary.
Trim and youthful in his early fifties, and a professor of law from
Dallas, Mills had taken the Karr case at a goodly financial loss.
Court-appointed attorneys in federal criminal cases received less
than sixty dollars per hour for their work. That fee might be 20
percent of what Mills would usually make. However, Mills was
intellectually intrigued by Madalyn Murray O'Hair and the
bizarre elements of the case—and the publicity wouldn't hurt his
law practice either, naturally.

Although he would never admit it, Carruth must have worried about what a skilled defense attorney like Mills could do to
his star witness—Waters's ex-girlfriend Patti Jo Steffens. The
fact was that Carruth had to make a silk purse out of a sow's ear.
Patti Jo was not a nice girl. She'd dabbled in pornography and
deviant sex with Waters. She'd done heroin. She'd stolen cars
with him. She'd bought him guns and stayed with him knowing
his history of homicide. She wouldn't leave him when she discovered bloody articles of clothing right after the disappearance of
Danny Fry. She even stayed the course after he had broken her
teeth with a pistol. (Carruth also knew that Waters had stabbed
her in the chest during a drunken fight in the early 1990s.)

Also, there was the distinct possibility that Patti Jo knew
much more about the Murray-O'Hairs' fate than she had admitted to the government. It was Patti Jo who had located the Cooksey Ranch burial site—land leased for deer hunting by a patron of
the cocktail lounge where she worked. And it was Patti Jo who

had rented the locker where Waters was to put the half-million dollars in gold coins.

There was yet another problem for the prosecution—a potential disaster that could completely destroy Carruth's carefully fashioned case. If Mills could find somebody with credibility who could positively say that they saw the Murray-O'Hairs alive after September 30, 1995, a jury would be hard pressed to convict Karr on *any* of the charges. And if Karr walked, then Waters surely would as well.

Unable to try Gary Karr for murder since there were no bodies, the government put the psycho ex-biker on trial for kidnapping and extortion in Austin's Federal Courthouse at the beginning of May 2000. Opening statements by both sides portended a well-tried case. Assistant U.S. Attorney Gerald Carruth presented the jury with a highly organized synthesis of the facts in the complex production. His basic request to the jurors was to "follow the money." Defense attorney Tom Mills emphasized the chronic problem the government faced: no bodies and only circumstantial evidence that the Murray-O'Hairs had been killed. If there were no victims, Mills reasonably asked, how could there be—beyond a reasonable doubt—a kidnapping or extortion?

It was to be parry and thrust—like all good courtroom dramas. Carruth, deploying a tried-and-true tactic of prosecutors the world over, wanted to humanize the victims—"to put faces on them" for the jury. He called two unusual first witnesses to accomplish this—the victims themselves. The rapt jurors were shown the last known public appearance by Madalyn and Jon Garth, a videotape shot at the University of Houston just weeks before their vanishing.

But regrettably for Carruth, humanizing Madalyn was not all that easy. "Prayer is insane. Children should not be taught to pray. It does them no help with anything," Madalyn grated into the microphone. When Jon Garth got up to address the students, Madalyn looked up at him lovingly with some obvious maternal pride—a plus for Carruth—but then Jon Garth spewed pompous platitudes with his Elmer Fudd lisp. It just was hard to make these people likeable. But in truth Carruth wasn't shooting for likeability. Given the Murray-O'Hairs' personalities, he simply hoped the jury would see Madalyn and her children as human— undeserving of their horrendous fate.

Next the government called Ellen Johnson, who was now running Madalyn's main organization, American Atheists. Carruth had managed to have the high-strung, nervous woman calm down before the jury, and more importantly, he was able to sanitize her dubious role in the affair. Johnson, for whatever reason, had never initiated a criminal investigation into the disappearance of the Murray-O'Hairs, even though evidence of foul play was considerable. (Notably, while the issue had not arisen at the time of trial, for some, Johnson was also a reasonable suspect in the possible theft of Madalyn's diaries and other items from the estate which Bill Murray alleged to have been pillaged.)

Regardless, Johnson's testimony was forceful and riveting for the jury, especially as she related the terror in Robin's voice when they last talked. She told of those terrible words that a distraught Robin choked out in their final conversation—"I know you'll do the right thing." Of course, as things turned out Ellen Johnson didn't "do the right thing"—but her knowledge of Madalyn's upbeat attitude after her court victory in San Diego and the resolution of the IRS tax problem gave weight to the government's contention that the Murray-O'Hairs weren't planning to flee the country—and that they certainly had no reason to hire Waters or Karr for "security."

Karr's ex-wife Charlene also gave testimony highly damaging to the defense. She was a tough witness who would stare down her ex-husband from the witness stand. She had secretly recorded a conversation with Karr, in which he admitted that

Madalyn, Jon Garth, and Robin had been murdered—and named Waters as their killer. Charlene also related how the wardrobe of her ex-husband suddenly became *GQ*-ish soon after the Murray-O'Hairs disappeared. The then jobless ex-con had purchased Armani suits, silk ties, leather jackets, and expensive shoes—worth easily in excess of fifteen thousand dollars, she estimated. She also remembered Karr trying to peddle two gold Rolex watches.

In keeping with the trial convention of female witnesses hammering the defense with coffin nails, the government's star took the stand. Patti Jo Steffens was dressed demurely. She was a handsome woman when she wanted to be, but her history was much less attractive. Carruth's strategy for defusing the problem of Patti Jo's past was to bring it up himself during his initial examination, thus taking away the power of surprise admissions in front of the jury—admissions that Tom Mills would surely force during cross.

With her past drug usage and other nastiness behind her on the stand, Patti Jo related her knowledge of Waters's history of violence toward her and others. She explained to the jury, in credible detail, Waters's hatred of Madalyn and his thirst for violent revenge after she published the atheist magazine article containing the maternal-urination episode. "He said wanted to snip off her toes," Patti Jo told the jury.

With confident recall, she told of renting a storage locker for him at approximately the time that the gold had been picked up by Jon Garth. She filled in fine points in the follow-the-money scenario that the prosecution had woven: Waters showing her a flawless solitaire diamond, his leaving her envelopes with nearly twenty thousand dollars in cash during the time when the Murray-O'Hairs were allegedly being held at the Warren Inn, and of course the gruesome tale of finding the bloody clothing after the abrupt exit of Danny Fry.

Articulate, with clearly superior memory, Patti Jo was not

going to be an easy witness to shake. Rather than go at her hammer and tongs, defense attorney Tom Mills seemed to pull his punches, perhaps since her testimony was really more damaging to Waters than to his client, Gary Karr. After reeliciting facts on her history with David Waters and jabbing at her being coached by the FBI's Donna Cowling, Mills let her go and called his short roster of witnesses for the defense.

In a bit of legal showboating, Mills had listed Madalyn, Jon Garth, and Robin as witnesses for the defense "if available." Unfortunately for his client, they were no-shows. However, Mills was still able to cobble together a surprisingly good defense from a couple of disparate witnesses. The first of these was an elderly bar owner from San Antonio, who claimed that Madalyn trundled into her establishment—which was near the Warren Inn—with the aid of a walker, along with a large man and a younger woman. She said that the women ordered Cokes and the man ordered a beer—they drank their drinks, Madalyn paid cash, and they left.

The other defense witness was far more powerful—able to potentially fell the prosecution with a single roundhouse punch. A born-again Baptist preacher from Georgia claimed that he'd *definitely* seen Madalyn, alive and well, in the fall of 1997. Dr. William E. Gordon told the jury that he had seen Madalyn wolfing down a plate of pasta in a restaurant in Rumania. He'd looked at her hard and long and didn't have *any* doubt about who she was.

During cross-examination, the second-chair government prosecutor got the preacher to admit he'd only seen pictures of Madalyn before his encounter, but Dr. Gordon was unshakable as to his description and the details of the Rumanian dinner interlude. However, he may not have been a neutral witness. The forty-six-year-old preacher had received his doctorate in divinity from the New Orleans Baptist Seminary, a fundamentalist religious organization (some might call it a Biblical diploma mill) with direct links to none other than Madalyn's old adversary and onetime crypto-cohort from the 1970s, the drummer-evangelist Bob Harrington. Unfortunately, the examining prosecutor didn't know this fact, or at least if he did, he didn't pursue it—and the defense rested on a sweetly doubting note.

After deliberating for three days, with a pretty spring weekend upcoming, the jury brought in a split decision. They found Karr not guilty of kidnapping—the linchpin of the government case. However, they did find that he was guilty of extortion, money laundering, and two lesser counts. Clearly the jury was flummoxed. Their verdict begged the obvious question: How could the extortion and money laundering have occurred if the Murray-O'Hairs weren't kidnapped? It was preposterous, but juries—as attorneys and judges know all too well—have a right to sire irrational verdicts.

The jury foreman was of the opinion that the Murray-O'Hairs could still be alive, given the testimony, especially that of the Baptist preacher. Other jurors thought that the missing trio had originally been planning to flee, and that somehow things went awry with their relationship with Fry, Karr, and Waters. One female juror, a middle-aged businesswoman, was said to have been romantically taken with the defendant himself—and didn't think that Karr was capable of killing people and chopping them up. Two other male jurors—a Dell Computer employee and a designer—were more skeptical of Karr's defense. Both believed that Madalyn, Jon Garth, and Robin had been murdered, and they expressed frustration with the Austin Police Department's inaction and the fact that the case was brought so long after the trio's disappearance.

However, finding Gary Karr not guilty of the kidnapping

count wasn't going to make any difference. With eight previous felony convictions for offenses ranging from rape to armed robbery, Karr faced life in prison without parole under the "three-strikes" statutes—if he was convicted on *any* count by the jury. When Judge Sparks handed down the expected life-without-parole sentence a few weeks later, he dryly noted that Karr's last release date from prison had been April Fool's Day 1995.

The Karr trial didn't settle the mystery of the Murray-O'Hair disappearance. Bodies would have to be found before the mists of myth and conjecture could be totally dispelled. But the trial did determine the penultimate question, which was: What happened to the gold? Where was the half-million dollars extorted from the Murray-O'Hairs? The answer would be so implausible that even the most rigid skepticism toward a theory of divine justice would have to rationally give way to other possibilities. A day after its acquisition by the murderers, all the gold would be gone.

Austin was a town with a mobile population and throngs of newcomers needing a place to store excess belongings, producing a binge of public storage-locker building with nearly two hundred separate storage facilities in and around the city. After killing Madalyn and her children, Waters had put the $500,000 in freshly minted gold coins in one such public storage locker.

It was Waters's girlfriend, Patti Jo, who had found and rented the small unit near the grungy cocktail lounge where she worked as a barmaid. Patti Jo had purchased the cheapest Master Lock available to secure the repository for the loot. Waters himself may have approved his girlfriend's buying a cheap lock, since an expensive lock is just as easy to breach with a bolt cutter and would bring more attention from thieves. At least that may have been Waters's thinking, since he was eminently familiar with such mind-sets.

Buying the cheap lock also could have been a simple lapse of judgment. By this point in the crime-line, Waters was juggling critical logistical problems and there is evidence that he was using heavy amounts of methamphetamine supplied by Karr via his biker contacts—maybe more than enough to impair his usually fine criminal judgmental abilities.

Whatever the case, within twenty-four hours of the Murray-O'Hairs' being murdered and the gold's being stashed, three young San Antonio–based pachuco-punks—Joe Cortez, Jaime Valdez, and Joey Cardenas—decided to come up to Austin and hit some storage lockers. Cortez had acquired a Master Lock skeleton key.

The plan was to go to a storage facility with minimal security, where one of them would distract the manager while the other two would race through the rows of lockers, trying the skeleton key in likely-looking locks. They didn't expect much. If they'd just shagged enough stuff—pawnable stereos and TVs maybe—to pay for gas and a good Saturday night on the town, their expectations would have been more than met.

The first self-storage facility they found matched their requirements for easy access, no security, and some cheap Master Locks. As Valdez distracted the manager, Cortez and Cardenas started opening lockers. One locker quickly produced a TV set and so did the next. Then, wanting to let things cool down, they went to another nearby storage facility to case it—but it didn't look as productive as their original site. When the trio returned, with Valdez acting as lookout, Cardenas and Cortez began running down the rows once again, hunting for the appropriate cheap Master Locks to try.

They quickly found one such locker—#1640. When Cardenas opened it with the skeleton key, he later said, "a ray of sunlight" hit a large black suitcase that was sitting dead-center in the otherwise empty locker. (Cardenas would later tell investigators that he would never have seen the luggage if it had been placed just a little farther back. The suitcase was jet-black and the locker was unlit—except for that single shaft of sunlight which illuminated the cache of gold.) Cardenas and Cortez barely could wrestle the suitcase into the trunk of Cardenas's car. It was heavy, man. Maybe it was like a couple of new car batteries or something.

In the parking lot of a Burger King they discovered what the luggage contained. The hungry trio of newly rich burglars celebrated by ordering some burgers and then drove back to San Antonio, where they stopped at a bookstore and bought a book on coin collecting. From there they went to Valdez's residence. They removed the gold coins from the plastic holding tubes and piled the treasure on the floor in the middle of Valdez's small bedroom. He went to the kitchen and got three big bowls. The amateur thieves split the gold up by taking handfuls of coins and piling them into their bowls. Cardenas would testify: "Sometimes you did one handful. Sometimes you did two. It didn't matter."

By the time the FBI caught up with them, some four years later, the gold was all gone. The boys said they had had some fun, though. Their testimony at the Karr trial, where they were government witnesses, told of a two-year punk wet dream of cars, plush rental houses, fifteen-hundred-dollars-a-night blowouts at strip clubs, jewelry, trips to Vegas, guns, and wide-screen TVs.

Of the half-million dollars in gold that cost Madalyn, her children, and Danny Fry their lives, only a single coin was ever recovered by the government. One of the boys had a 24-karat Canadian Maple Leaf made into a pendant for a favorite aunt. She turned it over to investigators.

TWENTY-FIVE

The Deal Is Done

In September 2000, David Waters was indicted by a federal grand jury in Austin, Texas, on five counts. He was charged with kidnapping, extortion, and robbery of the Murray-O'Hairs—but not their murder. The prosecution, again led by Assistant U.S. Attorney Gerald Carruth, had hoped that Waters's accomplice, Gary Karr, would cooperate in order to reduce his life-without-parole sentence. However, Karr—after initially singing to the IRS's Ed Martin—had hewed to "the code" and taken his sentence with his mouth shut.

Without any bodies, and given the lifestyle and behavior of Madalyn, her son, and her granddaughter, Carruth felt it would be infeasible to get a capital murder conviction against Waters in a trial. It seemed a reasonable conclusion—especially since it was possible that another squirrelly jury might be empaneled—and regardless, he'd still have to contend with the convincing Baptist preacher who'd spotted Madalyn downing pasta long after she'd been dismembered.

Actually, Carruth didn't need to get a murder conviction on Waters in order to have justice well served. Waters had already been sentenced to sixty years in Judge Wilford Flowers's state district court. His earliest release from that sentence could be in twelve years hence. Federal judge Sam Sparks, who would try the new charges against Waters, had sentenced him to eight years on weapons violations stemming from the bust on his apartment. Conviction on any of the new charges probably would be stacked consecutively—with the result that Waters, at fifty-two years old, would be unlikely to ever again see a day's freedom while on this earth.

For what would be Waters's final trial, Judge Sparks appointed attorney William Gates (no relation to the software Gates) to head up the defense. Gates was a fiftyish lawyer with a strong East Texas drawl that went with his big six-foot-plus frame, which he moved with the bulky grace that ex-football players often exhibit. Gates had grown up in Huntsville, north of Houston—an area dominated by the Texas prison system where correctional units speckle the pastoral landscape like gray carcinomas. His father was a psychologist with a law degree who worked at the different prison units as a counselor and administrator.

Thus one could say that Gates had exactly the right background for having an intuitive feel for David Waters's defensive legal needs—a knack that he was to demonstrate convincingly. Before getting appointed as Waters's counsel, Gates sat through the entire Karr trial. Since it was a dress rehearsal for the trial of his client, Gates could glean tremendous advantage by seeing how the prosecution presented its case, and where the strengths and weaknesses of the Karr defense were. In effect, he could replay the game as a Monday-morning quarterback, tailoring his tactics appropriately.

Gates was known to believe that he could win an acquittal for his client if Judge Sparks were to allow a change of venue from Austin to somewhere in the hinterlands, such as Waco. There Gates hoped to find a jury panel well stocked with fundamentalist Christians who'd have little sympathy for the Murray-O'Hairs. Gates planned to hammer hard at the star witness, Waters's ex-girlfriend Patti Jo Steffens. He thought that he could demonstrate that a relationship may have developed between FBI agent Donna Cowling and Steffens which was unseemly and would seriously damage the government's credibility. Gates also felt that he could reveal for the jury that Patti Jo was far more culpable than had been shown in the Karr trial.

However, the high irony—and still another paradox—was that Gates *didn't* want to prevail over the prosecution. If Waters was found not guilty, he'd then have to serve many years of his sentence from Judge Flowers in the hard-core Texas prison system where a prisoner might hoe cotton crops in the merciless Texas sun, while armed guards with shotguns rode horses and packs of hound dogs sat in the shade waiting for the command to run down an escaping inmate. No siree. This wasn't an appropriate retirement home for a convict of Mr. Waters's stature.

In fact, Waters wanted desperately to be put in the federal system—"Club Fed," as Gates was known to jokingly call it. While not a country club by any means, the federal prison system was tighter, cleaner, and had better medical help than Texas prisons—even if you could still die in a flash of random or planned violence, a shank quickly and expertly sunk horizontally between your ribs into your heart.

When Gates went over to take a look at the evidence against his client that prosecutor Gerald Carruth was holding at the U.S. attorney's office in Austin, he and Carruth commenced the delicate minuet that defense attorneys and prosecutors indulge in if they want to reach a plea bargain agreement rather than go to trial.

A plea bargain made sense for both sides. It would save taxpayers a large chunk of change. It would also spare Carruth even the remote possibility that Waters would win an acquittal. Carruth knew he'd done a good job of rehabilitating Patti Jo during the Karr trial, but he also knew that Gates, having seen her testify, might be able cut her up—especially before a conservative but conceivably antigovernment jury in places like the Waco out-back. Most importantly, though, Carruth had no bodies—no vic-tims—making all the charges subject to "reasonable doubt."

Gates, on the other hand, didn't want to go to trial and lose by winning. He wanted a plea agreement that would spec-ify that Waters would go to federal prison. Gates threw out some tasty chum for Carruth. He let the prosecution know that his client was suffering from what he termed a "terminal dis-ease"—hepatitis C. While hepatitis C was not technically ter-minal, without aggressive and expensive treatment—which would not be available to any inmate regardless of where he was imprisoned—the disease in all likelihood meant that Waters could die behind bars at a leisurely, agonizing pace as his liver progressively failed.

It was a scenario that did not bother Carruth in the least. His goal was to protect the public. He didn't want to see either Karr or Waters back in the free world. He and Gates decided on a twenty-year sentence. It was a good compromise—but contin-gent on recovery of the bodies.

It would take an extraordinary set of circumstances to effect jus-tice—a set of circumstances perhaps beyond conventional proba-bilities. If a veteran newspaper reporter hadn't become mesmerized by a long-shot story and been surfing wire copy on October 2, 1998, at precisely the right moment; and if a young but extremely able private investigator hadn't offered his services at a propitious time; and if a network news correspondent hadn't come up with the idea of a composite sketch, and had it executed by a skilled artist, *and* the brother of the victim hadn't been watching that late-night news program; and if three amateur punk burglars hadn't been ripping off storage lockers with a cheap skeleton key at just the right place and time; and if three top-of-their game members of law enforcement hadn't confederated their very individual talents—David Waters would have been free.

But he wasn't. On March 30, 2001, Waters came before Judge Sparks for a final sentencing. He had already completed his part of the deal, taking investigators to the secret grave site on the Cooksey Ranch deep in the Hill Country. But between January 27, 2001, when the remains of the victims were unearthed, and this last day in federal court, Waters had undergone a remarkable metamorphosis.

His thick, straight-back, male-model, salt-and-pepper hair had been shorn into a crude crew cut. Once handsomely masculine, his facial features were now exaggerated into a gnomish caricature, accentuated by a funky goatee and red-blotched prison-pallor skin. Waters looked frail and thin in the danger-orange jail jumpsuit he was wearing, but he glared ferociously at his courtroom audience, his head tilted back as if he were sighting down one of his beloved 9-mm Browning autos at the onlookers.

Prosecutor Gerald Carruth asked Judge Sparks to assess consecutive sentences for Waters, which the judge did. When Waters's second-chair defense attorney asked if their client could be incarcerated in the Peoria area, looking at Waters, Judge Sparks grumbled that he didn't care, "just as long as you are as far from me as possible." As the newly sentenced convict was removed from court, a cadaverous, elderly atheist screamed: "Ghoul. Filthy ghoul." Sparks made no effort to silence the man.

Outside, on the Federal Courthouse steps, the new queen of atheism, Ellen Johnson, held a press conference. She was droning political banalities to the gathered media when David Waters, leg-shackled and hand-manacled, emerged from the courthouse into the midday spring sunshine, escorted by two oversized federal marshals. As he was led to the prison transport van, Waters stared off into the distance—first looking across the street, then down the street, and finally up at the sky above the buildings of Austin. Distracted by Ellen Johnson, few of the reporters even noticed Waters, and none would appreciate the moment: Waters was trying to gorge his memory to capacity with the sights and sounds of a world he knew in his frozen heart that he was leaving forever.

TWENTY-SIX

Endings

What the last days and hours of Madalyn, Jon Garth, and Robin were like will never be known with certainty. Two men, both sociopaths to whom lying is a part of being, were the only witnesses to the final agonies of the trio. Each said the other did the killing and each related multiple, but still believable, versions of events to the point where even astute veterans of law enforcement could not be sure of what took place.

It can be said that it is *likely* that Madalyn and her children were kidnapped on Sunday, August 27, 1995. Apparently Jon Garth and Madalyn were working at the American Atheist Headquarters on Sunday afternoon. Ignoring earlier rings from the volunteer gardener, who wanted a drink of water, they did open the door to Gary Karr and Danny Fry, who were posing as deliverymen. Brandishing pistols, the two men herded the duo into a back area. Then their old office manager, David Waters, entered the building and greeted his captives. Even with guns pointed at her Madalyn was not cowed. She cursed at Walters.

Robin was at home. Walters knew their habits well enough that he banked on her calling and—if nobody answered the phone—she would come down to investigate. This is precisely what transpired, and Robin was taken hostage too.

From AAGHQ, the kidnappers drove the Murray-O'Hairs back to their Greystone Drive residence, where they were instructed to gather enough belongings for a few weeks away. Robin's Porsche 944—the red herring that Austin PD swallowed—was taken to the airport. Robin made Madalyn a sandwich, and the remains of the meal were left on the kitchen table.

Karr searched the Greystone house for jewelry and valuables and took the occasion to molest Robin in her bedroom. Shortly after the trio was loaded into a Ford passenger van for the drive to San Antonio. That night the three kidnappers and their three victims all stayed in one motel room along the Interstate just south of Austin. The group then moved into a second-floor unit at the Warren Inn—the motel-residence on the northwest side of San Antonio.

A routine developed fairly soon after the group arrived. Waters would order in food for everybody, mostly from an excellent Mexican restaurant across the street. It is likely that none of the captives was restrained all the time—at least initially. They could move freely about one of the two bedrooms in the apartment, but they were always guarded by at least one of their three captors. Waters also left a listening device in the bedroom where the trio slept.

The twenty-eight days of captivity at the Warren Inn were relatively civil for Jon Garth. He had agreed to cooperate with his kidnappers, believing their promises that they would all be set free after the gold came in. Jon Garth was allowed to go out with Waters to get groceries, medication for his mother, and to rent some videos. He even had Nintendo matches with Waters.

Circumstances for Madalyn were also comparatively benign. She was allowed to plan menus with Robin and cook in the minikitchen when they didn't order in. Her insulin and heart medication prescriptions were kept filled. She even took notes on her captors, which they found after they murdered her. (In one jotting she ridiculed Karr's lack of earlobes.) .

Living conditions for Jon Garth and Madalyn could have been worse—but not for Robin. Karr, an ex-convict newly released from prison after twenty years without women—a convicted rapist and kidnapper as well—began sexual predation on Robin immediately at the Warren Inn. With Jon Garth gone on one of his many excursions with Waters, Karr would force Robin to perform fellatio on him, while he kept Madalyn in the adjoining room. He told the terrified young woman that if she mentioned anything about their activities, he would kill her and her grandmother without hesitation.

On September 26, three days before Jon Garth was to pick up the gold shipment in San Antonio, the Murray-O'Hairs were moved from the Warren Inn to nearby La Quinta motel. Waters was worried about the prospect of getting the three obese corpses down the steps from the second-floor apartment unit at the Warren Inn. La Quinta had the proper requirements: two adjoining units on the ground floor where a cargo van could be driven almost up to the doorway.

On Friday, the twenty-ninth of September, Jon Garth took delivery of the gold at the bank and drove with the half-million dollars to a large mall parking lot where he was met by Waters. Waters transferred the gold to his vehicle and drove to Austin and placed the gold in the locker chosen by Patti Jo.

Karr and Jon Garth returned to the motel room. Over Madalyn's protests, the trio was bound with plastic ties on their wrists and ankles. They were told that this was being done so the captors could make a clean getaway. They would call the motel after they were clear of San Antonio and tell employees to look in room such and such.

Madalyn and Robin were quickly overtaken with dread, but Jon Garth remained optimistic. He told the women not to worry—so far their captors had lived up to their word and in a few hours they'd be set free. After he made his assurances, Jon Garth was separated from his mother and niece and moved to the adjoined room.

It was nightfall before Waters returned to La Quinta.

Almost immediately the captors moved to kill their first victim—Jon Garth. He fought tenaciously for his life. After smashing his head repeatedly on a night table—the trio were able to
overcome and suffocate the fatally naïve giant. They placed a bag
over his head since he was bleeding profusely from his nose and
Waters was worried about telltale stains on the carpet.

After catching their breaths, Karr and Waters went into the
adjoining room, where Robin and Madalyn were lying bound,
one on each bed. Waters, with Fry assisting, strangled Madalyn.
According to Waters's confession, she started screaming incoherently before she lost consciousness. Karr strangled Robin. After
she was dead, Karr supposedly complained to Waters that his fin-
gers were sore.

With the murders completed, the rented cargo van was
brought around to the front door of the adjoining rooms and the
corpses were wrapped in motel blankets for transportation. When
the killers opened the door to load the first body into the vehicle,
they froze. Two officers in police cars were chatting off to the
right side of the parking lot—perhaps after dining at the nearby
Denny's.

After regaining their composure, the killers loaded the
corpses beyond the line of sight of the patrolmen. The corpses
were transported to the large storage locker—now lined with
plastic sheeting—that Chico Osborne had rented for Waters in
Austin. Both Waters and Fry found themselves squeamish about
dismembering their victims. Karr jeered that he'd do it, but it
would cost them $25,000 per body. They agreed, and Karr set to
work with a large French chef's knife. The partially dismembered
corpses—legs cut off at the thighs—were loaded into separate
steel fifty-gallon drums and sealed.

The next day, using the ruse that they needed to find a
dumping ground for the barrels, Waters and Karr drove Danny
Fry to a riverfront area near Dallas where Waters executed Fry

with a single bullet to the head from his 9 millimeter Browning automatic. Karr, who apparently enjoyed the manual labor involved in butchering Homo sapiens, cut off Fry's head and hands, which they took with them, leaving the nude, headless, handless corpse on the riverbank.

Waters and Karr then returned to Austin, and shortly later transported the Murray-O'Hairs' bodies, and the head and hands of Danny Fry, to the burial site at the Cooksey Ranch. After a pit was dug, the corpses and body parts were dumped, doused with gasoline, burned, and covered with soil while still smoldering. Riding on what probably was a seventy-two-hour methamphetamine high without sleep, Karr and Waters drove the cargo van back to Austin with the barrels, which they left at a car wash.

• • •

In October 1983 Madalyn wrote in her diary about what was perhaps the last celebrity party to which she was invited—a bash thrown by her longtime admirer Larry Flynt. "Dick Gregory was there this week and Terry Southern, who wrote, *The Magic Christian,* and Dennis Hopper, who directed *Easy Rider.* The 'star' of *The Dukes of Hazzard* . . . I sat there with Timothy Leary and G. Gordon Liddy. Jack Nicholson came in." The diary entry smacked of Madalyn's lifelong affinity for braggadocio, but it also was a factual testament to the level of esteem and entree that she held with the powerful radical segment of American glitterati and intelligentsia, not to mention the millions of atheists and freethinkers embedded in the country's cultural landscape who saw her as a champion of their beliefs.

For those many, Madalyn was a heroine and martyr, even if more than a few were loath to say so openly. Larry Flynt, who once asked Madalyn to take over his $300 million publishing business, loves to tell the story about an exchange that Madalyn had with Johnny Carson during a commercial break when she was a guest on his show. Flynt said that Carson, off the air, confided to Madalyn that he himself was an atheist. She asked the megastar why he just didn't come out and say it publicly. Carson, who at the time had an extremely successful line of men's clothing and multimillions of nightly viewers, supposedly responded, "Who wants to buy a suit from an atheist?"

Flynt himself is candid about openly revering Madalyn for her fearlessness as well as brilliance, and he celebrated her in print as well as socially. One of the few times she publicly wept was when Flynt threw her a huge sixty-fifth-birthday party at his Los Angeles mansion. A "Who's Who of Hollywood," as Flynt put it, gathered to pay homage to the aging atheist high priestess. (Perhaps the only other time Madalyn was known to have cried openly was when she and her staff watched the Branch Davidian compound in Waco burn on TV.)

The porn tycoon had only one problem with his heroine heretic. "If I could fault Madalyn for anything it would be making her atheism her religion. She was as feverish as they [religious fundamentalists] would be." As a man not unfamiliar himself with experiencing white-hot hatred, Flynt has awe in his voice when he speaks of the courage of her convictions: "She was the most brilliant person I've ever known . . . and the most hated person in America. She could have given Osama bin Laden a run for his money."

While Madalyn was an idol of the elite Left, she had staunch allies in the mainstream too. Civil libertarians with a Jeffersonian bent always supported the atheist warhorse's battle for absolute "separation of church and state." While few liked many of her tactics, a diverse group of national leadership—from constitutional scholars to members of the Protestant and Jewish religious hierarchies to mass-media chieftains—supported her ideals and goals for religious freedom in America and delighted in her resounding, historic Supreme Court victory removing prayer from public schools.

Phil Donahue, the man who created a new genre of talk show programming with Madalyn as his very first guest, was an unabashed and lifelong devotee of the atheist doyenne. For nearly forty years, he was fascinated with her personality and its paradoxical, acidic character. "Madalyn Murray O'Hair was difficult to love. She was loud. She interrupted you. She would show you no deference. She was a zealot, but she was right. If you listened to her she'd make you stronger."

Donahue, like Flynt, was also struck by her valor and ever-willingness to take on the Establishment frontally, giving and taking no quarter. "Madalyn was fighting against public servants who believed they had a pipeline to God, and once you've got somebody who talks to God and God talks back, you're in trouble." Donahue continued, "Madalyn was victimized even more by the piety of America. She wouldn't have received this abuse in Europe. They understand hypocrisy. In America, the piety rises to a messianic level. Those who would pray for Madalyn are condescending. They're saying, 'I'm better than you. I'll take Jesus with me and I will win.' It is an anger in them that is the beginning of a war."

For her burial, Madalyn wrote, "I don't want some religious nut to shove a rosary up the ass of my body, or a communion wafer down its throat. I have told Jon and Robin that when I die, they should gather me up in a sheet, unwashed, drag or carry me out and put me on a pyre in the backyard and burn my carcass. . . . I don't want any damn Christer praying over the body or even putting his hands on it."

Madalyn was particularly fearful that her hated evangelical son, Bill Murray, might somehow get control of her remains. She needn't have worried that he did. Bill proved to be dutiful. After the skeletons of Madalyn; her second son, Jon Garth; and her granddaughter Robin had been through complete forensic analysis, the FBI brought them to an Austin funeral home that Bill had chosen. Per Madalyn's wishes, her remains were cremated.

The undertaker located a grave site in a nondenominational suburban cemetery on the outskirts of the city. The setting for the Murray-O'Hairs' final resting place was nondescript, bordering on bleak. Headstones were of modest size, if placed there at all, and few graves had flowers or remembrances. Crabgrass and hard-clay ground dominated.

On the morning of March 23, 2001, a small group of witnesses—mostly law enforcement officers, including prosecutor Gerald Carruth; the IRS's Ed Martin; and Donna Cowling of the FBI—along with Bill Murray and a preacher, gathered at the unmarked grave at the far end of the small cemetery. The grave diggers had been ordered to dig a deeper hole than usual for the concrete vault in order to discourage morbid souvenir hunters.

In the sarcophagus were three tan cardboard boxes with the trio's remains—the three inseparable in death, as they were for so much of their lives. Madalyn's ashes were placed at the head of the vault, the skeleton of Jon Garth in the middle, and Robin's at the foot. A few small bags of burned clothing and personal items—recovered from the secret burial place—had also been put with the cardboard boxes.

Following Madalyn's expressed wishes, no prayers were said over her grave. Bill wasn't even tempted. Most evangelical Christians don't pray for the dead. It would be useless. They believe the fate of the departed has already been sealed, and Bill had *no* doubt his mother was headed straight below. Perhaps it was so. But if there is justice and mercy in God's Heaven—then maybe not. It would seem that Madalyn had already done her time in Hell.

Author's Note

The primary source of information for this book came from extensive interviews with the players: approximately 140 interviews with just under one hundred subjects in fourteen states. Second in importance was the resource material which came from the extensive writings of Madalyn Murray O'Hair. Her published books and personal diaries were invaluable documents. Bill Murray's poignant autobiography, *My Life Without God,* provided me with many insights into his mother's historic Supreme Court victory banning prayer from public schools and his own tattered but fascinating childhood. Equally important was Paul Krassner's coverage of Madalyn in his brilliant and hyper-iconoclastic radical magazine *The Realist.*

The most important source of information surrounding the disappearance and murders of Madalyn, Jon Garth, and Robin was the superior coverage by John MacCormack of the *San Antonio Express-News.* That newspaper's website dedicated to the O'Hair story was an excellent repository of information—a touchstone touched many times. Robert Bryce of *The Austin Chronicle,* Austin's alternative magazine, also supplied much information on, and insight into, the story, and the website of *The Austin Chronicle* was outstanding as well.

Much of the data used in writing this book came from court documents, both "discovery" and trial transcripts. In fact, the two-thousand-page transcript of the Karr trial was the central document amongst many judicial proceedings used to write this book. Through the painstaking efforts of Ed Martin and Jerry Carruth, the trial transcript provided a lucid blueprint of an incredibly complex and horrendous crime. The FBI's response to my Freedom of Information Act request also produced a wealth of data on Madalyn's rise to prominence and lent good historical context. Actual recordings of the arguments at the Supreme Court for Madalyn's school prayer victory in 1964 were also primary and invaluable.

Acknowledgments

The process of authoring seems a collective enterprise in the sense that there must be good, helping hands along the way. Many years before I started writing this book my mentors buoyed me, and it is they whom I must thank first: James Williamson, who took the time to take a young boy fishing and in the process teach him through example about courage, discipline, and caring; Joe Jackson, who got me my first gig in Madison, Wisconsin, in 1970, and who helped change my ears, my mind, and my life so much for the better; "Aunt Lillian"—Liberty Katsikas, who always remembers and who has maintained a lifetime vigil of unconditional love. And, of course, "Uncle Nick"—Nicholas C. Culolias. Not a better man has lived.

I would also like to thank the following people and institutions for their generous assistance in the writing of this book, with genuine apologies to those whom I may have omitted by my oversight: Glenda Bailey, Southwest Texas State University, San Marcos; Alicia Belvin, Austin, Texas; Don Bonsteel, Enoch Pratt Free Library, Baltimore, Maryland; Tony Brackett, ABC News Archives; Robert Bryce, *The Austin Chronicle;* Dona Bubelis, Seattle Public Library; Anne Bushel, Rossford Public Library, Rossford, Ohio; Gerald Carruth, Assistant U.S. Attorney, Austin, Texas; Donna Castelli, District Clerk, Christian County, Illinois; Donna Cowling, Special Agent, Federal Bureau of Investigation, Austin, Texas; Jim Cross, USP Terre Haute, Terre Haute, Indiana; Walt Crowley, Seattle, Washington; Keith and Mike DeSa,

San Antonio, Texas; Jill DeVincens, New York, New York; Michael Dolan, Washington, D.C.; Phil Donahue, Westport, Connecticut; Bob Elkins, Wimberley, Texas; Dan Fesperman, *The Sun,* Baltimore, Maryland; Daryl Fields, U.S. Attorney's Office, San Antonio, Texas; Larry Flynt, *Hustler* magazine; Bob Fry; Anne Gaylor, Madison, Wisconsin; Barry Gilmore, Circuit Clerk's Office, Peoria County, Peoria, Illinois; Dr. David Glassman, Southwest Texas State University, San Marcos; Linda Graziani, Internal Revenue Service, San Antonio, Texas; Dr. Mark Hamilton, Ashland University, Ashland, Ohio; Ron Hamm, Peoria, Illinois; Martha Jan Hammer, Peoria Police Department, Peoria, Illinois; Diana Hersh, *Rossford Record Journal,* Rossford, Ohio; Samuel Sykes Houston, Federal Bureau of Investigation, Austin, Texas; Nick Howell, Illinois Department of Corrections, Springfield; Judge John B. Huschen, Woodford County, Illinois; Dr. Ja Jahannes; Gary Karr, Terre Haute Federal Prison, Indiana; Paul Krassner, *The Realist;* Leonard Kerpelman, Baltimore, Maryland; Mark Lambert, Southwest Texas School of Law, Houston; Richard A. Lanham Sr., Baltimore, Maryland; Joyce Lawrence, Dallas, Texas; Kevin Lyons, State's Attorney, Peoria County, Peoria, Illinois; Union County Public Library, Monroe, North Carolina; Peter Marin, Santa Barbara, California; Paul Marsa, Edison, New Jersey; Stephen Millies, *Workers World,* New York, New York; John MacCormack, *San Antonio Express-News;* Ed Martin, Austin, Texas; Maury Maverick, Jr., San Antonio, Texas; Lieutanant Doug Miller, Danville, Illinois; Terrance W. McGarry, Encino, California; Brady Mills, Department of Public Safety, Austin, Texas; Thomas W. Mills, Dallas, Texas; Evan Moore, *Houston Chronicle;* Emmett Murray, *The Seattle Times;* William J. Murray, Washington, D.C.; Derek Nalls, Arlington, Texas; Carol J. Newton, Woodford County, Illinois; Stephen Nordlinger, Baltimore, Maryland; Carol O'Brien, Cleona, Pennsylvania; Lynne Olson, Simon & Schuster, New York, New York;

Dr. Raymond Peat, Eugene, Oregon; Bill Pickett, Danville, Illinois; the staff at El Progreso Memorial Library, Olga Zamora, Leti Ruiz, Lucy Sandoval, and Sandra Arriola; Anne Ruggles, Peoria, Illinois; Patricia Reid, Internal Revenue Service, Washington, D.C.; Rene Salinas, Federal Bureau of Investigation, San Antonio, Texas; Jean Shrier, Peoria Public Library, Peoria, Illinois; Dr. Harry and Diane Smith, Reagan Wells, Texas; Cindy Tatton, Larry Flynt Productions, Los Angeles, California; Francis Tsay, The Free Press, New York, New York; Arnold Via, Grottoes, Virginia; David Villarreal, San Antonio, Texas; Dr. Paul Vitz, New York, New York; Valeri Williams, Dallas, Texas; Timothy Young of Arizona.

And especially Kelly Gionti, The Free Press, New York, New York, for the attention and effort she put into readying the manuscript, and her adroit help in breaking a crucial structural logjam. Thanks!

To those many sources who asked to remain anonymous, I reluctantly will honor their wishes but still extend them my thanks.

I'd like to express my special appreciation to Paul Krassner, for his kindness and help with details of Madalyn's early career. As well, my thanks to Dr. Ray Peat for all his meticulous and illuminating assistance regarding my inquiries about Madalyn's life and times in Valle de Bravo.

Particular acknowledgment and thanks must go to two gentlemen: Assistant U.S. Attorney Jerry Carruth and IRS Special Agent Ed Martin. Their patience with my ignorance always went beyond the call of duty. Undoubtedly their skill and dedication saved innocent lives, and as citizens, we're very lucky to have such men as public servants.

My deep appreciation and love goes to Patty and Greg Pasztor for their unflagging support for this book and their warm friendship over the many years. And to David Villarreal, who was always there, ready to bail me out of whatever troubles befell me. I salute you, brother.

Finally, I'd like to state my sincere gratitude to the man who has given me the opportunity to write these words and have them published, my masterful editor, Fred Hills. It's my understanding, even though he never mentioned it, that he edits a racing stable of excellent authors with commensurately exuberant egos. If so, regardless of his other obligations, he always deftly left me with the impression that my book was his sole task and joy.

Still, times are strange. Although we've unquestionably had an intense and rewarding two-year exchange of now countless phone calls, faxes, e-mails, letters, and FedExes, Fred and I have never met in person. It must be acknowledged that I wouldn't know my own editor from Adam if he walked up to me on the street. So Fred, if I ever make it up to New York, the brew's on me—face-to-face.

And above all, my thanks go to gracious Pan and all the other presiding Gods.

Index

PHOTO CREDITS

About the Author

TED DRACOS'S career has encompassed all aspects of media/communications. Beginning as a late-night FM radio host of jazz programming in Madison, Wisconsin, he went on to work as a recording engineer in Hollywood, laying down sound tracks for such groups as the Jackson Five and Diana Ross and the Supremes. Moving to the Northwest, he formed his own company specializing in environmental mediation and citizen organizing. He started his journalistic career as a contributing writer/photojournalist for the *Seattle Weekly*. As an investigative television journalist he has worked extensively in the area of social policy—scientific, medical, and the American justice system—for network affiliates in San Antonio, San Diego, and Minneapolis, as well as reporting, writing, producing, and consulting for ABC's *20/20*, Fox's *America's Most Wanted*, and Orion Telepictures' *Crimewatch*. His work has been featured in Condé Nast's *Self* magazine and the *American Journalism Review*, among other publications. As a college instructor of broadcast journalism, he was a member of the faculty at Incarnate Word University in San Antonio. Environmental educational programs that he developed are still functioning after more than thirty years in Washington State. A graduate of the University of Wisconsin–Madison, with a B.A. in history, he enjoys nothing more than a long walk on a quiet country road.